MW00629774

My Odyssey
with Donna

An Immigrant Filipino Family's Path to Success

May 26, 2024

To Dr. Petersen,
   With best wishes for
the future and gratitude
for the best podiatric I
recieve from you

Jose Pegon

Jose Peczon

Fulton Books, Inc.
Meadville, PA

Published by Fulton Books 2021

ISBN 978-1-63710-602-0 (paperback)
ISBN 978-1-63985-193-5 (hardcover)
ISBN 978-1-63710-603-7 (digital)

Printed in the United States of America

To my parents, Jose and Albina

To the love of my life, Donna
To her parents, Ramon and Dolores

To my children and their spouses, Walter and Rina and Lisa and Omar
To my grandchildren, Patrick, Sami, Michaela,
Haley, Brianna, and Charlie

To all the other members of my family

And to my friends

Acknowledgments

There are two versions of this book. The first is intended exclusively for family and close friends. The second is this, for general consumption.

Numerous individuals helped to make this book a reality.

Problems with the computer I used to write the manuscript would have been difficult, if not impossible, for me to solve alone. ALDER PECZON, my nephew, is invaluable in his availability, readiness, and expertise to resolve them.

The chapters on *My Role in the Evolution of Cataracts* and *Merging Streams,* renamed *Brush with History,* were edited by my associate, JANE A. WINCHESTER, MD, in my ophthalmology practice in Greenfield while we were both still in practice.

My medical school classmate, FELIPE I. TOLENTINO, MD, provided me with details in writing the chapter on "Serendipity and Philanthropy."

FREDERICO AGNIR helped in editing the chapter "A Memorable Gold Watch."

The book's front and back covers are designed by AIEL ORLINA, another nephew.

My sister ALBINA P. FERNANDEZ rewrote the chapter "Cruel Blow to the Family."

Throughout the entire stages of writing the manuscript, several people helped, in small and in large ways, to improve the final product. They are my classmate MUTYA SAN AGUSTIN, my brother BENIGNO D. PECZON, friends GAIL ROBERGE and TESSIE REYES, my cousin MIGNONET DAVID-CARLUEN, my niece GRACE P. ABLAN, and my grandchildren J. Patrick Tiongson and Michaela Amor Tiongson.

In particular, I want to acknowledge the magnificent contribution of my medical school classmate Lutgarda Abad-Vasquez, MD, who suggested some chapter names and the final book title after going through several variations. She is solely responsible for the idea of having two versions of the book, the private and the public editions. Her edits on most of the chapters are invaluable.

Frank Hilario edited the entire manuscript before it was submitted to Fulton Books. He was responsible for placing the chapter "Cruel Blow to the Family" to be the first chapter. It was originally the fourth.

Introduction

This is an autobiography, but the story is not just about me. Without two important women, this odyssey would not have been possible.

A common cliché says that behind every successful man is a woman. For me, there were two women—my mother, IMA, and my wife, DONNA. Both greatly contributed to who and where I am now. My mother steered me to a career in medicine, and she was solely responsible for my eventually meeting and marrying Donna, who shared my odyssey in life for sixty-five years.

Having said the above, I do not wish to belittle the contribution that my father, Tatang, had in my life despite the brevity of his influence in my upbringing because he died when I was but fifteen. However, his genes, in combination with my mother's, gave me the basic tools I needed to go as far as I was able to achieve.

Without Donna's dogged foresight that our future lay in a foreign land outside our country of birth, those genes would not have resulted in the home run that won the game for us.

Cruel Blow to the Family

On May 30, 1948, during the annual celebration of the San Fernando Town Fiesta in Pampanga Province, my father, JOSE PECZON SR., was shot and killed by a gang of criminals. The shooting took place right in front of our drugstore in that town, BOTICA PECZON, which was located just a few meters away from the municipio (town hall) along the town's main street. Our family ride, a converted surplus US Army jeep, was as usual parked in front of the drugstore. My younger brothers, BEN and PONCHIT, six and nine years old respectively, sat in the back seat of the jeep, while I, then fifteen years old, was in the passenger side in front. It was in the late evening, and the town fiesta was coming to an end. There were lots of explosions in the air from fireworks, a de rigueur part of the celebration. Suddenly, different popping sounds were coming from the back of the parked jeep. I knew that my father—as was his routine practice to check the spare tire hanging at the back of the jeep prior to driving off—was there, right where the weird sounds came from. To my shock and horror, I saw him falling to the pavement.

I quickly jumped out of the jeep and ran toward him, but before I could reach him, I experienced a searing pain in my left leg and fell facedown near him. I managed to crawl to his side. He was bleeding profusely, and I whispered to him that we should pray together. I searched for his gun, which he always carried with him, with the thought of firing back at those who hit us. Due to my wounds, I could not carry out my intention.

I remember the cacophony of human cries and shouts. People came toward us. Later I discovered that the local police chief, DICKIE

PANLILIO, took us to Pampanga Provincial Hospital. Because of the severity of the wounds inflicted on my father caused by several short-range shots all over his body, and my sister ALMA, who was shot in the head, the decision was made to transfer the mortally wounded to Clark Air Force Base Hospital in the nearby town of Angeles, touted as the best-equipped medical center outside the USA. It just had to be, for it was where sick and wounded American servicemen from all over Asia were sent for treatment. Since my wounds were not considered life-threatening, I was retained at Pampanga Provincial Hospital, which was not at par with the American hospital in terms of medical expertise and equipment but was deemed good enough for my case.

On my hospital bed, I soon became conscious of what had happened to me. I was bandaged over my left wrist and left leg from the buttocks down to the lower part of the thigh. My left leg from the knee down was numb, and I could not flex my toes toward me. Uncle RUBEN was the first person I could identify. He told me what happened. He mentioned that my father, with more serious gunshot wounds, was taken to a hospital in Manila where he could get better treatment.

That was a lie used to shield me from the more shocking truth of what happened to my family. Uncle Ruben was replaced by SITANG BELTRAN, our faithful family housekeeper, and LUCILA LEGASPI. These two worked at the BOTICA PECZON's The Cool Spot, the soda fountain section of the drugstore, made popular in San Fernando because of the beauty and charm those two girls exuded while serving customers. No other drugstore in the area had this feature. Coca-Cola, Royal Tru-Orange, root beer, and San Miguel Beer, served together with peanuts fried with garlic, pickled hard-boiled eggs, and balut (a boiled fertilized duck egg approximately five days before hatching, eaten in the shell and considered a delicacy) were some of the snacks I remember served by Sitang and Lucila. At the Cool Spot is where I first tasted and drank sodas but not beer. Drinking beer and other alcoholic drinks came much later in my life.

In the hospital, I remember the multiple injections of a painful medication that I later found out was *penicillin*. I came to realize that the wound in my left wrist was at the same level as the entry hole in my left buttock. Two shots must have been fired at me, aimed at the lower extremities but with no intent to kill me. *It was not my time to die.* In a few days, I was brought to the same Clark Air Force Base Hospital, where *Tatang*, Pampango for *Father*, and my sister Alma were taken right after the shooting to have an x-ray examination on my left lower extremity. The provincial hospital did not have this diagnostic tool that is now commonly available in all hospitals. The doctors at the provincial hospital probably wanted to eliminate the possibility that I might have had an injury to the pelvic bones and femur, the long bone of the leg. However, nobody made any effort to find out if any nerves were injured, but perhaps even if they did find out, they could not do anything about it.

In today's advances in surgery and understanding of human body regeneration, they will certainly look for severed nerves and rejoin them. No such thing happened to me. Consequently, I have been made to suffer from the permanent foot drop of the left foot that up to now I must deal with for the rest of my days.

An American nurse prepared me for the x-ray examination, first, by removing all my clothes I came in with and replacing them with a loose hospital gown. She noted that my male organ was wrapped in bloody bandages that she thought was also a result of the shooting. "Poor boy, he was hit there too," I heard her say. Apparently, she was not told that a week before that shooting, I had undergone a cultural rite of passage from boyhood to manhood by having a circumcision that was performed by our family physician, Dr. AQUILINO CANDA.

Now looking back at that remote past while writing this piece in the recreation room of my Southern California house in a gated community tailor-made for golfers, I cannot help but be more thankful for that unnamed American nurse's offer to me of a small carton of fresh milk and a chocolate cookie. I took her offer of this quintessential American snack gladly and consumed it with relish. Just as later in life, I took and have been taking gladly with relish what the nurse's Uncle Sam has been offering me and my family—the goodies of life as deserved.

I was returned to the provincial hospital, and in a few days, Uncles Ruben and Delfin brought me to Apung Taqui's house. It was odd that I was not brought to the house fronted by Farmacia A. David and that Ima did not visit me at the hospital. It was explained to me that she was in Manila watching over Tatang in a hospital where, like me, he was recuperating from his wounds. Soon Alma came to stay in the same house. I stayed in Apung Benig's bedroom and Alma in another bedroom. Many relatives and friends came to visit us.

I fondly remember the Panlilio sisters who came with a gift of a plane modeling kit. Their parents, Judge Panlilio and Imang Conching, were investors in Botica Peczon. My friend Marcelo Maniago (Eloy) came frequently, often bearing a local delicacy of freshly roasted young dove, *pitchon* in Kapampangan.

For quite a while, I was under the impression that my father was alive and was recuperating like me in a Manila hospital. It was not until a month later that Alma and I were told the truth. Both of us were finally taken to our house, fronted by Farmacia A. David. The town's parish priest, the Reverend Father Quirino Canilao, who had been enticing me to become a priest, calmly told us that our father had died. I do not remember crying. I think Alma did not cry too, but we both realized what a heavy burden Mother—*Ima*, we call in the dialect—had to carry from then on.

As days passed by, more detailed information came. I soon realized the enormity of the problems facing a beheaded family, how painfully traumatic this whole incident was to Ima and how she bore it with courage and dignity. I learned that Alma had sustained a gunshot wound right between her eyes. The bullet, probably a .22-caliber bullet, exited at the nape. The small-caliber bullet traveled the base of the skull but did not hit any nerve or blood vessel. Today, the scars from that bullet wound are hardly visible, and she demonstrates no physical or mental deficits.

I also learned that the family prepared two coffins after the shooting, one for Tatang, the other for Alma. Ben told me just recently, to remind me of that event, that he remembered being pulled by Pons to the floor of the jeep where he instinctively thought it was safer. Thus, out of sight, and with lower silhouettes, both were not hit by stray bullets. He was aware that so many people crowded in our house in Mexico.

The wake for Tatang was in the local church, but Ben never went there to view the remains. He could not remember the actual burial in the local Catholic cemetery either. I am convinced that he knew what was happening then, but because it was so traumatic, he wisely tried to erase it from his memory.

Reconstructing that incident, it appears that at least three gunmen were involved in that ambush-type killing. One gunman went to the front side of the jeep. He was the one who shot me in the left leg and left wrist. Alma, who was still inside the drugstore, was hit by a stray bullet, fired by a gunman who must have been standing a few feet away from the right side of the jeep. His wayward shot hit Alma, who was still in the drugstore. Ima and Zon were also still inside the store. Neither was hurt. The third gunman was stationed right behind the jeep and was the one who delivered the fatal multiple shots to Tatang. His shots also entered the jeep where my two brothers were sitting. It was fortunate that although the jeep was riddled with bullet holes, none of the bullets hit my young brothers before they scrambled to safety underneath the jeep.

A first cousin of my mother, whom we called IMANG BANING, later told us that the assailants were distant relatives of ours on the maternal side. We were told that they were asking for money that Tatang could not give because he did not have any to give them. It was easy to understand that because he was saving whatever disposable funds the family had, to buy a lot and build a house cum drugstore in Grace Park, Caloocan, a suburb of Manila, in anticipation of the time when we, the envisioned pursuers of our parent's dream of living a good life, leave home to get our college education. The drugstore would generate funds to subsidize our expenses.

The identity of the shooters and their real motives I will never know. I do not think any other in our family want to know either. Knowing who they were and what their motives were would not bring back Tatang. From the beginning up to the present time, I did not and I do not care to find out.

Tatang died at the age of forty-five, and he left a widow four months older than him with five young children to take care of—and who with grit eventually sent all five to college singlehandedly.

Although this incident was such an enormously tragic event for our family, especially for Ima, I get solace in the knowledge that the loss of Tatang, at such an early age, did not create a barrier for any of my siblings and me to reach for the stars. We all tried hard to excel in the respective careers that we chose, and all succeeded. I am enormously grateful that despite the economic setbacks our family suffered, I was able to go on to finish my education and ended up as an ophthalmologist and had the good fortune to find my life-time soulmate in DONNA I. VILLAFLOR, RN, while still in training at the University of the Philippines, Philippine General Hospital (UP-PGH). With her by my side, we made good the promise that SUCCESS IS WITHIN REACH OF THOSE WHO ARE WILLING TO WORK HARD FOR IT. With Donna's practice of nursing and my practice of ophthalmology, we found our places in the sun, albeit not in our homeland.

Consequently, we were able to help my larger family in some capacity, including the education of four young boys left behind by my younger brother Pons who died at a young age, at about the same age as our father, from sleep apnea, *bangungot* in our language. Additionally, I am so happy that we were able to provide a comfortable life for Ima, in a house built especially for her in a plush gated Quezon City subdivision, Ayala Heights. She lived to see eighteen great-grandchildren, the grandchildren of her children, Zon, Alma, Pons, Ben, and me. She died peacefully in her sleep at the age of 102 on August 10, 2004, with no symptoms of dementia.

My Roots

On the island of Luzon in the Philippines, in one of the largest and oldest towns in the province of Pampanga, Mexico, was where I was born on October 28, 1933. There were no hospitals then, and so I was delivered at home with my mother Ima attended to by APUNG TISIA. She was the wife of my mother's uncle CELO and was an experienced midwife. That residence was located right across the street from the Roman Catholic church.

My birth certificate was signed by my paternal grandfather, BENIGNO DAVID. One FORTUNATO COSIO was the registrar, but he did not sign the form. I don't know why. My middle name in that certificate is TADEO, not DAVID, contrary to cultural tradition then and now. In most instances, your mother's family name is your middle name.

From that first house, our family moved to a new house right next to the municipio, the town's municipal building. Three sisters preceded me, LUZVIMINDA (Luvy), JOSEPHINA (Pining), and CORAZON (Zon). I was the fourth child, the firstborn son. All four were born in that first house. After me came my sister ALBINA (Alma) and my brothers ILDEFONZO (Pons or Ponchit) and BENIGNO (Ben), one after the other, all born in that second house. My earliest recollection of childhood was in that second house

Paternal Side

I was named after my father, JOSE PECZON. Most of his friends called him *Pitong,* which was also the nickname I was called by many friends and relatives. My mother called him *Pepe.* My siblings and I called him *Tatang,* the Kapampangan word for *Father.* He did not have a middle name because he was an illegitimate child. His story needs to be told in some detail. The information I have of him came from different sources, but mainly from Uncle Ruben, my mother's youngest brother, and my first cousin BIENVENIDO LORENZO HIZON.

Tatang was born in Mexico, Pampanga, on April 8, 1903. His mother was SEGUNDA VITAL PECSON, whom we called APUNG GUNDA. Notice the spelling of my grandmother's family name, with an *s* instead of a *z* that my father carried. The change must have happened before I was born. There was something going on with or within the family at that time that made him change the spelling of our family name. He was educated within the public school system, which was just recently established by the Americans, five years after they acquired the whole archipelago from the Spaniards at the turn of the century via the Treaty of Paris (1898). Prior to that, there were only private schools run by Spaniards. While in high school, he was known as a runner and high jumper, winning a silver medal in the one-hundred-meter dash during one school athletic competition. After his graduation from Pampanga High School, he went on to National Teacher's College in Manila to earn a degree in teaching. After he obtained his diploma, he returned to Mexico to become a grade school teacher at Mexico Elementary School. Through the years, he climbed the ranks and later became the school principal (headteacher).

Apung Gunda married VICTOR LORENZO, with whom she had two daughters: ROSARIO, whom we called IMANG CHARING, and VICTORIA, IMANG TORING ("Imang" affectionate title for mother). She was widowed early in life. Regarded as a beauty, an amalgam of Chinese, Spanish, and Filipino blood, she was apparently pursued by many suitors. Among them was ADRIANO PANLILIO, the putative biological father of Tatang. He, too, was of mixed blood, a mestizo, half-Spanish and half-Filipino.

Adriano proposed marriage to Apung Gunda, but the Lorenzos opposed it. Maintaining family honor seemed to be the reason for this. IGMIDIO, Adriano's younger brother, was simultaneously courting VICTORIA, the youngest daughter of Apung Gunda. Victoria rejected him, probably because of the discomfort she felt while her mother was being courted by the older brother, Adriano. Igmidio was persistent. He did not easily give up. Following a small-town tradition at that time, he thought he could force Victoria to accept him in marriage by publicly embracing and kissing her in front of churchgoers while they exited from the Sunday morning Mass. This happened in front of the house that will become our first house/drugstore. In the Pampango language, the term for that unsavory tactic to capture a maiden's heart was *pangusut*. Most women subjected to that kind of social embarrassment and disgrace were forced to accept the men involved against their wishes because no one else would ever propose marriage to them. Already, they were considered as "damaged goods."

However, Victoria was not an ordinary Pampangueña. She still rejected this ardent suitor. Igmidio was now the one who was placed in a shameful and dishonorable predicament. A few days later, he took his own life with poison. This tragedy became the basis of a novel, *Lidia*, written by a famous Pampango writer named Juan Crisostomo Soto, also known as CRISOT, the father of Kapampangan literature.

Adriano eventually married CONSOLACION LIZARES of Silay, Negros Occidental. In Masamat, a barrio in the town of Mexico near the border with the provincial capital town of San Fernando, they built a mansion. With no children of their own, they tried to officially adopt JOSE PECSON as Adriano's own but were unsuccessful. I have no solid explanation for the refusal, but I am certain of one thing: That Tatang had no say on it. Why would he refuse to recognize his biological father? Why would he turn his back to a huge fortune from his father and his wife? I asked my mother about this, and her answer was, "I cannot tell you and please do not ask that question again." Mother knew best!

Adriano died in Masamat and was buried in a private cemetery near his house but was later disinterred and reburied in his wife's Lizares family burial chapel in Silay, Negros Occidental. It is interesting to note that Consolacion was a patient of DOLORES IBAÑEZ VILLAFLOR, the mother of DONNA, who would be my wife years later. As a nurse, she saw Consolacion frequently, giving her regular injections, probably calcium or vitamin injections that were popular at that time. Donna and I were already married when Consolacion died. Unfortunately, I was not yet fully aware of Tatang's undetermined parentage at that time. Had I known it, I surely would have presented myself to Consolacion. I can only speculate now that she would have happily embraced Donna and me upon our meeting and acquaintance.

As a child, I used to spend some time at the house of Apung Gunda, exploring the many rooms in the house and gathering delicious fruits from the yard. There was a huge mango tree at the back, some *dwat* (*duhat* in Tagalog) trees, tiny apples called *manzanitas*, *kaimito* (star apple), *atis* (custard apple), and *santol* (cotton fruit). There was a deep well that was the source of domestic water. I was afraid to go near that well because a babysitter told me that a *duende*, a mischievous elf, lived there.

Apung Gunda was religious, as were all the members of our immediate family. At her house everyone had to say the rosary before going to bed. When she visited us in our house, she imposed the same religious ritual. We were forced to kneel on the bare wooden floor while praying the rosary, but when she was not looking, the children did something else. My favorite was to have a maid scratch my back while I was sitting on my butt, which was more comfortable than kneeling on the bare wooden floor. Zon would kneel obediently, but I think Alma did not. Pons was too young to understand, and Ben was not born yet.

Soon after the war, Apung Gunda fell down the stairs in her house and broke her hip. She was never taken to a hospital, and anyway a doctor who made a house call said nothing could be done to rejoin the broken hip. She never walked again. To move her around the house, Tatang had a low-slung chair with wheels made for her. By this time, she was staying with us full-time until Tatang was killed by hoodlums in 1948. Thereafter, she was cared for again by Imang Charing and Cong ("Elder Brother") Carding. They left Mexico and moved to a small apartment on a side street along España Avenue in Manila, not too far from the campus of the University of Santo Tomas (UST).

It was at that apartment where she died. Before that, I was still in high school, on summer vacation, when I was asked to stay with her as a sitter. I assisted her in feeding herself and going to the bathroom when nature called. The night she died, she had a bad respiratory condition that made her cough uncontrollably. I awoke to give her cough medication. Upon swallowing the liquid, she went into more spasms of coughing, probably because some of the liquid medication went into her trachea instead of the esophagus. Suddenly she went into convulsions and became still. Dead. I woke everybody up. Fearing that rigor mortis would set in soon, Cong Carding asked me to sit on her right knee that was permanently flexed from the original hip fracture. Dutifully I did it and heard the cracking of the knee joint as I let my weight bear down to make the limb straight. She was buried at the family plot at the Catholic cemetery in Mexico. I was fifteen years old then, a junior at St. Joseph's Academy in Mexico, and soon to enroll as a senior at the Far Eastern University (FEU) High School in Manila, the capital city.

As a young boy, I remember sitting on Tatang's lap, facing him, while he read the local newspapers. With tweezers, I pulled all the hairs from his beard and mustache. He never flinched! Most men at that time went to a barber for a shave. I guess he neither had the time nor the inclination to do that. Most probably, he considered it a good time to bond with me more closely. When he was playing tennis with co-teachers, I was on the sidelines picking up balls, the *pulut* boy. From him, I got interested in the game.

He took me along in his hunting trips for birds, *pasdan* (snipes), and *dumara* (wild ducks). He was quite good with a shotgun. I was tasked with retrieving the hapless birds that had gone down and carrying them home. The family cook took care of cleaning and cooking them. It was not unusual to chew on those tasty birds and occasionally bite on a pellet or two that were still embedded in the flesh. I often wonder if unwittingly I ever swallowed any of them! I know they were lead pellets in those shotgun shells. At that time, no one knew that lead is a very toxic substance that can affect the central nervous system. Later Tatang bought me my own .22-caliber rifle, and I became quite a good shot with it myself. I also remember many camping trips with him, including the one to Mt. Arayat with a Boy Scout troop to which he was the scoutmaster. We went to Manila several times by train or bus to buy medicines for the drugstore. In Binondo, Manila's Chinatown, he took me to a few restaurants. Those were my first recollections of dining outside our house. He also introduced me to that quintessential American hamburger on a bun in a tiny hole-in-the-wall diner along a side street crossing Escolta in Manila's business district.

I vividly remember a bus trip with him to Baguio in April 1947 to attend a teachers' conference with his colleagues from other towns. During this trip, I noticed that several of the young female teachers were always cozying up to Tatang, which I can describe now as *flirtatious*. I did not make anything out of what I saw then, but now that I am older, I have come to realize that Tatang was quite a charmer to the opposite sex.

On the way to Baguio, the City of the Pines, a.k.a. the Summer Capital of the Philippines, we picked up a hitchhiking couple with a young boy about my age. They alighted from the bus during a rest stop in Agoo, La Union. I surmised that *that* was their destination. The boy got off the bus first and suddenly ran from the back of the bus across the street. He was immediately run over by another bus coming from the other direction. Oh my God! He must have died instantly. Tatang probably thought for a moment that I was the victim. He must have felt a huge sigh of relief when he saw me still on my seat on the bus, immobile and transfixed, after watching that boy run over by and crushed to death with the weight of that other bus. He took a collection from all the teachers on that bus, and together with money from his wallet, he gave the sum to the shocked grieving parents. Now that I am both a parent and grandparent, I can imagine what a horrific experience it is to see one's child killed in an accident like that.

Maternal Side

My mother was ALBINA CASTRO DAVID, born on December 16, 1902, in the barrio of Masamat in Mexico. She was nicknamed *Binang*, which was shortened to Bee, the name my father and close friends and relatives called her. My siblings and I called her *Ima*, the Kapampangan term for *Mother*. She was GRANNY to all her grandchildren, all of whom spoke English. She was the eldest of five siblings. After her came VICTOR, MALIGAYA, DELFIN, and RUBEN.

Ima's father was BENIGNO F. DAVID (1879–1939). We called him APUNG BENIG. He was the learned one despite limited formal education that did not go beyond grade two in elementary school; he had language competency outside of his native Kapampangan language: in Tagalog, Spanish, and English. He subscribed to all the major newspapers at that time. He became the town's secretary/treasurer and was the only notary public. (His signature is on my birth certificate.) The town also used his expertise as a self-taught surveyor and accountant. He was an active Mason, and the town priest denounced him for not attending Sunday Mass. He was probably the main source of my "genes" that later turned me into what I am now, an atheist. At the young age of sixty, Apung Benig died, most probably from a cardiovascular disease, because of heavy cigarette smoking and an untreated asthma.

My maternal grandmother was EUSTAQUIA G. CASTRO (1879–1977). She was APUNG TAQUI to all of us. What I remember most about Apung Taqui was that she kept an immaculately clean house. I remember frequently staying overnight at her house. She cooked the best fried rice, and we used to eat on a typical low table called *dulang* that was just a few inches higher than the floor made of bamboo slats. Only the main sala had hardwood floors. Her yard was neat; no weeds could grow. Uncle Ruben told me of the time he tried his best to grow garden grass in the yard, like the green grass-covered lawns of typical American houses he saw in magazines. My grandmother thought they were weeds. Methodically, she pulled out all of them, roots and all, to keep the yard neat!

At that house, Uncle Victor had a dark room on the ground floor to develop black-and-white photos. He took all my childhood photos. Uncle Delfin had a collection of rocks from one of his jobs in a mine in Mountain Province. The dark room and rock collection were targets for my curiosity. There were many banana trees, guavas, and other tropical fruits, not unlike the ones across the street at Apung Gunda's.

There was an icebox in the kitchen. One day Pons and I were playing hide-and-seek. I told him to go inside the icebox to hide, and I closed the airtight cover. Then I forgot Pons. Fortunately, one of the maids heard the noise coming from inside the box. When the lid was opened, Pons was already quite cyanotic. I almost killed my brother Pons playing that silly and obviously dangerous game.

There was a large birdhouse with several compartments to accommodate a dozen or more pigeons. Young pigeons, before they developed feathers, were a small part of our food chain. Called *pitchon* in our language, they were considered a delicacy.

Apung Taqui always had chickens and pigs getting fattened for eventual slaughter and sale at the local marketplace. Fresh eggs were provided by the free-roaming chickens. When I was going to medical school, my widowed mother had a meager income. Apung Taqui helped pay part of my college tuition by raising those pigs and chickens to be sold at the beginning of the school year. Many years later, finishing my residency in ophthalmology gave me the unique opportunity to surgically remove her cataracts before she died at the ripe old age of ninety-eight. Regretfully, intraocular lenses (IOLs) were not yet available then to restore sight to near-perfect.

Ima graduated from UP School of Pharmacy in 1928, before its conversion from school to college in 1935. After getting her pharmacy degree, she opened her first drugstore located in Mexico. With almost 100 percent certainty, I say Apung Benig financed that venture. The store was in a rented house just across the old Catholic church, which was in the middle of town. My parents had three daughters born in that house: LUVY, PINING, and ZON. Tragically, the first two died from pneumonia before reaching the age of two. That was an era before antibiotics were discovered. Zon was the first child to reach adulthood.

I was born there too. Apung Benig moved the drugstore to a new location because he thought that the original place was *malas*, bad luck. A new house was then built on leased land from the town, right next to the municipio. Again, Apung Benig most probably helped financially to build this new *botica*, a drugstore or pharmacy. FARMACIA A. DAVID it was called, and it occupied the front room on the first floor. There was a living room just behind the drugstore. Behind the living room was the dining room. At the rear were the kitchen and bathroom with a toilet draining into a septic tank in the yard.

There was no indoor plumbing. Domestic water came from a deep well dug in the backyard and a free-flowing artesian well in front of the drugstore across the street. In addition, there was also an outhouse emptying into the river that ran behind the house. Upstairs were the sleeping quarters. There was a small separate bedroom at the back. A larger L-shaped room took the front. There was a single queen-sized bed for our parents. All the children slept on the floor using *dase,* a rectangular mat made of woven palm leaves. Mosquito nets, *kulambu,* kept the mosquitos away but not the bedbugs, *suldut,* that inhabited the *dase.* There was no bathroom on this second floor of the house. At night we emptied our urinary bladders into *urinolas.* Those urinal pots were carried downstairs in the morning for disposal of their contents by maids. Our house was located to the right of the municipio. Alma, Pons, and Ben were all born in this house.

A large yard, blessed with fruit bearing trees—santol, caimito, *atis* (sugar apple), *saresa* (Jamaican cherry tree), and *camachile,* commonly known as Manila tamarind, separated our house from the municipio. This imposing building was an old Spanish-built structure with very thick walls of adobe. It was constructed in the early eighteenth century. The town mayor, treasurer, registrar, and other minor officials had their offices there. The office for the police force of two or three officers and the jail were there too. The building was obviously historic, but this was not appreciated by subsequent town officials who tragically had the municipio demolished and replaced with an ugly structure made with common cement hollow blocks across the street. What a shame! By that time, Ima had left Mexico. Our house was demolished at the same time as the municipio, as the whole area was converted into a marketplace.

Our house had a small icebox that was *not* always filled with ice. Refrigerators were yet to become available to the masses. Perhaps some rich families had them, but I am not certain of this. A family cook was assigned the job of buying fresh food from the market. I often was tasked with buying freshly baked *pan de sal* (common bread roll) from the local bakery for breakfast. Walking along the narrow street leading to the only bakery in town was no problem in the morning, but in the evening and at nightfall, the same street became a nightmare for my siblings and me because some maids told us about *duendes* (elves) that lived just over the high moss-covered adobe walls on one side of the street. An alternate route offered a similar hazard because of a large mango tree that was frequented by bats that obviously liked to feast on the ripening fruits. The strange noise they emitted was proof to us that the *duendes* were there too.

Meats, fish, and fresh vegetables were often bought by Ima from female vendors who came by the house bearing these comestibles in wide baskets *igu*, woven from thin strips of bamboo, which were adeptly carried on their heads. We also got a daily delivery of carabao's milk. During the holidays, there was always a flurry of buying and cooking so much food. I remember most vividly the cooking of *pastillas de leche,* a milk-based confectionery made famous in many towns of Pampanga. Sugar was added to the carabao's milk and boiled until it had the consistency of thick fudge, which was then shaped into bite-size bars and wrapped in thin white paper. My siblings and I always loved to eat this delicacy whenever we had the chance. While it was being cooked, we were often not allowed to partake any of it. It was intended only for the guests. All that we could eat was from what was left on the inner sides of the cooking pot and on the ladle.

I remember one town fiesta when an entire basketball team visited our house after a game. They were served this mouth-watering confectionery while my siblings and I watched from the side, drooling. To be fair, I have to say that on most occasions, we were given freedom to feast on the *pastillas de leche* (soft milk candy) to our heart's content. No wonder dental cavities were common among us children and adults too.

Aside from Farmacia A. David, there was OCAMPO DRUGSTORE on the left side of the municipal building. CANDA DRUGSTORE was a quarter of a mile away, past the bridge in the barrio of San Antonio, on a road leading to the towns of Sta. Ana and Arayat. Despite the three drugstores in this tiny town of Mexico, our store did well. We were not rich, but we were better off than most of the populace. The front of the drugstore became a meeting place for the town's elite that included the PANLILIOS, LAZATINS, LORENZOS, MERCADOS, DE LEONS, and HIZONS. The secret of our drugstore? Maybe it was the free coffee or the daily newspaper that was available for anyone's perusal. Here, the people also enjoyed discussing all the news of the day among themselves. It was at this drugstore where Tatang and I were listening to the radio when a broadcast was made that the Japanese had bombed Pearl Harbor on December 7, 1941, the onset of World War II in the Pacific.

The paltry monthly salary Tatang received as a teacher and later as headteacher (principal) at Mexico Elementary School was probably not sufficient to meet the needs of our growing family. With his experience in helping Ima run Farmacia A. David, he decided to set up a similar store in the town capital of San Fernando shortly after the war ended in 1945. The first such venture was to run a drugstore in the house/office of Dr. Ramos, a general practitioner, with the help of a hired pharmacist. This lasted a few months. I surmise that he saw the benefit of owning the drugstore alone for himself. He left that partnership with Dr. Ramos and set up BOTICA PECZON in another part of town. The pharmacist went with him. I spent many days in that drugstore and observed that it had a lot of clientele, probably because it was the only drugstore in town with a soda fountain that Tatang named "The Cool Spot." At that place, I gained valuable experiences with the customers and the medical problems they showed and shared, all of which became quite useful to me later in my medical career.

Tatang tried another business venture, this time in Manila. On a side street crossing Escolta, the Manila business district, he opened a small café. Cong Carding was the cook. I visited this place only once. It did not last long as Tatang decided to focus more on the drugstore business back home in Pampanga.

Shattered Lives

Tatang's life tragically ended on May 30, 1948, as the San Fernando town fiesta was winding down. He was killed by unidentified gunmen in front of Botica Peczon in front of our entire family. That day will forever be etched in my memory. (It is previously described in more detail in chapter 1.) This brutal act made Ima a widow at an early age of forty-five. Left with five young children, she did what had to be done, and that was to make sure that all of us got a full education, up to finishing college.

With inadequate income derived from just one drugstore, financial aid came from several sources: Apung Taqui's pig-fattening efforts and loans from Imang Guring (via Gloria Suba Beauty Parlor) and probably from other relatives too. That is how all five of us Peczons graduated from college. Zon got a degree in pharmacy from UST; I graduated from UP College of Medicine (UPCM); Alma finished as an English major from UP; Pons got an engineering degree from Mapua Institute of Technology; and the youngest, Ben, graduated from UP Los Baños College of Agriculture with a degree in sugar technology. Those degrees were all obtained in the Philippines. Later, Ben earned a PhD in chemistry, major in physical chemistry, at Purdue University in the US.

Looking back now, I truly regret that Tatang was not allowed to be adopted by his biological father, who showed a fervent wish to be part of his life. Would Tatang's life have ended differently? Would he have survived as long as his wife to witness and enjoy the successes that their progeny achieved? Would the great wealth he could have inherited from his biological father and his equally wealthy wife abet or hinder how my siblings and I looked to education to succeed in life? I can only speculate and imagine.

Six months after the death of Tatang, another cruel blow was inflicted on the larger family. My mother's younger brother Delfin was killed by a gang of thieves who were intent on stealing his brand-new Chevrolet sedan. Uncle Delfin was proud of that new four-door Chevy. In that car, he honed my driving skills. It had a four-speed manual transmission that I readily mastered to operate without stalling the engine. That was because I had previous experience in driving a motor car.

Shortly after liberation from the Japanese Imperial Army, American soldiers came to our drugstore in Mexico to buy home-made whiskey that my mother made from pure ethyl alcohol; she was a pharmacist, as I noted earlier. They would get drunk, and in this inebriated condition, they would take me for a ride in a US Army jeep, not just as a passenger but as the driver. I was only twelve years old! Tatang was upset with this, but he went along with it anyway. He probably knew that sooner or later I had to learn how to drive a car.

The story about Tatang will not be complete without my mentioning that my siblings and I have a half-brother, apparently fathered by him before he married my mother. PETER GONZALES presented himself to my mother during the wake just before my father was buried at the local Catholic cemetery in Mexico. My mother, true to her kind and understanding heart, accepted him without any question. Peter was not asking for anything other than the recognition that he, too, was a son of my father.

Pushing On

Later, traveling locally in the Philippines and abroad interested Ima a great deal. Twice she visited the US. The first time was in 1966, when my wife, Donna, our young children Wally, age two years, and Lisa, a year younger, were in our first year in the US as permanent immigrants. I was then working at Massachusetts Eye and Ear Infirmary (MEEI), where I was gradually building expertise by experience and gaining a reputation to achieve my dream of becoming a successful ophthalmologist with the wherewithal to provide a comfortable life for my family abroad. Ima helped us move to our first house at 17 Wellington Street, Winchester, Massachusetts, where we lived until 1968. She took care of Walter and Lisa while Donna and I commuted to Greenfield for my private practice, which I had started there. When we finally sold the Winchester house and bought a new house at 210 High Street in Greenfield, she was even more of a tremendous help to us.

There was a scary event just before we left that first house in Winchester. Coming home from work one afternoon, I saw a couple of fire trucks with lights flashing in front of our house. Ima, Donna, and the children already were outside on the street, and I thought our house was burning. My heart sank because we just sold the house and were ready to sign the transfer papers, and I was sure all of that was now lost. Fortunately, there was no fire, just a lot of smoke. It turned out that Ima had been cooking rice the traditional way in a pot over a gas stove. Automatic rice cookers had not yet been invented by the Japanese. She had left the pot on the stove and then went out to the porch to join Donna and the two kids who were playing outdoors. Accidentally the door closed behind her. There was no spare key left outdoors to open it. The rice on the stove started overheating, finally burning and leaving a lot of smoke inside. From a neighbor's house, they called the fire department, who forced the kitchen door open, shut off the stove, and blew all the smoke out through the windows. The blowing was what I saw when I arrived home. Finding out that my family was safe and nothing was ruined other than the pot of rice and a broken kitchen door, I was overwhelmingly thankful to the Winchester Fire Department.

Sometime in 1975 or 1976, Ima returned to the Philippines and came back a year or two later, along with Donna's parents. She was with us when we moved to our first Greenfield house at 210 High Street and again when we transferred to our second house at 11 Crescent Street.

While Ima was staying with us in Greenfield, two tragic events befell the family back home. Alma's youngest son, SAMUEL, drowned while trying to save a friend from drowning. This was a terrible blow also to Ima. This was followed a short time later by the even more unexpected and shocking death of brother Pons from *bangungot*. Medical knowledge now recognizes this as sleep apnea that leads to hypoxia, atrial fibrillation, and cardiac arrest. I offered to immediately buy airline tickets for both of us to be at Pon's funeral, but Ima refused. Stating that there was nothing we could change by going home, she instead asked me to save the money and make a promise to financially support Pon's family until all his four young sons finished their education. Donna and I readily agreed and eventually fulfilled that promise to the full, with help from Uncle Ruben, who invested the funds I left in his care. Happily, Ima lived to see all of them graduate from college. The youngest, ILDEFONSO, graduated from UPCM in 2000. He is now a practicing ophthalmologist in Metro Manila.

Ima became lonesome for all her other grandchildren who were left in the Philippines, so she returned home for good to the Philippines on November 29, 1981, and lived with Alma in a professor's cottage in the UP—Diliman campus. Later she lived with Zon in Grace Park, Caloocan. Pon's widow, Evelyn, and her four boys lived in a separate house in the same compound. She knew we would visit her there every year and so she would not miss us that much. Her presence there was a strong motivation for Donna, Wally, Lisa, and me to visit the home country every year, usually in December, when the weather was cooler in the Philippines and winter in New England was notoriously frigid. Celebrating her birthday on December 16 became an opportunity for the entire Peczon-David clan to gather and celebrate together. My brother Ben's birthday was the following day; this presented an opportune reason for a double celebration.

During one of those visits, we saw BEN and ELVIE, who had just built a house in Ayala Alabang, Muntinlupa, a recently developed luxury home community south of Manila. There was a house for sale not too far from their house, and after a quick inspection of the house and lot, we decided to buy it for 1.2 million pesos ($26,000 today). That turned out to be quite a good buy. It was intended for Ima, but she refused to live in it because it was too far from the rest of the family in Grace Park, Caloocan, now a city. We immediately had it rented for two years, but when the lease was up, we could not get another renter because there was no phone line to the house. We did all we could to secure one but to no avail. A friend told me he knew the president of the Philippine Long Distance Telephone (PLDT) company, the only Philippine telephone company at that time, who might be able to help—but he did not. However, the following summer in Greenfield, we got a long-distance call from a real estate broker in Manila who said that he represented a client who was interested in buying the property with a good offer—five million pesos. That was a neat profit in two years, and so we accepted it. The buyer turned out to be the PLDT president himself. He wanted the house because of its proximity to the Ayala Alabang Polo Club. Not unexpectedly, there were multiple phone lines the day after the sale!

With the proceeds, we bought a property at the prestigious Ayala Heights in Quezon City and made plans to build a house, specifically intended for Ima, who I thought would welcome it gladly. "I do not need it," she said, arguing that she did not want to leave Grace Park. Obviously, she did not want to be away from a large segment of our family living there, but I was insistent that she move out. The pollution was increasing, and safety was rapidly deteriorating. During the rainy months, her bedroom was flooded frequently, leaving a lot of mold in its wake. That, to me, was the main cause of her frequent bouts of upper respiratory tract infection. The neighborhood was also increasingly becoming physically unsafe. There were numerous instances of petty crimes like thievery, but there were also more serious crimes like armed robbery. A frightening event occurred one day when Arthur, Zon's husband, was followed into the house by robbers. They kept all the members of the house in a bathroom while they ransacked the place. Thankfully, no one was hurt.

Finally, I just told Ima that those two families would have to be relocated too. With my assertiveness, she finally consented to leave Grace Park when the Ayala Heights house was finished. I returned to

Greenfield, smug with the knowledge that my persuasive reasoning finally had won her over. However, I found out that she had spoken to Uncle Ruben and asked him to tell me that she really did not agree with my plans for the family. In her usual nonconfrontational manner, she did not want me to return home to Greenfield "empty-handed." So I had to speak to her again by long-distance to make her understand that it was better for everybody. I was determined to build her a new house, a better one, in a much better neighborhood. And she *had* to live there.

The other two families followed my insistent plan with little resistance. Shortly after Ima moved to 23 Jose Abad Santos Street, Ayala Heights, Old Balara, Quezon City, Evelyn sold her Grace Park house and built a new one in New Intramuros. Arthur and my sister Zon sold their house too and built a new one in Tierra Pura. My sister Alma and her family lived in Tierra Bella. All three houses were within a couple of miles from Ayala Heights.

Ima was happy, and I had fulfilled my promise to her. Those bouts of coughing from upper respiratory tract infections disappeared! During one of the many annual, later biannual, visits there, she told Donna and me that she had never been so happy in her entire life. She said, "Never in my wildest dreams did I think that I will have a house as comfortable and as beautiful as this one you have built for me." It gave Donna and me a lot of pride that we succeeded in doing this for her, but I teased her with a reminder that she did not want it the first time. She had a good sense of humor and took this joking graciously.

In that house, Ima spent the rest of her long and happy life, albeit without her beloved husband, surrounded by her family, who always celebrated her birthday on December 16. These annual celebrations became a tradition for the entire Peczon-David clan to enjoy each other's company at least once a year.

That glued the clan closer together. For me, there was total satisfaction that I was able to do this for a mother who represented an ideal one, who cared so much, not only for her own family but for anybody who needed help. I never heard her say anything bad about anyone. She was always cheerful despite the very traumatic loss of people close to her: her first two children, father, mother, brothers Victor and Delfin, husband, son Pons, and grandson Samuel. As she gracefully lived to a very ripe old age of 102, she was given excellent care by three caregivers, PARING, ALMA, and TENTEN. Finally, she just went to sleep peacefully for eternity on August 10, 2004. I am sad that Tatang did not live long enough to be always alongside Ima, enjoying life that spanned over a century. I am certain that he would have been proud of what my siblings and I had accomplished. And Ima's life would have been much happier.

To honor and memorialize the lives of Tatang and Ima, my surviving siblings and I decided to build a library at Mexico Elementary School. With other relatives, we built a two-story Peczon-David Family Library (Learning Resource Center) that was inaugurated and officially turned over to the school on January 12, 2006. This was the first such learning center donated by private citizens to a public school in the province of Pampanga. It also became a model for other similarly civic-minded groups to do the same for their hometowns.

Ima's Retirement House

Ima was born in a small house made of bamboo frame and nipa roof. She was first in her family to finish college and travel abroad, principally to the United States. She spent the last two decades of her life in a house Donna and I built for her in a plush, gated community in Quezon City, surrounded and cared for by a loving extended family and three caretakers. Ima never had symptoms of dementia. At the age of 102, she passed on to the great beyond peacefully in her sleep on August 10, 2004.

Early Years

Before I went to school, I had a lot of fun at St. Joseph's Academy, an old building in the center of our town of Mexico, Pampanga, just across the plaza from our house that was right next to the municipio. Attached to one end of the school was an incredibly old bell tower that was part of the old Spanish-built church that was destroyed in an earthquake over a century ago. As a young boy, I used to climb that tower with friends through a dark, winding adobe spiral staircase, reeking with the smell of urine, not from humans but from resident bats who liked the dim, humid place. Mindful of the danger that snakes might lurk in the dark recesses, we were careful to watch our steps. For a few centavos, my friends and I rang the bells during baptismal celebrations, weddings, baptisms, or funerals of parishioners, but many times we just rang the bells for free. From that vantage point was a panoramic view of the town that lay before our eyes. On many occasions, we just went there to enjoy the view and solitude while eating any kind of fruit we freely gathered from nearby trees.

There was one huge tamarind tree in the back of the main building. The young fruits of this tree, still without seeds, were quite sour, but we liked that taste, especially when coupled with uncooked *baguk,* fermented tiny shrimp that we bought from the local marketplace. I was unconcerned about possibly causing any health issues with that raw condiment. Ignorance is bliss!

Kindergarten

My kindergarten and grade 1 school days were there at St. Joseph's Academy. A religious order of Benedictine German nuns ran the school. Among my first teachers was Sister FELIX, who was very tall and probably blond and blue-eyed. There were quite a few of these German nuns, but by the time I entered grade 1, most of them had been replaced by Filipina teachers.

At St. Joseph's Academy, I remember vividly my participation in a school show in which I recited a poem by Kate L. Brown:

> *In the heart of a seed, buried deep so deep,*
> *A dear little plant lay fast asleep!*
> *"Wake!" said the sunshine "and creep to the light!"*
> *"Wake!" said the voice of the raindrop bright.*
> *The little plant heard and it rose to see,*
> *What the wonderful outside world might be.*

The curtain fell, but I just stood out there, unmoving, until someone pulled me out to the sidelines. Perhaps I wanted to stay in the limelight much longer than my short declamation called for.

Elementary School

I started my grade 1 year at St. Joseph's Academy and the rest of it at Mexico Elementary School, where my father was a teacher and later principal. The latter school was farther away, perhaps a fifteen-minute walk.

Tatang was the local Boy Scout leader. Not old enough to join the Boy Scouts, I joined the Cub Scouts, but I participated in most of the older boys' activities that included camping in nearby Mt. Arayat. Attending some of the upper-grade classes that Tatang taught, I remember going to his geography class of grade 4 only to find out that I knew more about the subject matter than any of the older children. I was only in grade 1.

Going to school meant walking the distance from our house in the center of town to the school located in the outskirts of town between Third and Fourth Streets. The distance was probably just about half a mile. Initially, a babysitter always walked me to school. During recess, most of my classmates bought whatever goodies were sold outside the school gates, like *camote* (sweet potato), sugarcane (to bite and munch), fruit, *apulid* (local water chestnut), and *hopia,* a bun stuffed with a sweet bean paste. I rarely had any of those; instead, my babysitter took me under a big mango tree inside the schoolyard. Under the shade of the mango tree, she spread a blanket and had me lie down to consume milk prepared at home that was in a bottle with rubber nipples attached. With no refrigeration available, the milk was made from condensed milk from a can with the appropriate amount of diluting water.

My mother had the best intention that I get the proper nutrition, not knowing that the sugar in the condensed milk wreaked havoc on my teeth. Thus, recurrent toothaches from numerous cavities are parts of my early childhood recollection. Some classmates called me a mama's boy, not an inaccurate description in that situation. Probably only a few of those other kids' parents could afford to buy condensed milk. Most well-to-do families in town sent their kids to private schools in San Fernando, the capital town of Pampanga.

The male teachers usually wore suits made of white linen, locally called *de hilo*. With an appropriate tie, they looked neat, but it must have been uncomfortable, especially during summer days. Women wore dresses. Tatang often rode a bike to school, and occasionally, I got a free ride at the back-passenger seat; it was uncomfortable because it was just bare metal with no padding. During the rainy season, we used umbrellas or locally made *turong*. This was a wide cone-shaped hat, three or four feet in diameter, made of nipa palm, and it was quite effective as a rain gear except during windy days when it was difficult to keep it in place. So it was not unusual to use a single banana leaf in place of an umbrella or turong. The leaf was effective for the purpose, and it was disposable.

Banana trees were useful in several other ways. Not only did they provide the sweet fruit, but the *puso*, or heart, made a tasty vegetable dish when chopped finely and sautéed with garlic, onions, and vinegar. The leaves were used as umbrellas, as I have just described. Strips made from the dried bark, *tiban*, were used as sturdy twine or rope. Fresh trunks, when joined with strips of bamboo, made a dependable and unsinkable raft that we used during floods to navigate swollen rivers and flooded rice fields. Pieces of the trunk separated from each other were used to shield seedlings planted in a garden. It was also used as plates to serve food.

When going to picnics, *binalot* was a favorite. This was freshly cooked rice wrapped in young banana leaves. Usually, a hard-boiled egg and *adobo*, a combination of chicken and pork marinated in vinegar and soy sauce with garlic and peppers, were embedded in the rice. Fresh tomatoes and *begucan*, or shrimp paste, cooked with pieces of pork, garlic, and a bit of sugar, made for a tasty treat.

Walking to and from school was often terrifying for me because of the many dogs left free to roam the streets by their irresponsible owners. I was attacked more than once but fortunately never bitten, probably because I was just lucky, but I know of many kids who were not so fortunate. Up to now, I have a phobia of dogs.

The houses of Apung Taqui, my maternal grandmother, and Apung Gunda, my paternal grandmother, were both located along Third Street on the way to school. Many times, I stopped by any of them to have a snack, pick some fruits from the yard, or use the toilet.

Bellyaches and diarrhea were common among children my age because sanitation in the whole town was not good. Most houses did not have septic tanks, and toilets were simply outhouses on bamboo stilts, with pigs underneath to take care of the human waste. It was not unusual to see a pig running around the streets with a "golden crown" on its head. No wonder intestinal parasitism was rampant among us who played barefoot most of the time.

In medical school, I learned that *Ascaris lumbricoides*, the most common worm infestation among Filipinos, has the following life cycle: "Human feces contain ova of the worm. They hatch into larvae in the moist ground. Larvae have the capacity to penetrate bare skin, go into the bloodstream, and eventually settle in the intestinal tract, where they mature into adult worms to lay more eggs to complete the cycle. Sometimes the worms end up in the lungs, brain, and liver."

As children, we were fortunate that we only had the intestinal worms that caused a lot of stomachache and probably anemia (low red blood cell count). Periodically Ima would give us *lycopodium oil* by mouth. This killed the worms, but they had to be extruded with a purgative. It was sheer torture to have to go through that routine once or twice a year.

Looking back, I now realize how lucky we were not only to escape any serious complications from this worm infestation, but we also survived its drastic treatment! This is in no way a condemnation of Ima, who was a pharmacist, but it is just a statement of fact; at that time, knowledge and treatments of diseases were meager.

Learning in grade school was easy for me. In most subjects, I had good grades. My lowest grades were in music. I remember Miss GAUDENCIA GARCIA, our music teacher, who got so frustrated and irritated in teaching us how to properly sing Christmas carols. The entire class did very poorly, and I did worse than the others. In arithmetic, now called mathematics, I always came in first. I think it was in grade 4 when our teacher asked several pupils to go to the blackboard in front of the class and write in numerals a number he called out—eleven thousand eleven hundred eleven. I was the only one who figured it out by writing 12,111. It was the first time for me to solve a problem like that, but my teacher was skeptical. He told me that someone must have told me about that number before.

At graduation from grade 6, I came in second, salutatorian, to ADORACION COSIO (Doric), class valedictorian. Doric's father was also a teacher at Mexico Elementary School. They lived along Third Street, not far from the school. She was a dark, pretty girl and very smart. I was attracted to her and always hoped to walk with her going home from school. In January 2006, at the inauguration of the Peczon-David Family Library at the school, she came as an invited guest. In my informal speech formally turning over the library to the school, I mentioned this puppy love I had for her. She was quite surprised but flattered, I think, and the audience got a big laugh out of it.

I was in second grade when the World War II came to the Philippines. During the Japanese occupation, schooling continued. We had special Japanese teachers to teach Niponggo, and I became quite good at it. My ability to read katakana, Japanese characters, was put to good use in our drugstore because I was able to read labels of Japanese medications that were the only ones available until the end of the war.

Games, Toys, and Friends

The whole outdoors was our playground. We went to the rice fields to catch fish, frogs, and *camaro*, a type of cricket that was edible, especially when prepared a la *adobo*. You would think I am exaggerating when I say that the fattest ones were found under dried carabao dung that was usually shaped like a chocolate cake!

Our fascination with insects included the gathering of spiders during the evening when they came out to start spinning their webs. We housed them in matchboxes in which we fashioned individual cells with blades of grass, six cells in most standard-sized matchboxes, *casa fuego*, "house of fire" in Spanish and Kapampangan. Those prized spiders were pitted against those caught by other friends. For the spider fights, we placed two of them front to front on a twelve-inch-long stick, usually made from a dried-up rib of a coconut palm frond. We did not have to get these from the tree itself, for there was none in the inland areas like Pampanga. Instead, we just got the sticks from locally made brooms, *palis ting-ting* in Kapampangan. The stronger and larger spider naturally easily conquered the smaller and weaker fighter. The loser ended up in a silky cocoon spun by the winner, and the owner of that spider got to keep it to be stored in the cell of the winning spider in the matchbox. That provided food for the winning spider, lasting for several days. That was better than watching a cockfight that involved sharp knives and blood!

Bottle caps, *tansan*, were collected and prized. We used them in playing *teching*, a game in which an equal number of bottle caps from each player was placed within a circle drawn on the ground. Using another *tansan*, each player tried to hit as many of them with a single shot. Those that were moved outside the circle became the property of the player.

In summertime, when school was out, we used the many corridors, stairs, and classrooms of St. Joseph's Academy to play "pirates." Following the example of ERROL FLYNN, popular as a swashbuckler in pirate movies, we tied narrow bands of clothing around our heads or necks to look like pirates depicted in those movies. For fencing, we used narrow strips of bamboo with pointed ends and a shield to protect the hand. Eye protection? Never was a thought given to that. As an ophthalmologist, I repaired many injuries from those kinds of toys. Today, I shudder to think about that.

Walking around the streets with arms around each other's shoulders was the norm. There was no sexual identification associated with it. Aimlessly roaming around town, whenever I spotted nails, screws, or any metal pieces on the ground, I picked them up. With these, I constructed a tree house on a huge *saresa* (Jamaican cherry) tree in our yard. I would spend many hours there with friends.

We would gather the *saresa* fruits from the tree. I recall them being about half the size of small grapes, and they were sweet. Many other fruit trees in the town provided us with healthy snacks: *santol*, *camachile* (Manila tamarind), *sampaloc* (tamarind), *caimito* (sugar apple), *siniguelas* (Spanish plum), *dwat* (Java plum), mango, papaya, *bayabas* (guava), *atis* (custard apple), and many others.

Guava trees had other uses. The strong branches made the perfect material for slingshots. We chose appropriately Y-shaped branches and cut them down to size. Strips of rubber, from a discarded inner tube of a tire, attached to opposite holes on a piece of leather taken from an old shoe, made for a sturdy, long-lasting slingshot. Bullets were fashioned from clay that was abundant in the area. Marble-sized rounds, *bedoques*, about half-an-inch in diameter, were first left to dry in the sun. Most often, we used those slingshots to shoot at targets of interest, like old bottles and tin cans, but we also used them on helpless birds for no apparent reason than to show prowess. Looking back, I realize now how cruel and destructive that was.

Guavas also provided a crude antiseptic in the ritual of circumcision. Young leaves of the tree were chewed and kept in the mouth of a young boy about to undergo a rite of passage to adulthood. The circumcision was performed by a local guy with no surgical skill other than having experience in performing this operation earlier on many young boys my age. Again, from the guava tree, an appropriately shaped branch was shaped to look like an anvil that fitted exactly right under the prepuce of the boy's penis. With a sharp razor, he placed the blade just at the right spot, and with a quick blow with a piece of hardwood on the top of the razor blade, the circumcision was done. The boy spat the guava leaf juice from his mouth onto the wound, and bandage was applied. Believe it or not, all that was practiced widely, and I do not know of any serious complications from my friends. Maybe they just did not tell?

Town Fiestas

My buddies enjoyed pulling pranks to annoy people.

During a town fiesta, a lot of barrio folks came into town riding in carabao-drawn carts. Those slow-moving but strong animals were the backbone of rice farming in the area. A farmers' wealth was measured by the number of carabaos he owned. Rice harvests from the nearby and far-flung barrios were brought to the town market in those carts. Often, those beasts of burden relieved themselves in the middle of the street. During the fiestas and holidays, there were a lot of folks on the street milling around gaming tables to try their luck in bringing more money home. Some do manage that, but many more returned to their homes in the barrios with less cash in their pockets.

To make matters worse, many of them became victims of our youthful exuberance. One such devilish prank was the use of firecrackers. We wrapped a firecracker in a waterproof cigarette-pack foil and inserted the fuse in the middle of a cigarette stick that served as a delayed-action fuse. The cigarette was lighted and then planted in the middle of a freshly laid chocolate-shaped carabao dung. We moved away several hundred yards, hiding behind fences, waiting for the explosion. Imagine the surprise and anger this caused the hapless farmers who came to town in their Sunday best, peppered by this smelly chocolate-brown carabao feces all over their clothes! Of course, we, the perpetrators, were never discovered. Laughing with boyish glee, we gave ourselves high fives.

More than once, we pulled that same prank, minus the carabao chocolate cake, of course, inside the church too. We went to the choir loft at the back of the church as the Mass was being celebrated and left this firecracker-cigarette improvised explosive device (IED, used extensively during the Iraq War) somewhere in the back of the choir loft. We then calmly walked out of the church as the Mass was coming to an end. You can say that some Masses ended in an explosive *Ite missa est,* "the Mass is ended" in Latin. Work of the devil? Perhaps!

I mentioned Errol Flynn, the swashbuckler in many pirate-oriented movies. To see these movies, we walked five kilometers from Mexico to San Fernando, where the bedbug-infested movie houses were located. Most of the time, we did this barefoot or wearing wooden shoes. The Peoples Theatre, one of the movie houses there, was located right next door to the Suba Beauty Parlor that was owned and operated by the wife of my uncle Delfin, GLORIA SUBA. Most of the movie house attendants were her customers. They recognized us, and many times we got into the movie house *free.* No extra payment for the bedbugs too!

I displayed youthful exuberance, not just in games or pranks with other playmates, but I also seemed to have this penchant for discovery and inventiveness in everyday things. An example of this was an episode during my early high school years in St. Joseph's Academy. This was the day when my mother confined me to bed in our house because I was sick with whooping cough. When I got better, I started getting bored. This led to a discovery of a small handheld mirror used by my mother to fix her hair in the morning. My room was in the upstairs bedroom, the windows of which were open to the street and plaza below. I started playing with this mirror, reflecting the afternoon sun to the academy building across the plaza, which made a perfect target. I imagined myself as FLASH GORDON using a death ray to shoot at the bad guys in the bell tower and in the many rooms of the academy. I inadvertently or perhaps purposely aimed my death ray gun at the window of the classroom where I would have been in, had I not been sick. I imagined myself sending signals to my allies inside that room by trying Morse code of short and long flashes of light in and out of the room. I was having such a good time that I did not notice the school principal marching to our house and telling my mother what was happening. I did not know that I was disrupting the whole class. I readily owned up to the crime as charged and did not repeat that death ray game again. My mother mildly berated me for this. In fact, both my parents never had to rein me in for my youthful exuberance, and I never made them angry enough to punish me. This trait of adventurism and exploration I have carried on to this day.

There was one time when my father criticized me for not properly securing the swinging doors that barred entrance to our garage where our family jeep was kept. My father assigned me that task that I did each night. One day, he pointed out my carelessness in securing the two barn-door-type swinging-door panels. That evening, I decided to do my best by using the ample length of a metal chain that was used to secure those doors together. I came up with an intricate interwoven link that was difficult to discover where the end of the chain started and where it ended. It was better than an ordinary keyed lock! In the middle of that night, my father woke me up to ask me to go down to the yard with him to unlock the chain. The jeep was needed to transport a member of the family to the hospital in San Fernando for a medical emergency. With a flashlight held by him, I easily unlocked the intricately linked chain. He, or anyone else that night, could not figure out how I was able to secure that chain "lock" without an actual keyed safety lock. My father proudly gave me a nice pat on the head for the job well done. Reflecting on that incident, I bet he was quite embarrassed that I outwitted him and all the other adults that night. Since that episode, I never got another complaint that I was doing a sloppy job.

Helping with Farm Chores

It was not all play and no work. During those early years, the same as it is today, breakfast, lunch, and dinner, required ready-to-cook rice. We did not always have *abias*, Kapampangan for *rice*. Often, we could only get *pale*, which are the unhusked grains harvested from the amber fields of rice plants in the farms. The needed removal of the hard coating of each grain was efficiently done in rice mills, but those were not always in operation. To solve the problem, thus, we resorted to a more primitive but effective way of removing the inedible coating of each grain by placing them in a wooden mortar and repeatedly pounding them with wooden pestles. Mortars were cut out from a one- to two-foot-wide single tree trunk measuring about three to four feet high. The pestles were made from the smaller branches of the tree measuring three to four feet long and three to four inches in diameter. Three people stood in a circle around this mortar, and each one took turns wielding a pestle to repeatedly pound on the grain placed in the open end of the mortar until all the grains were stripped of the hard coating. It was done in a rhythmic, synchronized way so as not to hit the mortar at the same time. It was not just work. It was fun, and it provided exercises to the arms and upper body. There was no need to go to a gym. My sister Zon and I did this, together with our family's favorite factum factotum, CATALINO BONUS, Ima's first cousin.

Another job was helping to extract sugar from raw sugarcane harvested from nearby fields. This happened early during the Japanese occupation when we evacuated from our house in the center of the town to a small barrio, San Miguel, about five kilometers away. The house was shared with members of the extended family: the Hizons, Imang Charing, Cong Carding, Cong Bidong, Atching Anna, Apung Gunda, and others.

There was a primitive but efficient sugarcane mill on the premises. It consisted of two hardwood lumber fashioned into cylinders of similar dimensions, each one three feet long and about a foot in diameter. The two were joined together at the top with cogs so that they could roll against each other as a single unit. One of these cylindrical wooden cylinders was attached to a long bamboo pole that, in turn, was connected to a yoke fitted to a carabao's neck. This all-around-beast of burden went round and round in circles to turn the wheels against each other. Raw sugarcane stalks were fed between the moving wooden cylinders, releasing the sweet juice from the canes. My job was to help catch this sweet nectar in a metal pail and transport it to a nearby large cast-iron cauldron placed over a roaring wood fire. Adults constantly stirred the boiling sugarcane juice until it turned thick and brown. While still hot, it was poured into cuts of bamboo stem with one end of each cut open, the other closed, in the natural nodes found in this most useful species of grass: *Bambusa* spp. The sticky fluid formed into *bagkat* inside the bamboo containers. When cooked correctly, it remained a liquid with the consistency and sweetness of honey but with a darker brown color. The same hot liquid was also poured into coconut half-shells. There, the hot liquid became a hardened cake called *panocha*. This was used as a sweetener in making all sorts of desserts for which Pampango cooking has been well known for.

Pampanga was even then the center of sugarcane plantations in the island of Luzon. There were many commercial sugarcane refineries. Cartloads of canes from various barrios were carried to these sugar centrals. The nearest central to our house was in San Fernando, five kilometers away from Mexico. My friends and I often waited for those slow-moving, carabao-drawn carts filled with freshly harvested canes. We would pull out one stalk each from the back of the cart without the farmer's notice. Gleefully, we would cut and discard the undesirable top end of the cane and start peeling the tough outer skin of the cane with our bare teeth to get to the sweet and juicy part. Eating raw sugarcane like this is *mamangus* in Pampango. I did not know then that if carelessly done, it could cause damage to the teeth enamel in addition to contributing to the formation of cavities.

Milking goats was also a daily routine for my sister Zon and me during the Japanese occupation. Absent the baby formulas that are so common today, this freshly extracted milk from a herd of goats, penned inside a fenced area in front of our house, was boiled and poured into a feeding bottle with a nipple attached. This supplemented the nutritional requirements of baby Ben whose primary source was Ima's mammary glands that were providing increasingly smaller amounts because of aging. In medical school, I learned that goat's milk is a good substitute for human milk because the two resembled each other in many aspects. Lucky for Ben, the goat's milk was better than the condensed milk supplement I got when I was his age.

Speaking of milk, we consumed a lot of carabao's milk that we also purchased from farmers. This milk had a copious amount of fat and protein, as can be expected from a large animal like the trusted farmer's best friend, the carabao. It was usually sold in a standard-size ketchup bottle. For eating, after boiling, it was poured over freshly boiled rice and was usually paired with *tuyo,* a common variety of fish already dried. An even better combination was with charcoal-roasted sweetened and salted thin strips of carabao meat, *pindang damulag.* This delicacy came from butchered older animals that had exceeded their useful life as beasts of burden. It is like beef jerky. The milk made the best kind of flans, *pastillas de leche, tibok-tibok,* and other Pampango delicacies that are still available today.

Another activity was in making *samat.* Apung Taqui prepared this concoction made from the *samat* (betel) leaves for which the bar-rio of Masamat ("has plenty of *samat*"), where my mother was born, got its name. It was made into a roll like a miniature doughnut after a thin layer of lime, *api,* was spread evenly on one side of the leaf. In the middle of the doughnut, a piece of betel nut *luyus* was placed. My role was peeling the fibrous coat around the betel nut with a device called *kalakati,* one blade of which was wide with a sharp cutting edge, and the other just a narrow, sturdy piece of metal contoured like the shape of an average-sized betel nut. The resulting product is called *maman.* My grandmother kept these in a small pouch made from any fabric available.

She, like all the women in town, including my mother, chewed on this betel nut-*samat*-lime combo, turning their saliva almost bloodred in color. The teeth also became tinted with the same color. The juice was not swallowed but later spat out, looking like blood from a tubercular patient. I believe that cocaine was present in small amounts in the betel leaves and nuts. The lime was just a spice. Peruvian Indians, living high up in the Andes, chewed on coca leaves for the same reason. Cocaine, the name of the narcotic, is derived from those leaves. Drug addiction was present (in Pampanga) even then, and it was part of the culture. No laws could be passed to limit that. Eventually, the practice gradually disappeared because of the high rate of cancer of the mouth in those women.

Youthful Business Attempts

I had an interest in making money early on. The earliest I can remember is as a shoeshine boy. With some pieces of pine wood locally called *palo de china,* I made a shoeshine box and filled it with different tins of colored shoe polishes, two brushes (one for black, the other for brown), and some rags. I did not do the actual manual labor. ABELARDO NAVARRO, a classmate at the elementary school, did that. Like a budding entrepreneur, I was the one who solicited business by offering to shine the shabby-looking pairs of shoes of men who came from the barrios to the town plaza during fiesta time on the Fourth of May or during Sundays to attend Mass. I collected the fees and paid Abelardo later. This venture made us some pocket money during the dry season. In the wet rainy season, most men went barefoot, which meant meager earnings. Most people were shoeless anyway even in dry months, and so, we never got to feel rich from this boyish venture.

Renting out comic magazines was a more profitable activity. Nobody else did this, so I had no competition. I had dozens of the popular ones during that time, like SUPERMAN, WONDER WOMAN, TARZAN, DICK TRACY, FLASH GORDON, and many others, including Classic Illustrated editions. I displayed them on a billboard type of stand that I placed in the waiting area in front of our drugstore. In time, most of those got pretty worn out by the many children who enjoyed reading them. I probably got a lot of centavos from that venture, but had I kept those old comic magazines in mint condition, they would probably be worth a small fortune now. I must admit I was *not* a WARREN BUFFET!

At the start of the Japanese occupation, my sister Zon and I gathered the fragrant *sampaguita* (jasmine) and *ylang-ylang* (perfumed tree) blossoms. Strung with thread, we sold those flower necklaces to the Japanese soldiers who were lined up in front of one of the largest houses in town. We did not know then that these soldiers were there buying the services of *comfort women.*

Toward the end of the occupation, I had a thriving business buying and selling cigarettes with Japanese sentry guards. I do not know why those soldiers let me buy their quota of cigarettes because the money used at that time was worthless. I, too, made a mistake of reselling the cigarettes to locals who paid me with the same worthless paper money. I should have bartered them for food or handmade toys!

Ima's drugstore was also a source of income for me, a foreshadowing of things to come. She had patrons who needed insulin shots. She showed me how to administer both subcutaneous and intramuscular injections. She handed me a list of diabetic patients for insulin injections in their houses. My younger brother Ben performed this same service to the patients after I had left for Manila to attend college. He had a bike to make his rounds go faster. A few came to the drugstore to get intravenous injections of calcium gluconate that was a popular medication at that time. It was believed to help tubercular patients. With my knowledge of medicine now, I am certain that any benefit that treatment provided was purely a placebo effect. At least, it did not do any harm. I, on the other hand, benefited from the early training to become an expert in doing intravenous injections even before I became a teenager.

You might say that I was a MR. HYDE, as in the famous novel written by ROBERT LOUIS STEVENSON, but I had a DR. JEKYLL side too. I was an altar boy. With appropriate altar boy attire, I assisted in the celebration of the Roman Catholic Mass and memorized many prayers in Latin. Earlier on, we were always immersed in the ritual of the Catholic faith, with nightly reciting of the rosary, regularly going to confession and receiving communion, and annually celebrating Lent and Christmas.

In the celebration of the weekly Mass on Sundays, I served as an altar boy. At communion time, I was the one who put a small silver platter under the open mouths of pious believers, and I would recite, "*Domine, non sum dignus, ut intres sub tectum meum, sed tantum dic verbo, et sanabitur anima mea*" ("Lord I am not worthy that thou should enter under my roof, but only say the word, and my soul shall be healed"). I said this short prayer for each of the communicants, the number of whom may be in the hundreds on special occasions, as during town fiestas.

I also learned how to fuel a charcoal-fed contraption where incense was placed to produce an aromatic smoke around the altar to give it an air of holiness. This imparted a sense of sacredness in the house of God.

When I went on to premed in UP Diliman, I was one among a small group of altar boys to Father JOHN DELANEY, SJ, who regularly said Mass in the newly constructed circular chapel, the first of its kind, with the altar in the middle rather than in the apse section of the church. I was still a follower of the Roman Catholic faith until I got to medical school when I began questioning the teachings of the Church in the face of abundant scientific information that flooded my daily life. Gradually, I veered away from the religion that I grew up with. Finally, when I was starting to practice ophthalmology in Greenfield, Massachusetts, I became a dyed-in-the-wool atheist.

High School

Most of the elementary school graduates in my class went on to Pampanga High School in San Fernando, the capital of the province. My older sister, Zon, was enrolled at the St. Joseph's Academy High School that was just a few steps away from our house. That was where I enrolled, too, one year behind her. Classes in this high school were small, less than two dozens for each year. Most of my friends were in this school too. First year to third year in high school were easy for me. In all subjects, I was at the top of the class, including religious instructions.

However, more than once, I was sent out of the classroom because I was "too disruptive," according to one teacher. The truth was that I was bored with the classes, which probably prompted me to frequently tease the girl sitting in front of me. However, one episode in English class was an embarrassment for me because I was unable to answer a question from the teacher, ILUMINADA PANLILIO. Luming, as she was often called by relatives and friends, asked the class the meaning of the word "jail-less." Nobody was able to give the answer, including me, who was supposed to be a know-it-all. That was really embarrassing.

It must have been during my freshman year in high school when I learned how to drive a car. That started when the US Armed Forces liberated the Philippines from the Japanese in 1945. My first experience came from some US servicemen who allowed me to drive their army jeeps. I was twelve years old then. This was reinforced by more driving lessons from Uncle Delfin when he got a brand-new Chevy.

In 1949 my sister Zon graduated from high school and went on to enroll at the pharmacy school in UST in Manila. Ima sent me along with her as a companion. As a senior, I enrolled at FEU High School.

Poultry Business

We lived along Tenth Avenue, Grace Park, Caloocan, a suburb of Manila. There, Uncle Ruben and Imang Pacing operated a family-owned poultry farm for our sustenance and expenses. My role in this operation was to feed the thousands of layers that were always clacking for food. At least that was what we thought.

Early each morning, I rode public transportation, usually a jeepney, a converted US Army jeep, to go to the nearest wet market, Blumentritt in Manila, which was about a ten-minute ride from the house. There, I searched and bought the cheapest fish that I could find. A *bayong*, a carryall bag made of woven palm leaves, full of these half-rotten fish, I brought home to Tenth Avenue. Usually, I rode at the back of the jeepney because the odor from those fish was just too offensive to the other passengers.

Back at the poultry farm, I processed these smelly raw fish through a hand-operated meat grinder. The fish I mixed with chopped *kangkong*, water spinach, a cheap but nutritious vegetable. I added and mixed rice bran and old powdered milk, the grinding and mixing all done by my own two hands! The hens obviously loved this.

The chore consumed the whole morning and was finished in time for me to wash up, change clothes and commute to FEU in Manila to attend my senior year classes that started at 1:00 p.m. and ended five hours later. That senior year went by quickly. My grades did not place me at the top of the class but were good enough for me to qualify and be accepted to the UP premed class in Diliman. This was a two-year preparatory school, a requirement to enter medical school. (Even then, UPCM was considered the best medical school in the country, and the best way to get accepted there was through the UP premed course in Diliman,)

In hindsight, I believe that my good academic performance was in large part due to having more time to keep my nose between book covers rather than socializing with friends. Truthfully, I did not have any social life at all. And I made friends with none of the girls in my class. Obviously, who would be interested in being friends with a guy who reeks with the smell of rotting fish, chicken excreta, and with no money to boot? Donna, the future love of my life, unwittingly, was to be the beneficiary of my monk-like existence.

The FEU president Dr. VIDAL TAN handed me my high school diploma in 1950, the first step in the ladder to the kingdom of promise. The same distinguished mathematician was the president of UP in 1957 when I received my college diploma from UPCM. That was the second rung in the ladder. He was one of the two principal sponsors when Donna and I exchanged vows of marriage in 1958. That was the third rung.

The War Years

I was eight years old, a grade 2 pupil at Mexico Elementary School, when in 1941 World War II in the Pacific intruded into our lives. Through the radio and newspapers, Tatang had been following developments happening in Europe and the rest of the world. One Sunday morning, December 7, on the radio, we heard about the bombing of Pearl Harbor, and a few hours later, live sounds of war—airplanes and explosions—coming from the direction of Clark Air Force Base not too far away came to our sleepy little town. From that day, we spent many nights huddled in an air-raid shelter: a hole dug out in our backyard covered with cuts of timber to hold a thin layer of soil cover. It probably could have stopped bullets from small arms fire but not a shell from a cannon or a bomb from an airplane. Tatang had his bird-hunting shotgun by his side, ready to defend his family, as it were; Ima was nursing four-day-old Ben and taking care of the rest of my siblings. Pons was two years old. He frequently cried, protesting the primitive surroundings. All of us were afraid that his cries would alert the enemy, leading to our unimaginable end.

There was a large glass container filled with a boric acid solution and pieces of gauze stored in the dugout. In case of a poison gas attack, all of us were instructed to soak a piece of gauze into that boric acid solution and place it to cover our mouths and noses. Looking at a vantage point now, I am sure that attempt to ward off a toxic gas attack would have been totally useless. In any case, at that time, it gave us a little sense of extra security.

In a short time, Tatang realized that his trusty shotgun, loaded with ammunition intended for bird hunting, was more of a liability than an effective weapon to fight the invaders, who were obviously armed with modern assault rifles, so he wisely stored it hidden somewhere inside the house. I cannot forget the sound of those Japanese rifles. There was an initial short high-pitched sound followed by a louder boom. Civilians who heard this called the guns *pik-bung*, a truly apt description of this weapon.

A lot of soldiers, both American and Filipino, with their vehicles, suddenly appeared at the center of town. We learned later that these troops were part of the retreating forces from the North, those that General DOUGLAS MACARTHUR had ordered to consolidate in Bataan and Corregidor Island. Many of them probably died in battle, and those who surrendered after a brave but futile defense of those two last bastions of Filipino-American military might became unwilling participants in the infamous Death March from Bataan to San Fernando, Pampanga (a distance of forty kilometers).

At Apung Taqui's house along Third Street, Uncle Ruben also dug an air raid shelter in the yard. It was stocked with a lot of canned goods gathered from supplies left by retreating Filipino-American forces that were never completely consumed, surviving the entire three-year duration of the war. At Apung Gunda's house, no such preparation was done.

There were a few civilian casualties in town the day Japanese planes came to drop bombs. One of the victims was EDEN, the oldest sister of my classmate DORIC COSIO. Their house was four houses away from Apung Taqui's abode, probably a distance of no more than three hundred yards. By that time, all military units had left the town for Bataan, and so it was inexplicable why those bombs were dropped on civilian areas. The municipio next door would have been a better target, but it was spared. Otherwise, our house would have suffered collateral damage, probably causing great destruction to the purely wooden structure, not to mention what it could have done to all of us hiding in that bomb shelter only a few feet from that building.

Evacuation

After that bombing, the family decided to leave our house. The municipio was too near for comfort. The distant barrios in the middle of rice fields were considered safer. "Evacuation" became a popular word among the townspeople. It was pronounced *bacuit* in Kapampangan because Pampangueños have no letter *v* in their alphabet. Our family, together with Apung Gunda, Imang Charing, Cong Carding, Cong Bidong, and Atching Aning, all went to Barrio San Miguel, about two kilometers away from the town center. We stayed in a large house built entirely of bamboo. There was no indoor plumbing, but there was a deep well nearby where water was fetched in large cans, formerly containing kerosene, and transferred to earthen jars indoors. There was an outhouse in the backyard.

Apung Taqui and her family moved to Masamat, which was the barrio where Ima was born. Most of her relatives lived there. It was about two kilometers equidistant from San Miguel and the center of town.

In the middle of a cane field in that bamboo house in San Miguel, food was in ample supply. I participated in the harvesting of sugarcane and converting it to usable sugar. There was enough rice. Fresh eggs were provided by free-roaming chickens. Plenty of fish were caught from the rivers and rice fields. Pigs were plentiful. Fruits and vegetables, of course, were abundant and varied. I also saw farmers make rope out of narrow strips of bamboo that were twisted together to make extraordinarily strong, albeit stiff, rope. I even learned how to join ends of those ropes by weaving them into each other rather than just by tying them into knots.

Rumors were thick in the air about the return of many American forces who were to repulse the enemy. We gleefully and innocently believed that a special army of African American soldiers, who had excellent night vision, it was claimed, had landed somewhere and were not too far away to save all of us.

It was not clear to me how the decision was made to return to our house in the center of town, but we did. I guess we were resigned to the idea that Uncle Sam's forces were not coming to save us at that time, but we clung to the promise of General Douglas MacArthur, "I shall return," after the Fall of Bataan and Corregidor. It was accepted that the Japanese Imperial Forces had the upper hand at this point, and the family elders thought that we might as well make the most of it. By that time, the town was completely occupied by a company of Japanese cavalry whose horses were so much larger than the local ponies. The municipio was occupied by the troops as their head-quarters, and our house next door was where the commander of the unit, along with his aide, was billeted. Captain Sakuma and his sec-ond-in-command, Lieutenant Kamatso, took over the upper floor of our house while my parents and our maids became part-time ser-vants to these officers.

It was interesting to observe how the Japanese bathe themselves. A large empty metal barrel used to store gasoline was converted into a hot water tub. The lid was, of course, cut off. Water filled it almost to the brim. It was placed over a wood-fed stove. The officers were the first to enjoy the steaming hot bath. After them came the other soldiers, probably in the order of military rank. All of this was done in the yard between our house and the municipio. (Much later in life, with Donna, I enjoyed this same exquisite Japanese bathing custom in famous onsen ryokan hot-spring inns around the base of Mt. Fuji in the company of our best friends, TAISUKE and KAZUMI KUBOYAMA.)

The first year of the Japanese occupation was not too oppres-sive, thanks in part to the lack of opposition to the occupation and to the benevolence of the captain. A West Point graduate, he was fluent in English. He read books to Zon, Alma, and me. He showed us pictures of his family and children. I had the impression that he was against the war with America but had no choice except to obey his emperor. The lieutenant was a samurai type, stricter, more militaris-tic, and obviously imbued with the *bushido* code of ethics. I remember making errands for them, like buying freshly baked *bibingka* made of hand-ground rice (*galapung*), eggs, and coconut milk. This *galapung* was placed in a plate-size earthenware lined with banana leaves and cooked over red-hot wood charcoal placed below and above it. It was a local delicacy that the Japanese officers savored.

Each morning, people were required to go to the center of town facing east to greet the Japanese emperor (his image) and to sing a patriotic march. Up to now, I can still remember part of one song—*"Miyo tokai no sora akete, kyokujitsu takaku kagayakeba"* and ending in *"Waga Nipon no hokori nare."* The ending is translated to "what is happening in my country" in English. It is probably akin to US Marines singing, "From the Halls of Montezuma to the shores of Tripoli." There was *radiotaiso*, calisthenics, which was vigorously practiced by the Japanese soldiers themselves. Civilians were encouraged to do the same. There was always an armed guard near the front of our house to provide security for the officers inside. People passing by were required to stop and bow to the guard. Those who did not follow this procedure were often stopped and given a sharp slap on the face.

The Bataan Death March

I did not realize it at the time, but the Bataan Death March passed near our town some five kilometers away in the provincial capital of San Fernando. Several Filipino soldiers were clandestinely saved from the marching ranks, such as when the guard was not looking. One of them was my godfather, a medical officer in the Philippine Army. Dr. MANUEL PANLILIO was an alumnus of UPCM, the same school where I graduated from later. He was married to another physician, Dr. HERMINIA BASA, who later became a distinguished obstetrician and who wrote a textbook in obstetrics with my classmate FE PALO-GARCIA. Many years later, both Panlilios became my patients for cataract extractions and implantation of intraocular lenses. My godfather did not want to talk much about his experience in that war when I tried to ask him what it was like to be in Bataan and participate in the Death March. Perhaps it was too horrible for him to try to remember. Tatang and Ima always had him as a visitor whenever he was in town. I believe that it was partly because of him that my parents wanted me to be a medical doctor.

The Japanese ordered the early opening of schools, and so there was just a brief interruption of our education. In grade 3 and grade 4, at Mexico Elementary School, I learned to read and write *Niponggo*. This ability to read some Japanese was extremely helpful to my mother in her drugstore. When Tatang and I went to Manila to buy supplies for the business, this skill was put to good use in the reading of descriptions and instructions before the buying of Japanese-made medicines that made up the bulk of available medications, especially in the second and third years of the occupation.

Unlike other areas in the Philippines, where an awful number of atrocities were committed, our town mercifully suffered very few of those. However, when the invading troops were replaced by occupation forces, the attitude of the Japanese soldiers to civilians changed. They became crueler to the population because there was a rising guerrilla activity against the invaders.

One terrifying day during the entire Japanese occupation sticks in my mind. To ferret out guerrillas, the Japanese ordered all adult males in town, Tatang and other adult males in our family included, to get inside the fenced St. Joseph's Academy campus, located just across the town plaza from our house. One by one, in single file, the men were ordered to get out of that campus, cross the plaza and stand in front of a man seated at the main entrance to the municipio. This man who was suspected of being a guerrilla had been previously tortured in the municipio jail. For several days and nights, we heard the agonizing cries and groaning of this hapless individual.

Now, on this terrifying day, he was made to sit on a chair with a hood over his face showing only his eyes through two small holes. If he made a certain prearranged sign to the guards that indicated that the man in front of him was a guerrilla, it was tantamount to a death sentence. That suspected guerrilla was immediately taken to a local cemetery where he was summarily executed after he was forced to dig his own grave.

There were no trials, and no other witnesses were called to verify the verdict of this one tortured soul! Fortunately, Tatang was not among those defenseless victims who numbered about half a dozen. Almost miraculously, this tortured man, later identified as ANACLETO

BELTRAN, survived the war. His son later became one of my best basketball buddies. I wonder if those who were pointed out as guerrillas by him were indeed guilty as charged. It is not too far-fetched to say that this man did not know who the real guerillas were, but he had to make quick decisions just to save his own skin. Is it possible that he pointed out some men he just did not like? Significantly, no retaliation was made to him or any member of his family for the rest of the occupation and in peacetime.

Other terrifying events happened on a few other occasions. Guerilla forces raided the town one night and fired multiple shots at the Japanese soldiers occupying the municipio next door. With our house not more than a few meters from that fortified building, a few wayward bullets hit our house. The first time this happened, we were totally unprepared. We just cuddled in the bedroom farthest away from the front of the house and prayed. After the first guerrilla attack, Tatang hired laborers to erect a four-foot-high wall made with large pieces of adobe stones taken from the bodega ruins next door to cover the entire front of the drugstore. In subsequent guerrilla attacks, we quickly ran downstairs to hide behind that fortification. It felt a bit safer, but it was still scary.

In the more peaceful time that followed, I traded with many Japanese sentries to buy and sell food and cigarettes. It made me a good profit in Japanese-issued currency papers that were almost worthless. I described this activity in an earlier chapter dealing with my early years as a budding entrepreneur. I will also briefly mention here my sister Zon, and I sold fragrant *sampaguita* (jasmine) and *ylang-ylang* (perfumed tree) necklaces to Japanese soldiers who visited the local "comfort house" to satisfy masculine desires. Perhaps the availability of comfort women in town was the principal reason no rapes occurred, and therefore, none reported on civilians.

General Douglas MacArthur Returns

Liberation from the Japanese invaders was becoming more evident in 1944 when, first one airplane, then swarms of US naval air-

planes started to appear in the skies. Our town was close to Clark
Air Force Base, built and formerly used by the Americans and now
occupied by the Japanese. By this time, Japanese soldiers in town
were reduced to a small force of no more than a platoon. Perhaps
there were a dozen soldiers. The rest had left, probably sent with the
large force of reinforcements to repel the returning Yanks in Leyte.
The municipio was abandoned, and the few remaining soldiers fortified themselves in a smaller house, made mostly of stone, along the
second street farther away from the center of the town.

My friends and I watched aerial dogfights that almost always
resulted in Japanese planes being shot down. One of my playmates
was hit by a stray bullet. He did not survive the wound. There was one
aircraft that went down in the rice field not too far from our house.
Curious, I ran with many townsfolks to the crash site to find that it
was a US plane. The dead pilot was a young blond man. Someone
took his dog tag, and this was attached to a marker where his body
was buried right next to his plane. His remains were later dug up by
US occupation forces, Mortuary Affairs Branch. Presumably, he was
buried with all other American casualties of this war in the American
cemetery just outside Manila.

All contents and parts of the plane that could be used were
harvested. Guerrillas took the machine guns and ammunition. The
silk parachute was divided among many to make into clothes. The
K-rations were eaten on the spot. It was my first taste of cheddar
cheese from a tin can. All of the metal from the aluminum-made
plane was taken away and melted to be converted to pots and pans.
Fuel, remaining in the intact tanks, was also taken to be used in
lamps.

The Clark Air Force Base was known as one place where kamikaze suicide pilots flew their bomb-laden planes on their final one-
way journey to try to sink as many US naval ships during the battle
for Leyte. These suicide planes inflicted more damage to the US Navy
than the Japanese Imperial Navy did in the Battle of Leyte Gulf. It is
entirely possible that I saw some of these planes as they flew out of the
base that was only thirty-three kilometers from our town. American
planes, identified with stars and stripes, came in larger numbers in

the following days and weeks. With information we got from people who had access to short wave radios, we soon became familiar with their names: North American Aviation P-51 *Mustang*, Republic P-47 *Thunderbolt*, and *Lockheed* P-38 twin-bodied fighter-bombers. Planes marked with the Rising Sun started to show less in number, and in a few weeks, they completely disappeared from the skies over our town. Soon American ground troops started to arrive.

The sign that our town had finally been liberated was the arrival of a single jeep armed with a Browning M2 .50-caliber machine gun manned by a lieutenant and his driver. No shots were fired. That was one of the most joyous days of my life and of members of the family and all other inhabitants of the town. The center of the town soon became crowded with people who surrounded the two US soldiers. We lustily sang "God Bless America" to them. General Douglas MacArthur's promise, "I shall return," had been fulfilled!

The local Japanese garrison was abandoned. The Japanese soldiers scattered to the countryside, but they were soon hunted down by guerrillas. Later in the days and weeks that followed, we saw men carrying sacks that contained heads of these hapless soldiers. They were placed in the front yard of the ancestral house of Manuel Panlilio, my godfather, who survived the Bataan Death March. It was just a coincidence that the house was temporarily used by the guerrillas. Such is the cruelty of war.

Tatang and Ima became friendly with many American servicemen. I remember a Captain RALPH GANNING, Lieutenant NORTON, and a sergeant who regaled me of stories from his hometown of Omaha, Nebraska. Two American WACS spent a night in our house. They were probably nurses assigned to a field hospital erected somewhere in San Fernando. Ralph exchanged several letters with my parents after the war. The lieutenant had a photo taken with my entire family in front of the elementary school. That is the only family portrait in our possession. The sergeant from Omaha supplied me with chocolates and other goodies in exchange for my cleaning his jeep. My first unofficial driving lesson was from an inebriated Yankee soldier.

From the radio and newspapers, we learned of the dropping of atomic bombs, the Little Boy on Hiroshima on August 6 and the Fat Man on Nagasaki on August 9, 1945 (Wikipedia). Less than a month later, September 2, on the USS battleship *Missouri*, General MacArthur and his aides accepted the formal surrender of Japan to the Allies.

Pursuing a Career in Medicine

After graduating from FEU High School in Manila in 1950, I applied for admission to the premed program at UP Diliman, located in Quezon City. With good grades from St. Joseph's Academy and FEU, there was no problem in getting accepted.

During my first year at premed, I lived in a dormitory at the UP Diliman campus. The "dorm" was not a dormitory in the strict sense but was the private residence of the ROTC (Reserve Officers Training Corps) commandant. It was a donated US Army metal Quonset hut located in Area 5. I shared a room with several other students like me who brought their own beds. Mine was a surplus US Army folding canvas cot. I do not remember how much the bed space and three meals cost, but it must *not* have been cheap enough for Ima to easily afford because, in the second year, I was already living outside the campus, moving to our house on Tenth Avenue, Grace Park, Caloocan to reduce the expenses. That was not much of a sacrifice for me, and it did not affect my grades.

We were the first group of students who had classrooms in the newly built Liberal Arts Building, and I became acquainted with many different people my age who came from all over the Philippines. Some freshmen chose individual classes with specific instructors in mind, but I opted for a block schedule. These were recommended classes for those enrolled in the premedical course. Many freshmen in this same block I chose later became classmates in medical school proper and became my friends. Among them were MUTYA SAN AGUSTIN,

Lauretta Cillan, Sylvia Roa, Elsa Ramirez, Butch Regala, and Wilfredo Yutuc. Some did not go on to medical school and made it well in other fields. Among these was Roger Austria, who became a psychologist and now lives in Wisconsin.

The premed program was heavy in mathematics and science subjects, but there were also subjects in the arts, like English, Latin, and another foreign language. I did well in English but just barely got by in Latin, a required subject, and in Spanish, an optional one to complete foreign language requirements. Now that I am older and wiser, I wish I had placed more effort into learning Spanish. As a practicing ophthalmologist in Massachusetts, I learned a few Polish words and phrases that were very useful in taking care of many Polish people in Franklin County. I now realize how important it is to be able to speak other languages.

Mrs. Benitez was the name of my English teacher. She gave me a grade of 1 (Excellent) in the course because I made an oral presentation of the big bang theory in class that really impressed her.

Physics, chemistry, mathematics, logic, botany, and zoology were all easy subjects for me, and I got mostly 1 or 1.5 grades (3 was Passing, 4 Probation, and 5 Failure; 4 and 5 are entered on the record with red ink). I remember Professor Tenmatay in Chemistry fondly. I became his favorite when he asked the class how to light a candle inside a sealed glass bottle. I was the only one with the correct answer, which was to use a magnifying lens to focus the sun's rays on the wick.

In zoology, we had a very interesting European professor. He was among many white Russian Jews who were admitted as refugees from the Nazis by President Manuel Quezon. He was among the first to recognize the coelacanth fish as a prehistoric animal found in the deep trenches of the Philippine archipelago. He made us dissect and learn the anatomy of a shark and a cat. Another member of that group of Jewish refugees was a professor in pediatrics, Dr. Eugene Stransky, an Austrian, when I entered medical school.

Most of our classes were in the new and modern Liberal Arts Building, but a few were in old US Army Quonset huts, which were extremely hot during summer and even worse during the rainy months because rain made so much noise on the metal shell that normal conversation could not be carried out. We could not hear the lecturer and vice versa; he or she could not hear any of the students who asked a question or was answering one.

In addition to the academic subjects, we had to take a physical education (PE) class and participate in an ROTC class. To this day, I have no idea why we had to participate in ROTC to complete the requirements for admittance to medical school, but we had to do it. Two sets of uniforms were required, khaki for parade purposes and fatigue for maneuvers, but we never had to do one of the latter. Mostly, we were taught how to stand rigidly at attention, march in a straight line in matching moves, and make crisp right or left turns while carrying a wooden rifle in preparation for the parade at the Luneta in Manila during the Independence Day celebration that was held on the Fourth of July at that time. Those who chose the artillery battalion got a chance to fire blank cannon shells. Students enrolled at the UP College of Arts and Music filled the ranks of the marching band.

The prettiest coeds were selected to be corps sponsors. One was TERESITA ABUEVA, a beautiful coed who lived in the area where my dorm was, and I used to walk just behind her to watch her well-shaped legs and hips swaying, like most nubile teenagers do. I never had a chance to talk to her, and even if I did, I may have been so nervous and would not have known what to say to her. Later in life, I had interactions with her older brother, JOSE ABUEVA, who became president of UP. He visited Boston on a fundraising tour, and I was one of the hosts assigned to help in his mission. I was already quite successful in my practice in Greenfield at that time and knew many UP alumni in the area. Dutifully, I introduced him to these people by hosting a dinner in a famous restaurant in Boston. A couple of years later, during one of my regular visits to the Philippines, I personally asked for his presence to grace the inauguration of the MIYAKE EYE OPERATING ROOM at the PGH Eye Department, which Dr. FELIPE TOLENTINO and I helped to create. He flatly refused without giving me a reason.

PE included swimming. To me that was a huge problem because of my inherent fear of drowning. Behind our house in Mexico,

Pampanga was a branch of the Pampanga River that often overflowed its bank during the rainy season. All my friends learned how to swim there. One drowned. That left a lasting phobia of swimming for me. For graduation from premed, each student was required to swim two laps across the Olympic-size swimming pool. Try as I might, I could not do it, but I was saved by my best friend WILFREDO YUTUC during the final PE examination. When my name was called, Willy jumped into the pool! The instructor did not bother to look closely. Willy and I had the same build and same haircut and were both Pampangueños. He was an excellent swimmer. That took care of that pesky requirement. Up to the present, I cannot fathom the reason to require medical students to be able to swim or to be trained in ROTC to become physicians. The Hippocratic oath does not include anything remotely related to those provisions.

To a limited extent, I helped Uncle Ruben build a house right beside the main house in Grace Park. He used most of the lumber from the poultry house after that family business was abandoned. I helped in cleaning that lumber to make it suitable to be used in the house he was building. Much of the lumber had been coated with dried-up chicken droppings. Again, the ever-ready free labor force of Bapang Cati, Cousin Willy, and I were tasked with removing all that chicken excreta on the lumber.

Uncle Ruben asked me to get copies of his transcript of records as a premed student in UP. Those records were a prerequisite for admission to the FEU School of Journalism. Dutifully, I went to the administrative building and filed the forms needed to get his records. When I returned the following day to get them, the clerk cheekily said, "Did you know that Ruben T. David is a communist?" I was a bit bewildered, but upon looking at the transcript, her attempt at making a joke became clear to me: All the grades were in red ink (4 for Probation, 5 for Failure)!

Obviously, Uncle Ruben was not meant to be an MD because that was not where his talent was directed at. He had been coerced by his sister, who was my mother, to take up medicine because of her intense desire to have a doctor attending to Farmacia A. David. She could not wait for me to come to the scene. Uncle Ruben told me that the same tactic was used on his older brothers, Victor and Delfin, who both tried but failed. At the FEU School of Journalism, admission officials wisely ignored Uncle Ruben's failing grades in premed. He quickly proved that they made the right decision. For me, even as a young boy, I knew I was headed for a medical career because of my early exposure to medical practice, starting with giving ordinary intramuscular injections and quickly advancing to learning administration of infusions given intravenously. To be truthful, I must confess to my initial consideration to go into Engineering because of my natural curiosity about how things work. To Ima, I give full credit for steering me to the right path that led to an unbelievably successful and satisfying career in ophthalmology that I can describe as follows.

One, I was a pioneer in a technology in ophthalmology that is now practiced worldwide, introducing intraocular lens implantation in the eye during cataract surgery. *Two*, I gained the respect of my colleagues in the US and Philippine ophthalmology field. *Three*, I enabled the merger of two hospitals in Massachusetts, where everybody else had failed to convince the two hospitals to combine operations. *Four*, I became a very popular ophthalmologist in my country and in the US.

In that same tiny house, built by Uncle Ruben, I took Donna to see where I lived when I was in the senior year of medical school. Seeing how meager our family resources were and how honest I was in *not* covering it up, I captivated and won my future wife's admiration. The rest is history, ours!

From Grace Park, Caloocan, I commuted to my classes in Diliman, Quezon City, by bus, just like I used to do during my senior year in high school at FEU. There was not much traffic, and the commute rarely went more than fifteen minutes. It cost ten centavos each way. My other expense was for lunch that I usually took at a place in Diliman called Little Quiapo, so named because there were many small stores and eating places there, just like in Manila's famous Quiapo District. Sometimes when I had a little more money, I ate at the home economics cafeteria just behind the Liberal Arts Building, where the food was fancier but cost several centavos more. That was also a place to ogle at pretty coeds who enjoyed being noticed by the boys anyway.

I remember many times when I developed diarrhea after a meal, whether I ate it in Little Quiapo, at the home economics cafeteria, or any other restaurant I dined in. I was lactose intolerant then, as I still am, a condition I did not recognize at that time.

Religion still played an important part in my life then, principally because of a Jesuit priest named JOHN DELANEY, who was the UP chaplain. He was extremely persuasive in the way he presented Catholicism to the congregation in his homilies. He explained the origin of many of the religious practices in the offering of the Mass. For example, he said that the round host, believed by the faithful to represent the body of Christ used during the sacrifice section of the Mass, represented a coin so that the congregation in olden times would not forget that their contributions were being used by the church in a meaningful way.

Many students went to his daily celebration of the Mass, and I was among them. I even served as an altar boy. After the end of the two-year premed course, I prayed every day that I would be accepted to UP Medical School. It was unthinkable for me to have to attend a medical school other than UP, the premier medical school of the country then and even to this day. Not to mention that I was acutely aware that the tuition in the state-owned UP Medical School was much lower than that in the private universities. I could not bear the shame of placing more financial burden on Ima if I were not accepted at UP.

In the US, there was a doctor who lived in Dove Canyon, where Donna and I retired, who regaled our golfing friends with the declaration that bright medical students from rich families enrolled at UST where he graduated from and that bright students coming from families with limited means went to UP. He was correct!

At the end of the two-year premed, I was on vacation in our hometown. A family friend, a nurse working at PGH, visited our house and informed Ima and me that she saw my name included in a list of students admitted to the freshman year of UPCM. My prayers had been answered!

Laying the Foundation
of Public Service

One hundred of us were in the freshman class of 1952. Most came from the premed preparatory program of UP Diliman. There were a few from Silliman University and Ateneo de Manila. A lone American, ROBERT HENDRICKS, came from across the Pacific Ocean to join the class. Eighty-six graduated in 1957, with a failing rate of 14 percent.

A class in anatomy was the first lecture we had as freshmen. Professor MARCIANO LIMSON, who looked so menacing what with a Bell's palsy on one side of the face, opened the class very dramatically by calling on one bewildered freshman, POLIENO CESPON, asking him to describe the topography of the female breast. When Cespon failed to answer in time, the professor said, "Have you never seen a female breast before?" That was an indication to me that there was a lot to learn.

In particular, it indicated that all of us had to be prepared to know as much as possible about the subject matter at hand to avoid embarrassment in case your name was called to answer a question from any of the professors. For me, this was a high hurdle to jump because I did not have any textbooks in any of the subjects, so it became a challenge. It spurred me to learn as much as I could by going to the library as often as possible, borrowing from classmates willing to loan their textbooks to me, and taking copious notes during lectures. This was my situation during the entire four years of undergraduate education in medical school. Our family income was thinly spread out to me and four other siblings who were attending either high school or college. There was barely enough for each one of us. Despite this shortcoming, I kept up with the rest of the class, making good scores in all examinations. Never was there an examination that I did not pass. Most of the time, I scored in the 75th percentile of the class. For this, I thank my parents for the genes that they endowed me with.

Learning everything about human anatomy was not just by listening to lectures in classes by professors and instructors, but it was also hands-on or actual dissection of human cadavers. Four students, determined by family name in alphabetical order, were assigned to a single cadaver. In my group were CONSTANTE DE PADUA, FE PALO, and LUZ POLICAR. This group stayed together throughout the four years, including the third and fourth years that were mostly clinical work.

(I will digress a little bit to mention that Fe Palo and I became good friends. Her mom was also a pharmacist who graduated with my mom in the second class of UP School of Pharmacy in 1928. Later in her professional life, Fe became a professor and head of the PGH Department of Obstetrics. She was coeditor of the *Philippine Textbook of Physiologic and Pathologic Obstetrics*, with my godmother, Dr. HERMINIA BASA-PANLILIO. Fe was the attending obstetrician when my daughter Lisa was born on September 19, 1965.)

Classmates who came from outside Manila stayed in boarding houses near the UP Manila campus. I stayed at our 318 Tenth Avenue, Grace Park, Caloocan, house. A classmate, NICHOLAS VELARDE, lived nearby on Eighth Avenue. We often commuted to and from school together, played tennis together, and became close friends. Exposed to many hours in the Anatomy Department full of cadavers preserved in formaldehyde, the odor stuck to our clothes. It was not strange to notice fellow passengers in jeepneys who gave us disapproving stares, probably wondering why we smelled that way. If they had known that often I carried pieces of preserved organs in my knapsack to study at home, including a whole human skull, they would have freaked out. During that time, I lost my appetite for eating meat. (But I got over it in due time.)

At home, I carved out a tiny sanctuary on the upper floor of our Grace Park house, enough to accommodate my canvas army cot and a reading lampstand, which I fashioned out of pieces of lumber and plywood to give me some privacy. Personal possessions were stored under the cot inside a box. On my cot, I read everything I needed to learn from borrowed textbooks and reviewed my meticulously taken notes from lectures. Due to the discipline that I devoted to studying beforehand, it was not necessary to "cram" for most examinations.

By sophomore year, all of us were required to wear a traditional all-white uniform. At this time, we no longer smelled like formalin-preserved cadavers that we had to dissect and examine in the freshman year. Riding in jeepneys, we still received stares from passengers, especially from the young females, but this time it was most likely because of the white uniform that identified us as future doctors! In the junior year, we started hanging stethoscopes around our necks as we made rounds in the medical/surgical wards with seniors, interns, residents, and consultants. We displayed them when outside the hospital too. Of course, we liked to advertise our status as medical students to the whole world. The admiring stares from young and pretty females were unmistakable. We basked in the glory of joining the ranks of doctors! It would have been easy to make dates with many available females, but I only had eyes for a student nurse whom I had met at the PGH medical wards. Furthermore, I did not have any money to go on dates!

Life as a medical student was not limited to just studying all the basic and clinical aspects of how to be a physician. There was also a social life that invited itself to be explored. Up to this point, my social life was limited to a small circle of friends in the sleepy little town of Mexico, Pampanga. In Grace Park, Caloocan, it was mostly work in the family poultry business and studying to graduate from high school and on to UP Diliman for the premed course. I had never had any regular girlfriend, although I was friendly with at least one, HILARIA MERCADO. She was a pharmacy student enrolled in UST. Part of summer, she apprenticed at Farmacia A. David. It became obvious to me later that she was attracted to me, but I did not take advantage of it. We attended a few informal dances. That was all.

Joining a fraternity was a big deal. Upperclassmen, belonging to two competing fraternities, were actively recruiting prospective plebes. After gathering background information, I decided to join the Phi Kappa Mu Fraternity. This was mainly the result of the advice I received from a cousin, QUIRINO DIZON, who was two years ahead of me and a member of that fraternity. At that time, he was courting my older sister, Corazon. We were second cousins, but that did not deter him. He promised to give me "protection" during the hazing process that was known to be brutal.

He kept his word. Delivering flowers to girl fiends of upperclassmen, shining their shoes, and enduring occasional physical punishment were all I needed to be accepted to join the ranks of Phi brods (brothers)! Some in my group got harsher treatments.

There was some advantage of becoming a fraternity member. We helped each other study better. Hanging around each other gave me a view into their coping world. One fraternity brother, VIRGILIO VELASCO, introduced me to the future love of my life, DONNA I. VILLAFLOR, a student nurse. Another brod, RUSTICO TONGCO, had a four-door Chevrolet sedan. He was generous in sharing this chauffeur-driven car with us.

Another experience etched in my mind was attending the Annual Medical Ball held at Manila Hotel on January 14, 1956. Brod ANATOLIO CRUZ and his date and Donna and I were a foursome riding in a Philippine Armed Forces jeep that his dad, who was an active officer in Philippine Armed Forces, allowed him to use for the event.

There were unpleasant incidents, however, that bothered me as a fraternity man. It was the tendency of upperclassmen to use severe physical pain in hazing incoming freshman candidates. I did not believe and refused to participate in this activity. Later in life, I became even more critical of this behavior, such that I advised my son, Walter, and grandson, Patrick, *not* to consider joining any college fraternities. Neither of them did. Periodically, I read of deaths resulting from brutal hazing. I consider this a type of gang culture.

Later in my professional career, I found pride in being a member of a fraternity that tried to give back to the alma mater. I was among the first frat members to contribute $5,000 to build a Phi House dormitory, which was the brainchild of Brod IMAN LAT. It was the first and the only existing dormitory on the UP-PGH campus.

Many classmates regularly visited the UP Diliman campus. This was usually during Christmastime when we participated in the Annual Lantern Parade. Arbor Day was another special event. Volunteers came to plant trees. At present, the UP Diliman campus boasts of many large acacia trees that provide much-needed shade and ambiance to UP Diliman people and visitors. Some of these trees were probably products of our volunteer efforts.

MUTYA SAN AGUSTIN and I had a special friendship that remains strong up to the present. She married classmate Virgilio Velasco, who, I mentioned earlier, was the brod who introduced me to Donna. Teasing Mutya often, I was guilty of. There was nothing romantic going on between us, but many classmates concluded otherwise. Once I asked her to shorten my white pants for me to use in tennis. She did, and her mother wondered why. (Mutya went on to become a professor of pediatrics, clinical epidemiology, and family and social medicine at Einstein, where she established the primary care residency program in pediatrics and internal medicine at Montefiore Medical Center and North Central Bronx Hospital, both in New York City.)

Sports continued to be a part of my college years. Tennis was my favorite. Within the main UPCM campus, there was a tennis court. In front of it was a small cafeteria and recreation place with two bowling alleys using duckpins and smaller bowling balls. I was good at tennis, not so at bowling. A second tennis court was in the PGH (Pandora Tennis Club) compound, right at the back of Nurses Home. It was mostly reserved for residents and faculty members. I began playing there during internship and residency not only to enjoy the game but also to impress a certain student nurse who I knew was watching. I enjoyed playing for her attention.

In the fourth year, we were called CLINICAL CLERKS. This year was a prelude to becoming INTERNS one year later. We took care of patients who came almost in endless queues to the Outpatient Department. There I learned how to perform simple surgical procedures. Examples include removal of ingrown toenails, excision of lumps in the breast, circumcisions, and repair of simple lacerations. In the wards, we helped interns take care of more seriously ill patients. Taking case histories was a skill we needed to master. Simple laboratory tests, like blood counts, urinalysis, and fecalysis (examination of stools) we also performed. In addition, we rotated to different specialty hospitals around Metro Manila, like National Orthopedic Hospital (now known as Philippine Orthopedic Center) specializing in the skeletal system, San Lazaro Hospital for infectious diseases, Philippine Tuberculosis Hospital (that dreadful infectious disease was very common then, as it is today), and Philippine Psychiatric Hospital. Medical students from the other medical schools (there were only two others aside from the University of the Philippines at that time: the University of Santo Tomas and Manila Central University) rotated in the same hospitals.

I remember, with some pride, a group class lecture in one of those hospital rotations. There was a senior consultant who gave a lecture on neuroscience. At the end of his lecture, he asked the class if there were any questions. Nobody raised a hand. "All right," he said, "I'll ask a question. Why is the eye regarded as a window into the mind? I'll pay five pesos for a good answer." Nobody raised a hand either. But five pesos was a good amount at that time. And I knew there was a female student from UST who was there. She came from a rich family from our hometown, and I must confess that I had an attraction to her, but I was too timid to become close to her even though she was friendly. Boldly, to impress her, I raised my hand and gave this answer, "From an embryologic standpoint, the eye is derived from an outpouching from the primitive forebrain. The retina and optic nerve come directly from this brain tissue. Therefore, we can conclude that looking inside the eye is like looking directly into the brain." That answer impressed the consultant, who promptly pulled out a five-peso bill and handed it to me. That made me so proud. I am sure that the female medical student from my hometown was impressed too!

One classmate, FELIPE TOLENTINO, found his future wife, FLORA LIMCAOCO, during his rotation at San Lazaro Hospital.

Internship was the fifth year as a medical student. We were not licensed yet, but we took on the duties of full-fledged physicians. Interns were housed in special dormitories. We were taking twenty-four-hour rotations when on duty spending long sleepless nights and days assisting in major surgical procedures, delivering babies, treating minor and major injuries in the Emergency Room, taking full responsibility for treating serious medical cases, and giving intensive care to postoperative cases. There was one instance where I missed a free meal at the dining room, and I did not have enough funds to buy food elsewhere. To prevent hypoglycemia (low blood sugar), I resorted to gulping small bottled samples of cough syrup that I knew contained a lot of sugar.

Other assignments were considered a lark. Ambulance duty was one. The only responsibility was to determine whether a patient had a life-threatening condition that warranted a ride in the ambulance to the hospital. Another easy rotation was the inspection of restaurants for public health purposes. We were assigned restaurants around the city to inspect for unhygienic conditions. I do not know if this practice was of any value, but we got nice free meals whenever we certified a restaurant. Gratitude? Of course, it was. Corruption? Maybe.

Christmas celebrations in the Philippines start in September. Medical and nursing students both prepared for a Christmas show in December. There were musical and dancing numbers that had to be choreographed and practiced by talented members of each class for a much-anticipated Christmas Eve show. Medical and surgical wards were decorated. We practiced Christmas carols. Friendly and hospitable professors invited us to visit their houses for caroling. For me, it was my first exposure to imported food I had never tasted before: Italian salami, Spanish ham, and Swiss cheese. The huge and spacious houses were indeed each a revelation to me.

To one of these Christmas programs, I invited my grandmother, Apung Taqui. I remember her coming to PGH in a traditional Maria Clara outfit, complete with butterfly sleeves. She was accompanied by my sister Alma. They traveled from our house along Tenth Avenue, Grace Park, Caloocan. Undoubtedly, they took public transportation. Automobiles were way beyond our financial resources at that time. That was the first time that I introduced Donna to two members of my family. Alma later told me that both she and Apung Taqui gave Donna high marks of approval.

Internship at PGH was an arduous task, often going without sleep for twenty-four hours or more. The hospital was always swamped with patients, many times overflowing onto the corridors, lying on nothing but thin mats or blankets over the cold cement floors. We took care of seriously ill patients, delivered babies, applied casts on broken legs and arms, assisted residents in major surgical cases, and performed minor surgical procedures ourselves. There was much to do, which was an unparalleled opportunity for us to learn so much in medicine at such an early stage of our training.

The question may be legitimately asked: "How was this situation viewed from the standpoint of patients who came from the huge indigent segment of the population?" I can categorically say that it was good for most of them because we were the best qualified medical students, selected from a large pool of applicants. Those who performed poorly during the freshman and sophomore years had been winnowed out. The only other choice for these patients was to have no medical care at all or be treated by *albularios, derived from the Spanish herbolario, herbalist in English, who practices folk medicine.*

However, there was no doubt in my mind that some patients were probably harmed from insufficient supervision of us from full-time, more experienced, and older physicians and surgeons. Sadly, this inadequate supervision still exists today as I write this, in the year 2020. For several years now, I have made it a personal crusade to improve this situation by asking to be chairman of an ad hoc committee in the University of the Philippines Medical Alumni Society in America (UPMASA), looking to improve this glaring weakness in an otherwise world-class medical education and training at UP-PGH in the land of my birth. To me, the solution is to have FULL-TIME CONSULTANTS, at least among heads of departments, who are given salaries and be allowed full-time private practice anywhere on the

UP-PGH campus; that will allow them to see their private paying patients, thereby giving them the opportunity to earn an income comparable to physicians in private practice elsewhere. They will be required to be available 24/7 to see their patients side by side with nonpaying charity patients with interns, residents, and fellows.

Currently, full private practice is allowed only in the private wards, certain operating rooms, and a special office building, QualiMed. This building was originally the out-patient department building. It was converted to offices for rent to UP-PGH faculty and staff members. This was a development of the Mercado Medical Group who built similar office buildings and medical clinics all over Luzon. QualiMed—that is the brand name. Before QualiMed, the building was named Faculty Medical Ambulatory Building (FMAB). Mystifyingly, QualiMed does not allow interns, residents, and fellows to observe consultants treating their private patients. Moreover, majority of patients are concentrated in the PGH Outpatient Department.

For over a decade now, I have met with many deans, UP Manila chancellors, PGH directors, and UP presidents; so far, I have failed to change minds. I now feel like Don Quixote jousting a windmill and have given up. Perhaps, not completely yet. I recently met with former UP president EMIL JAVIER while attending a meeting of a group of dedicated former UP Los Baños alumni (February 2020), as an invited guest of my brother Ben, who is the founding president of CAMP; Dr. Javier is the founding chairman. CAMP is the acronym for Coalition for Agriculture Modernization in the Philippines, a group whose purpose is to advocate and promote sound agricultural policies and programs, which include massive utilization of climate-resilient and environmentally friendly agricultural innovations and improved governance and management systems to help advance the livelihoods of Filipino farmers and fisherfolk. I can readily empathize with all that. In reference to the problem, I see at UP-PGH, Dr. Javier said that the UP board of regents will approve any program that is advocated by a regent who represents the medical community. He should know; Dr. Javier is a former UP president. I have shared this information with some UPMASA members who have the same vision as I do to help our alma mater retain its role as the leading teaching hospital in the country while also improving the care of indigent patients. I believe that there should be no difference in the quality of care between paying and nonpaying patients.

The problem with the current training of physicians at UP-PGH is that there is always inadequate supervision because the consultants who are officially on the rolls of staff members have their offices outside the campus. They must take care of their own private patients first before they can go to PGH to respond to requests for help from residents and fellows, who in turn supervise the interns. The legendary traffic problem in Metro Manila makes the situation much worse, almost impossible in many situations.

At the end of that year of internship, I had learned so much and helped so many people and felt so much psychic reward that if the hospital were to ask me to repeat that year as an option, I would have done it without any hesitation at all.

Internship, however, was not all work and no play. With youthful exuberance, we also indulged in some stupid escapades. One involved our own classmate, RESTITUTO NOCUM, who was a loner and did most of his work at night. Most days, he would sleep soundly in the Interns Quarters. One day while he was deep in slumber, a bunch of us wicked interns started to slowly roll his bed outside to the nearby basketball court. On the way out of the dorm, a lady came along and inquired what we were doing. We told her to keep quiet. We thought she was one of the *lavanderas* (wash ladies) delivering clean clothes to Resty, as we called him. It turned out that, indeed, clothes were being delivered to him—by his mother!

Diplomas were handed out at a ceremony at the UP Diliman campus, Diliman, Quezon City. Our diplomas were handed out by UP president Vidal Tan, the same distinguished academician who handed me my high school diploma when he was president of FEU in 1950.

UPCM class of 1957 did not end its relationship with UPCM when we received our diplomas. Aside from serving our own people for those who stayed in the home country and other people of the world for those who left abroad for further training or more rewarding work, we, as a group, distinguished ourselves as community physicians, educators, researchers, innovators, and sometime philanthropists, who contributed greatly to the alma mater and the human race as a whole. I take pride in being ordained as class president for life by classmate MUTYA SAN AGUSTIN-SHAW (which I accepted in friendship and mutual admiration) during a reunion in Maui, Hawaii, to celebrate our UPCM Class Thirty-Fifth Anniversary. With the cooperation of most classmates, I believe that, among classes from other years, our class has had the greatest number of reunions, averaging once every two years. At a mini-reunion at Conrad Hotel in Manila on February 20, 2020, a classmate, RAMON GUSTILO, gave me a copy of his autobiography, *Heart of the East and Tempo of the West*, with his signature and message: "Hi Joe, In appreciation of being the 'Glue' of Class '57." That meant a lot to me.

Thanking Our Stars

During the third year of medical school, students are first introduced to clinical medicine by making the rounds of hospital wards and observing firsthand how common diseases manifest in live patients. During one of these visits to Ward 5, the main medical ward at PGH, my classmate, Mrs. PURA TORRES, the wife of Dr. LUIS TORRES, chief of the PGH Urology Department, directed my attention to a beautiful student nurse giving an injection to a female patient. I only saw her from the back, noticing the killer legs leading up to a very shapely hip that was connected to the rest of the slim body by a tiny waistline.

I was not bold enough to just walk up to her and introduce myself, but luckily, another classmate, Phi brod VIRGILIO VELASCO (Gil), must have seen me drooling and told me that he knew that dazzling student nurse and would be happy to make an introduction. Without any hesitation, I eagerly said yes. So both of us walked up to the hospital bed where the student nurse was attending to a patient. Gil said to her as she turned to face us, "Donna, I would like to introduce my brod Joe Peczon." The first time I saw her face, she took my breath away. I was smitten! What I noticed most attractive was how her upper lip formed such a graceful angle with her slightly upturned nose. There were a few pimples, not dimples, that made her face even more attractive. The nameplate on her crisp white student nurse uniform identified her as "DONNA I. VILLAFLOR." Not wanting to distract her from what she was doing and possibly getting her into trouble with the ward head nurse, I briefly said that I was so pleased to meet her and walked away. The year was 1955.

The student nurse was twenty-two years old, and I, the medical student, a year older.

There were specific times during the weekend when student nurses could receive visitors. At the first floor, a visitor would go to the receptionist seated by a small table on the left side at the foot of a large staircase leading to the second and third floors of the building, write the name of the student nurse on a piece of paper, and then wait in the large reception room on that first floor. Nurses Home was located on the PGH campus facing Taft Avenue. Behind the dorm was Pandora Tennis Club, where I spent many afternoons playing tennis with classmates ALEX BERBA, WILLY YUTUC, NICK VELARDE, RUSS TONGCO, EMY RIVERA, CENON CRUZ, and BOY VILLASEÑOR and some professors including Dr. JOSE BARCELONA (hospital director), Dr. ARTEMIO JONGCO (pediatric professor), residents Dr. GERMAN CASTILLO and Dr. ISIDRO BENITEZ, and others.

Donna would come down after a few minutes to join me to find seats in a quiet corner in the spacious reception room, where other couples like us tried to get acquainted with each other. Other young men like me were mostly UP medical students, but some were from outside the UP-PGH campus. After several meetings this way, we progressed to being able to get permission from the Nurses Home supervisor to go out for dates. Donna's classmate NORMA GUERRERO (Noy) was extremely helpful. Because her father was a very popular surgeon, Noy enjoyed a certain influence over many of the nurse supervisors and had the privilege of taking Donna out of the dormitory as long as Noy returned with her before curfew.

Under this convenient arrangement, we took many leisurely walks down Herran Street, now renamed PEDRO GIL, toward Dewey Boulevard, now renamed ROXAS BOULEVARD (after President MANUEL ROXAS), that fronted the famous Manila Bay. We watched the sun disappear beneath the gentle waves of Manila Bay while sitting under coconut trees on the wide cement wall separating the sidewalk from the gentle waves lapping on the rocks below. We talked about our backgrounds, parents, siblings, friends, news of the day, popular song hits, and so on. Sometimes we would see a movie at the nearby Gaiety Theatre. Going there and returning to our dorms in UP-PGH, we held hands, a practice we preserved for the next sixty-five years. Today, half-jokingly, I tell my grandchildren that we did this for romantic reasons initially, but later we did it for the more practical purpose of mutual support to prevent dangerous falls!

Every month there was Social Night at her dormitory. Officially, the nursing curriculum included the social development of the students. Student nurses invited their favorite persons to this social event that was always held at the reception room, where visitors were entertained. During this Social Night, there was dancing accompanied by music from a phonograph player. Disc jockeys were not popular then. Among more affluent schools or social clubs, popular bands like TIRSO CRUZ and his dance band provided the music. Donna invited me to most, if not all, of these monthly socials. In addition, we communicated with each other by passing messages written on small pieces of paper carried by messengers who were usually classmates. In our case, it was mostly Noy. I remember one such message delivered to me coming from Donna. The note said, "There are kisses for you waiting at Nurses Home at 5 PM." Sure enough, when I got there at the appointed hour, Donna, grinning from ear to ear, was waiting, and she handed me a small package of chocolate KISSES. I was expecting something different!

UPCM also had a similar social event. It was larger and was held only once a year. This was the much-anticipated MEDICAL BALL that was usually held just before graduation. It was attended by all the graduating interns and many of the undergraduates. I invited Donna to one in 1956 that was held, as usual, at Fiesta Pavilion of Manila Hotel. Tirso Cruz and his famous dance orchestra provided the music. During this dance, I gave Donna my fraternity pin as a sign that we were going steady. This meant that we dated only each other and no one else. My Phi pin was now utilized for a noble purpose!

Clinical clerks went on duty for twenty-four hours, just like interns. Student nurses went only on eight-hour shifts; morning duty was from 7:00 a.m. to 3:00 p.m., afternoon duty was 3:00 p.m. to 11:00 p.m., and night shift was 11:00 p.m. to 7:00 a.m. When Donna was on the afternoon shift, I usually found time to take a break from my own duties and waited for her to be relieved at 11:00 p.m.

We would walk to the dining room and have a late dinner together, then I would walk her to Nurses Home. Most of the time late, meals in this hospital dining room were *champurrado,* a porridge of rice with chocolate, paired with lightly salted fried dried fish, *dilis.* Sometimes it was EENT *sisig,* a concoction of chopped pig's head parts minus the bones and brain. It was called EENT by the medical students and nurses because it contained the ears, eyes, lips, tongue, and all other edible parts of the pig's head. It was marinated in vinegar, onions, garlic, salt, and pepper. Sometimes it was deep-fried fish, most commonly shark or other inexpensive kinds of fish. The best thing that could be said about those meals was that they were *free.*

Money was always in short supply for me. Often, I had to borrow money from my sister Alma to afford to go on a date with my student nurse. With the limited budget, I usually took her to an ice cream parlor on Taft Avenue just in front of the PGH gate. Sometimes we went for *foot-long* hot dogs at BROWN DERBY, a popular watering place for medical students and their dates. When I was feeling rich after selling medical samples to a local drugstore in front of the hospital, we went out to dine at a Chinese restaurant along the Escolta or Avenida Rizal streets farther away.

One date I will never forget. After the usual movie and dinner at our favorite Chinese restaurant, we headed home along Taft Avenue to PGH, riding the ubiquitous jeepney. A taxi ride was out of the question—it was the fare. Along the way, I suddenly developed severe intestinal cramps. It must have been something I ate or drank for dinner. Today I am certain it was lactose intolerance. Donna was not affected, but I had an awfully hard time trying to clamp down on my anal sphincter so I would not soil my pants and really embarrass myself!

Informing Donna of my predicament, before the jeepney stopped in front of PGH and Nurses Home, I told her that I had to leave her alone to walk back to the dormitory while I made a mad dash to Ward 3, where I knew there was a restroom. I made it just in time. Whew!

One time, Zeny had a party at their house in Project 4 in Quezon City. She invited two other student nurses, CORNELIA CORNISTA and

Evelyn Gueib. I invited three brods from my class, Cenon Cruz, Russ Tongco, and Gil Dacumos. Russ Tongco's four-door sedan was our only transport. It was amazing how eight people were able to fit in that car. Donna ended up sitting on my lap during the ride back to their dorm. She weighed no more than ninety-eight pounds at that time, and so it was no big deal. I do not remember much about the party, but I still vividly remember that car ride with my favorite student nurse sitting on my lap! You can't blame me if I was feeling amorous.

We also went to a lot of picnics that were organized and given free to clinical clerks and interns by United Drug. As I mentioned earlier, we got a lot of free samples from United Drug and other manufacturers. Those were supposed to be given free to patients, but for poor medical students like me, those free samples were a source of much-needed funds!

In one particular picnic, Donna was unusually quiet and aloof. I could not figure out what I did wrong. Even after we went back to PGH and I walked her back to the dorm, she would not tell me what was troubling her. However, when she got inside the door of the dorm, she abruptly turned and said that perhaps we should *not* see each other again. That was a ton of TNT dropped on my head! I was really depressed but could do nothing about it until I could talk to her again the next day. It turned out that she was very disturbed when I told her that the woman I will marry must be a Roman Catholic. She was a Protestant Baptist! At that time, I was not yet an atheist. Learning that this was the problem, like making a correct diagnosis of a patient's ailment, I found great relief, for now I knew that her apparent coolness toward me was not from something dastardly that I had done. Very quickly, I was able to find the proper management to win her back.

Annually, Christmas at PGH was highlighted by a traditional show at Science Hall. All departments of the hospital, nursing department, and the medical school all contributed parts to the program. I introduced Donna to my family during one of these celebrations. I invited my sister Alma and Apung Taqui, my grandmother, to the show. Alma paid for the light snack we indulged in after the show. Shortly after this introduction to the family, I took Donna to Tenth

Avenue, Grace Park, Caloocan, where I lived in a tiny house built by Uncle Ruben with some help from me. By that time, he and his family had moved to a posh new house along Dita Street in Makati.

I helped build this house. That was how I learned carpentry and masonry work. This one-story house had two bedrooms, a dining room, a kitchen, and a toilet. The raised floor was made entirely of bamboo slats, each slat being about one and a half inches wide, the slats separated by one-fourth of an inch to provide free circulation of air from the space below to the living areas above. This was a poor man's way of having air-conditioning without the use of electricity. Apung Taqui cooked and kept house for my sisters Corazon, Alma, and me. Earlier, I told Donna that I lived in this tiny house made with bamboo floors, but I guessed she was not prepared to see that the house was indeed tiny and that the floors were made of bamboo slats. I was wrong. She later told me that it was my honesty in *not* pretending to be rich that won her heart completely. She knew at that moment that I was the guy she wanted to be her lifetime partner! No one can ever accuse her of marrying me for my money—I had none!

Donna met the rest of the family at the house of Uncle Ruben along Dita Street in Makati. This happened during a family celebration following my graduation from medical school in April 1957. With her easy demeanor coupled with her physical attractiveness, she won the admiration and affection of everyone in my family. Some of my close friends started jokingly calling me *Joenna* instead of just plain *Joe*.

After finishing my clinical clerkship, from Manila I went home to spend summer in my hometown of Mexico, Pampanga, before returning to PGH to become an intern. Almost upon arrival at home, I became extremely sick with chickenpox. I remember the chills, high fever, and intense headache lasting almost a week. Each spike of chills and fever was followed by fresh crops of clear-fluid-filled vesicles all over my body, including the eyelids, scalp, palms of my hands, and soles of my feet. Our family doctor, TOMAS GUEVARRA, whose office was our own family-owned drugstore, took care of me. All he could do was to provide symptomatic treatment, as there was no treatment for that virus at that time—there is still none at present.

After a rotation in pediatrics, I learned that chickenpox was usually mild in children but could be deadly for adults because of complications like carditis and pneumonitis. I had the disease when I was young, and so my immunity was not permanent. After this infection as an adult, my immunity became much stronger and permanent. When the acute phase was over, my sister Alma helped me write and send a letter to Donna to let her know about my illness and how much I missed her. It was so sweet to get a response from her promptly that, without a doubt, made my recovery period short!

Donna's mother, maiden name DOLORES ILAGISON IBAÑEZ, *Nanny*, as she was called by Donna and her two brothers, was on hand on capping day, which was graduation day for the nurses. In 1956 Donna received her BS in nursing from UP-PGH. Her parents from Bacolod came to attend this important milestone, and I was introduced to them for the first time. Before this, I had met Donna's older brother RADY, who was two years behind me in medical school. Her younger brother EDWARD, I did not meet until later. Donna happily confided to me that I made a good impression on her parents. They treated us to ice cream at our favorite ice cream parlor in front of PGH. They must have known that my wallet was as thin as an empty envelope!

After graduation from the PGH School of Nursing in April 1956, Donna left for her home and family in Bacolod. As she boarded the steamship *Governor Wright* at one of the piers in the Manila port area, I was left standing alone, longing to make the trip with her but could not. Coincidentally, at that time, PAT BOONE had a popular hit song, "Harbor Lights":

> *I saw the harbor lights*
> *They only told me we were parting*
> *The same old harbor lights*
> *that once brought you to me...*

Up to now, I get nostalgic when listening to that ballad.

We communicated with each other by mail that took days and sometimes weeks to be delivered. Phones were available but in a limited scope. There was one phone line to the Interns Quarters at PGH, but it was always busy as can be imagined with so many interns living there. Donna had to rely on a phone in the house of her former piano teacher across the street from their house. On top of this limited availability of a phone connection, the charges were almost beyond what I could afford. It was a lonely and miserable time for me. Fortunately, the enormous amount of work of PGH interns kept my mind off the constant longing for her, and I focused on the work at hand, being aware that I had to make good grades to place myself in a good position to get accepted into the competitive EENT (Eye, Ear, Nose, and Throat) Department. This feeling for her was an apt comparison to the popular Ilonggo folk song "Dandansoy." This boy longed for his sweetheart, who had to return to her hometown of Payao. Later, in our golden years, her pet name for me was Soy.

No longer than two months of stay in Bacolod, where she reviewed for the nursing board examinations, Donna returned to Manila. She successfully passed the examinations and earned an RN (registered nurse) after her name. Promptly, she found a job as school nurse at Adamson University located along San Marcelino Street, which was just a short walking distance from PGH. This made it possible for me to visit her almost daily at her job. She lived at a nearby dorm run by Philippine Normal School. After a few months, she landed a plum job at the PGH Surgery Department as an operating room nurse assigned to the Neurosurgery Department. The operating room nurse supervisor had high regard for her skills and attitude and assigned her to a demanding job as the regular nurse assistant to the famously temperamental and only neurosurgeon at that time, Dr. Victor Reyes. This job provided her free housing at the PGH Dorm 5 that was exclusively used by PGH graduate nurses employed by the hospital. The beauty of this was that I was in PGH Dorm 3, which was *next door*, used by PGH interns and residents. This fortunate arrangement made it quite easy for us to see each other almost every day.

Our love for each other blossomed, and it was inevitable that marriage became a frequent topic of our conversations. She wanted to get married just as much as I did.

Till Death Do Us Part

With Donna as a PGH operating room nurse and I as an intern and later resident in ophthalmology at PGH, we had all the opportunities to see each other as often as we wished, which was almost daily. As a graduate nurse, she stayed in Dorm 5 with all the other PGH graduate nurses. The dorm was just a basketball court away from the intern/resident quarters where I was billeted. As expected, our relationship blossomed.

With the same intensity, we both desired to get married, but there was an impediment. There was no doubt in my mind that she would be my perfect partner for life. However, I harbored a trepidation that my lack of a solid financial base could be a detriment to a happy marriage. In addition, I had wanted to help my mother to the best of my ability by starting a private practice after I finished my ophthalmology residency.

I was earning a bit more than the meager salary of a PGH resident, two hundred pesos a month, equivalent to $50 then, with free food and laundry, by moonlighting as an assistant to Dr. GEMINIANO DE OCAMPO in his office and hospital. This was a common practice at that time, and Dr. De Ocampo, who was the head of the Eye Department, must have seen my potential. It was obvious to me that he was grooming me to practice with him permanently after completing my residency. I thought this was a good opportunity for me too, yet I was not totally convinced that Donna and I could get married while at the same time helping to support my mother, who was the sole earner for my younger siblings who were still in college. Alma was at UP Diliman (Quezon City), Pons at Mapua Institute of Technology (Manila), and Ben at UP College of Agriculture, now UP Los Baños (Los Baños, Laguna).

Serious discussions about marriage took up most of the time we were together. Probably sensing that I was not ready to commit myself to a married life at this juncture, she told me that she wanted to get on a US exchange visitor program and to apply for a nurse's position in the US. Reluctantly, I agreed, and I even went to the extent of helping her fill up application forms. At that time, it was a piece of cake to land a job at a hospital in the US, which regularly sent representatives to Manila to recruit nurses. She signed up with Cook County Hospital in Chicago.

During a short vacation that I spent with my mother, Ima, in my hometown in Pampanga, she asked me why I was moping around, unusually quiet, and obviously not happy. Mothers seem to observe these things and have the instincts to try to help. I told her about the plan that Donna and I had made. "Do you love each other?" That was the only question she asked. Answering her in the affirmative, she said, "If you let her go to Chicago, you will never see her again. If you really love her, you should get married now. Do not worry about your siblings. We will find a way to get them through college just like you." My mother gave me the best advice in my life! I cut my vacation short and returned to Manila as fast as I could! (Had she not said that in a definite language, I could have lost Donna forever and would not be where I am today.)

Sitting on a swing built for two that was located in front of her dorm, where we usually spent countless hours talking about events of the day, I told Donna what Ima said, and then I proposed to her. It was nothing dramatic. There was no engagement ring to offer her. I could not afford even the tiniest diamond anyway. As I had anticipated, she accepted my proposal to tie the knot.

(Twenty-six years later, while already living the good life in Greenfield, I finally bought her a flawless one-carat diamond engagement ring. It is never too late for that! I do not remember what she told me, but I remember the beautiful smile she always gave me when I made her happy.)

It did not take too long for me to go on my first flight in an airplane, Philippine Airlines (PAL) C49, a two-engine propeller-driven plane used extensively in the last war as a workhorse in the US Air Force. Donna had alerted her parents in Bacolod about my *pamanhikan*—that is, to ask permission to marry their daughter. Her father, whom she called *Daddy*, RAMON MAGONG VILLAFLOR, waited for me at Bacolod Airport. He took me to their house at 54-A Libertad Street, Bacolod, riding in a chauffeur-driven rented car. Her mother, *Nanny*, was waiting there.

Her grandfather, RAYMUNDO VILLAFLOR, was there too. He and I tried to strike a conversation but did not get much headway. He spoke neither Tagalog nor English. I only knew a few words in Ilonggo, and I had forgotten most of my Spanish that I learned in premed school. It was too bad because in that language of the first Europeans who colonized our country, he was fluent. It was also too bad that it was the last and only time I saw him. Donna last saw him again when she returned to her hometown after graduation from nursing school in 1956. He died eight years later at the age of 102. Both Donna and I were in Boston when this happened.

There was no problem communicating with Donna's parents. Both college-educated, of course, they were fluent in English.

Nanny prepared a typical Bacolod feast, mostly fresh seafood cooked by the family cook and housekeeper, TERESA.

That night, I slept on a bed in the same bedroom occupied by my future father-in-law. As I had expected, he asked me how I was going to support his daughter after we got married. Without any prior rehearsal, my answer was that I would do my best as a budding ophthalmologist. My memory fails me now because I do not remember whether I slept at all that night. Was I imagining what was in store for us all in the future?

We set the wedding date for September 6, 1958, on her twenty-fourth birthday. We chose the closest venue from PGH, the Ermita Catholic Church.

Nanny helped Donna with the wedding gown that was made by their *modista* in Bacolod who previously hand-made all of Donna's wardrobe in the past. Mrs. Gianzon and her sister-in-law helped too.

This was in an upstairs bedroom in the Gianzon house just across the street from Uncle Ruben's house along Dita Street, Makati, where I stayed during the last year of my PGH ophthalmology residency.

The bridal car was lent to us by one of the bride's colleagues who was working in the same PGH operating room.

She marched down the aisle, holding on to Daddy's arm, who in turn gave her hand to Jose D. Peczon, MD, waiting at the altar. The only two sponsors, Dr. Pura Torres and Dr. Vidal Tan, smilingly endorsed the turnover. At the Bayview Hotel, not too far from the US Embassy in Manila, we spent our first night together. In the morning, we took a train to go to Baguio, the most popular honeymoon destination at that time, where we spent a couple of nights at the Pines Hotel. On the way back to Manila, we stopped by my hometown to visit Ima.

With limited funds between us, we rented a bedroom in the house of Mr. and Mrs. Antonio Gianzon. Each of us continued to work at PGH as we prepared to travel to the US for further training in our respective fields.

In March 1959, six months after our wedding, Donna left for Chicago as planned. In Chicago, she did her best not only to cope with the loneliness of separation from her husband but also tried to quickly adapt to the bitterly cold and windy Chicago winter. She wrote a letter to her best friend Nelie Arao-Antigua, confessing how miserable she was, longing for her Joe.

In November 1959, after a separation of eight months, we were together again. She had been able to get an appointment for me as an intern in West Suburban Hospital in Oak Park, Illinois. I could not get a better appointment, although I had already completed two and a half years of residency in ophthalmology. Without realizing it then, internship in that hospital proved to be a significant opening of a door to pursue our Filipino dreams:

That I would become a successful ophthalmologist earning enough to have a comfortable life, provide good education for our children, and be able to help those in need just as our parents envisioned.

That eight-month separation was the longest that we were not together. A shorter separation of three months was in the summer of 1960 when I took a basic science course in ophthalmology, the Lancaster course, in Colby College, Waterville, Maine. These separations were the only times we were not together during the next sixty-one years of married bliss.

UP president Vidal Tan was to play notable parts in our lives in the Philippines and the US. That was the reason why we chose him to be one of our two principal wedding sponsors. He was the president of FEU when I graduated from FEU High School. I have a picture of him handing me my high school diploma in 1950. Seven years later, in 1957, this time as UP president, he handed me my diploma in medicine. Before that, Donna got her BSN diploma from him in 1956.

For a few months, Donna worked for Dr. Tan's family, providing 24/7 nursing care to Mrs. Tan. Donna stayed in their house in Cubao. I visited her there regularly. After our wedding, Donna resigned from this job. Zeny, one of her best friends, took over.

Dr. Tan loaned us the funds we needed to purchase the airline ticket for Donna when she headed out for Chicago. This loan was repaid in full by diligently sending monthly installment payments to a contact of Dr. Tan, who lived in Delaware.

There in Chicago, the seeds of our destiny to spend our entire lives together were nurtured. The two most important women in my life, Ima and Donna, made me see the light. I remember one of the earliest poems I memorized and recited in a kindergarten class extravaganza: "In the heart of a seed, / buried deep so deep; / a dear little plant / lay fast asleep; / wake! said the sunshine / and creep to the light; / wake! said the voice / of the raindrops bright" (by Kate Brown).

Sharpening Medical Skills

During internship, almost all of us had an idea of what would follow after graduating with the MD initials after our names. Those at the top class ranking had the best chance of getting accepted to any department at PGH for any specialty training of their choice. The Surgery Department was considered a prime choice. To get a better chance of getting accepted in a department that had the most promise for me, I applied for a less competitive specialty: EENT.

More than 75 percent of the class did not go through this route. Instead, they went abroad to get appointments at hospitals in the United States of America, at a fortuitous time when there was a great demand for foreign medical graduates. A large proportion of the remainder of the class who stayed behind to get residency in a specialty department at PGH, eventually went to the US for further training. I am not aware of any classmate who immediately went into private practice as a general practitioner in his/her respective town or province. However, many of those who went abroad eventually returned to the Philippines. That was my original plan, too—to finish my residency training at PGH, go abroad for further training, and then return to serve the country of my birth.

I am not sure how many of my classmates applied to the EENT Department that had only two positions open every year. In 1957, FELIPE TOLENTINO and I were accepted to those two positions. There were two sections in that combined department—the eye and the ENT subspecialties. Upon acceptance, a coin was tossed to determine who had the first choice. I won, and I chose the eye section; Felipe had no choice but the other section. When we both went to the US for more postgraduate training, he switched to train in ophthalmology, which was his primary goal in the first place.

Dr. Geminiano de Ocampo was chief of EENT at that time. In his wisdom, he petitioned the UP board of regents to split the department into an independent Eye section and a separate ENT section. This was approved, and so, after two and a half years of training, Felipe finished as chief resident in otorhinolaryngology, and I, in ophthalmology. We did not have to complete the five-year postgraduate training course at the previous EENT Department. Both of us went to the US for further postgraduate work in our respective fields, the subspecialty of glaucoma for me and retinal and vitreous diseases for him. Both of us took the Lancaster course in basic ophthalmology. From there, I became chief resident of ophthalmology at Boston City Hospital (BCH). After this residency, I received further training in a subspecialty as a clinical research fellow in glaucoma at MEEI in Boston. To wit, my training as an ophthalmologist, before establishing a permanent private practice, spanned a total of seven years after graduation from medical school.

Let me go back to those two and a half years at PGH. The first year was mostly assignments in the PGH Outpatient Department, where hordes of patients needing eye care would receive what they needed. With little supervision, we learned how to do refractions to fit patients with properly graded lenses for them to see clearer. It was by trial and error, actually, and inevitably, we made some errors during the early months. Fortunately, these did not lead to permanent damage. At worst, the patients had to spend more money to replace the wrong lens power we had ordered to be fitted by an optician.

I remember the older sister of one of my classmates, Mutya. The lens prescription I gave for her bifocal corrective lenses was the right one for distance but not for near vision. I had given a lens that was too powerful for the reading distance she needed. From early mistakes, I learned quickly how to do more accurate refractions.

We took routine care of simple eye conditions, such as infections of the eyelids and blocked tear ducts. We also performed minor surgical procedures like repair of eyelid lacerations, removal of small benign and malignant tumors, removal of foreign bodies on the surface of the eye, and incision with drainage of sties (abscesses). We assisted senior residents and consultants in performing cataract removal, glaucoma surgery, and extraocular muscle procedures to straighten misaligned eyes. There were many cases of enucleation (removal of the entire eye). Many of these were in young children who suffered from a highly malignant tumor called *retinoblastoma*.

We took turns as junior consultants in ophthalmology in the always busy Emergency Room Department. I vividly remember one case. This was a young boy who complained of a *puing*, or foreign body, in one eye. He presented a history of accidentally running into a wire-mesh kitchen door. I found a piece of wire had pierced the center of his cornea. With fine forceps, I grasped the end of the wire and pulled it out. It was much longer than I thought. Immediately, fluid from the anterior chamber of the eye came gushing out, producing a condition called *flat anterior chamber*. Alarmed, I called the senior resident, Dr. ROMEO FAJARDO. I followed his advice to merely place a pressure bandage on the eye and wait for a couple of hours. Indeed, after that time, the chamber started to refill. On the young boy's follow-up visit the next day, all was normal except for a tiny scar in the cornea that did not produce any significant loss of vision. As we became more experienced, we gradually transitioned to taking care of more complicated procedures.

Dr. Geminiano de Ocampo must have noticed my potentials early on. He invited me, and I readily accepted, to work part-time in his private practice as an assistant. De Ocampo Eye Hospital was located along UN Avenue (formerly Isaac Peral Street), near the corner of Taft Avenue, where PGH was located. It was an easy walk for me from PGH to his clinic.

He had the largest ophthalmology practice in Metro Manila at that time, catering mostly to the upper crust of society. Not only did I welcome the salary he gave me, which augmented my income as a PGH resident, a monthly salary of two hundred pesos that was equal to $50, plus free meals in the hospital dining room; additionally, and pricelessly, he also gave me a firsthand look at how a prominent ophthalmologist managed his private patients.

I learned a lot about medical science from Dr. De Ocampo. He was a pioneer in corneal transplantation and encouraged all residents to engage in research. At that time, rejection of the donor corneal tissue was the main reason for the failure of the transplant. Corticosteroids were not yet available. He postulated that using cornea from an entirely different species could be a possible solution. Perhaps, donor tissue from an animal farthest away related to man could be less prone to rejection.

With official approval from him, I performed my first clinical research study in my career. I credit Dr. De Ocampo for setting the stage for me to be inquisitive and unafraid to seek solutions to problems that are not yet solved. Choosing completely blind eyes that were scheduled for enucleation anyway, I transplanted corneas harvested from fresh fish and chicken eyes. For a few days, the transplanted tissues thrived, but after several more days, the tissues completely disintegrated due to the natural rejection response, which is the bane of all tissue and organ transplants. At present, this rejection response to tissue transplants from human eyes has been largely controlled by more effective medications, such as corticosteroids and nonsteroidal anti-inflammatory eye drops. Although my experiments did not produce the positive results that I was seeking, the results provided the answer that Dr. De Ocampo had pondered for some time.

Unfortunately, the results of my research I did not write up for publication in a peer-reviewed medical journal because I was not yet aware that a clinical trial with a negative outcome had an equally important role in the dissemination of new knowledge. Years later, while working with Dr. WALTER MORTON GRANT in Boston, I learned that a previously reported negative result can be just as important as a positive one when one is performing a clinical research project.

In the second year of residency, I did my first case of cataract operation. Cataract, a clouding of the human lens, was and still is the leading cause of blindness not only in the Philippines but throughout the world. Any ophthalmologist worth his salt must be proficient in this operation. Dr. GLORIA LIM, among the most dedicated of the department's consultants, assisted me during the operation. The surgery was completed without any complications. In celebration, the following day, I bought a bunch of lunch of stuffed milkfish, *relyenong bangus,* and rice for the entire eye OR staff.

In my last month as chief resident in ophthalmology, I was confident enough to remove cataracts in both eyes of my dear grandmother, Apung Taqui. In fact, in later years, I performed this operation with the implantation of an artificial lens in one of Ima's eyes at Farren Memorial Hospital in Turners Falls, Massachusetts. She became one of the first fifty such cases I performed; I reported the favorable results of those cases at an ophthalmology meeting of the New England Ophthalmological Society (NEOS) in Boston. I did a similar operation on her other eye at Eye Referral Center along TM Kalaw Avenue in Manila. At the same place, I did similar operations on my sisters Zon and Alma. Thus, I can claim to be among a small cadre of ophthalmologists who have performed cataract surgery on three generations of mothers in a family: grandmother Apung Taqui, my mother, and my sister Zon.

Two cases during my residency highlighted the deficiency in supervising medical trainees. First was a young lady with a puncture wound in one eye that ended up in enucleation (removal), when a simple repair of the wound might have been more appropriate. Without any doubt, the presence of a consultant would have saved that eye. A second case occurred when I followed a mandatory two-week rotation in surgical pathology. While there, I was assigned to examine a tiny piece of tissue from the ENT Department, labeled "biopsy of vocal cord lesion." My report to the ENT Department was "squamous cell carcinoma." This was confirmed by Dr. BENJAMIN CANLAS, the head of the Pathology Department.

A few days later, from the same department, I received the entire larynx of this same patient! I was horrified that such a radical procedure was performed based on my pathology report alone. There had been no communication between the ENT and Surgical Pathology Departments. There should have been a discussion among the heads of the two departments and the residents before performing such a radical procedure, which inevitably changed this patient's life in a profound manner forever. With great relief, after examining the entire large laryngeal box carefully, I found evidence of the local spread of the cancer. The decision for doing the surgery was justified after all, but it could have gone the other way.

The two and a half years of residency training, coupled with part-time work as an assistant to Dr. Geminiano de Ocampo, added to me what I thought was sufficient knowledge in ophthalmology to start my own private practice; however, the vow I made to Donna to be together with her for a lifetime took precedence over everything. To be with her was the most compelling reason for me to go abroad. What I did not know was that there were huge gaps in my bank of knowledge about the eyes that only became apparent when I became exposed to advanced ophthalmology in America.

After my PGH eye residency, I traveled to the US to join Donna, who was then working as a neurosurgical OR nurse at Cook County Hospital in Chicago. It was she who got me an appointment as an intern at West Suburban Hospital, Oak Park, Illinois. It was a step down for me, but it was the quickest way to be with my darling wife again.

Unaware of it then, a door of opportunity was before me to open. I met Dr. GEORGIANA THEOBALD, a highly respected author of a textbook on ocular pathology. She and Dr. HAROLD KIRK were partners in private practice in Oak Park. Both were extremely helpful to me. They took me to monthly meetings of the Chicago Ophthalmological Society. They both recommended that I take the Lancaster course in ophthalmology. Dr. Theobald even loaned me her own personal binocular microscope, which was needed in the ocular pathology part of the course. I took care of their private patients who came to the hospital for emergency care, and I assisted them in scheduled surgical cases. Those were added learning experiences for me; it was also the first time I witnessed how American ophthalmologists took care of their patients.

Knowing Dr. Theobald led to my attending the Lancaster course in summer of 1960. That was an intensive course in basic ophthalmology that filled a void in my training at PGH. From there, I got an appointment as chief resident on Ophthalmology at BCH and eventually as a clinical research fellow at Glaucoma Consultation

Service (GCS) of MEEI, Howe Laboratory, Harvard Medical School (HMS).

As chief resident of the BCH Eye Department, I was allowed by Dr. ROBERT ALPERT, chief of the department, to attend a one-week course in ocular pathology at Walter Reed Military Medical Center in Bethesda, MD. There were more doors to open and to explore beyond.

While serving as a resident physician on the staff of BCH, there were opportunities to interact with residents from other departments. One was a doctor from England, ROGER BANISTER, famous as being the first man to break the four-minute barrier running in an officially sanctioned one-mile race. We attended the same neurological grand rounds and ate at the same hospital dining room.

Significant opportunities to learn new things presented themselves when I attended monthly clinical conferences at MEEI and of NEOS. There I learned how residents and fellows presented cases, something that my PGH experience did not provide. I also came to know Drs. PAUL CHANDLER and W. MORTON GRANT, who were pillars in the subspecialty of glaucoma and coauthors of the classic textbook *Lectures in Glaucoma*. That led me to be interested in that subspecialty of ophthalmology. My insular mentality had broadened!

Lofty Aspirations

The eight-month separation when Donna was in Chicago while I remained in Manila was the loneliest part of our lives. It was, of course, assuaged by diligently writing to each other, encouraging ourselves to be brave as we could be while waiting to be reunited again. We knew the future would be bright for us if we made this sacrifice. We were fearless. We were confident of our love for each other and in each other's intellectual capacity to learn new things. Almost sixty years later, I wrote her a letter on her birthday and said, quoting Christopher Marlowe in his poem "The Passionate Shepherd to His Love," "'Come live with me and be my love, and we will all the pleasures prove.' You consented and we went on a marvelous journey together." Then I enumerated all the pleasures in life we enjoyed.

Let me digress a bit to describe my first trip outside the Philippines.

I boarded a four-engine Pan Am plane to Hong Kong, where I bought a hand-tailored full-length woolen winter coat and a top-of-the-line Canon range-finder camera. After this much-needed shopping, I flew to Tokyo, where I stayed another twenty-four hours. No shopping was done there. At the hotel in Tokyo, I must have made a waitress at breakfast dumfounded when I ordered a hamburger. I did not know about the usual breakfast fares at that time. That was the only meal I could think of that sounded sophisticated. She brought it to me, nevertheless. I took a tour of Nikko, just outside Tokyo. That was my first experience of subfreezing winter temperature, still quite cold despite a full-length woolen winter coat over my warmest made-in-the-Philippines woolen suit.

On November 21, I boarded a four-engine Boeing 707, as it happened the first jet flight ever across the Pacific by Pan Am or any other airline at that time. How lucky can you get! All the passengers were toasted with a bubbly drink. It was my first taste of champagne, and we were each given a certificate as we crossed the International Date Line on our way to Seattle, Washington.

Upon my arrival at O'Hare Airport, Donna met me with a couple of her friends who provided the car to bring us to the YMCA hostel in downtown Chicago. I remember having my first Chinese dinner in the US at the Nan Yan Restaurant located just outside the loop—bitter melon with pork and shrimp. Our room at the hostel was small. We had to share a common bathroom down the hall with other guests. The price was right, though—$4 a night! Breakfast the next morning was in a cafeteria where I first experienced the most varied breakfast fare I had ever seen in my life. We had no inkling that much more elaborate and sumptuous meals waited for us in the future.

In Chicago, Donna stayed in her dorm at Cook County Hospital. I resided in the intern's quarters at West Suburban Hospital. Two or more times a week, we met at my hospital. Donna stayed over in my room, where no females were allowed. In the morning, she left the room via the fire escape! One night Dr. KARAMATAS, an OB resident and my roommate, came into the room to change clothes. We chatted a bit while I was in bed with Donna beside me, hidden under the blanket. She was not noticed. Weighing a mere ninety-eight pounds, she hardly made a bump under my blanket!

My stipend at the hospital was $200 a month. I believe Donna made a bit more than that at Cook County Hospital. To supplement my meager income, I moonlighted by offering barbering services to interns and residents, charging a dollar a head. A larger source of income was the fifteen dollars paid by the hospital for each autopsy permit I was able to get from the family of a deceased patient. The hospital needed a certain number of autopsies to comply with federal hospital regulations, and I was the only one among all the interns who could speak fluent English, albeit with a Filipino accent. All the others, including Thais, Koreans, Turks, Greeks, and other Filipinos, did not speak as fluently. The ward nurses noticed that. So I was made the de facto intern to be called when an autopsy permit was needed.

Aside from that, I was the expert in locating hard-to-find veins for IV infusions. Nobody else was called by the pediatric ward nurses for this kind of procedure, especially for drawing blood needed for lab examinations. My previous experiences treating impromptu patients, which were good for training purposes, at the family drugstores in Mexico and San Fernando, Pampanga, and PGH, all in the Philippines, came to the fore!

Exactly how did I become an expert in doing this? I started young as a twelve-year-old. My family's drugstore, Farmacia A. David, in my hometown Mexico, Pampanga, not only sold medicines to the public but also served as a clinic for a UP graduate, Dr. Tomas Guevarra from nearby Sta. Ana, who had his private practice on the premises. I was given the task of giving injections, such as penicillin shots, which was the only antibiotic available then, and insulin. Each morning, I would walk around town, giving diabetic patients their daily insulin needs. I quickly learned how to give medications intravenously too. At that time, it was a common practice to give calcium gluconate IV infusions, presumably for better health and as an adjuvant treatment for tuberculosis. This skill became sharper when my father opened Botica Peczon in San Fernando, the capital town of Pampanga. There were a lot of Chinese businesses there; consequently, there were a lot of Chinese nationals who came to the drugstore, each bringing a little white pill that I was asked to give as an intravenous injection. I dissolved the pill in a spoonful of boiling distilled water, heated over an alcohol lamp. I then aspirated the solution in a syringe and injected it intravenously. Arm veins in these folks bore numerous needle marks, some of which were of my own creation from previous injections. I was paid with a few coins, toys, *hopia,* a popular sweet bean cake, and most often, with firecrackers.

While in medical school, thinking back, I realized that I had really but unknowingly been a drug pusher! This skill I demonstrated early as a medical student at PGH. During my first rotation in surgery, our instructor, Dr. Isidro Benitez, noticed that I was not paying much attention as he demonstrated the technique of doing IV injections. I told him I already knew how to do that. "Show me," he said. Of course, I did it on the first try. When assigned to pediatrics, I learned how to draw blood from infants by inserting a needle into the neck veins. You can say that I literally went for the jugular!

The extra income enabled Donna and me to buy our first automobile, a VW Beetle, model 1959, via installment. Cost—$1,500. Monthly payments—$15.

With my background in ophthalmology, I was the intern called for patients with emergency eye problems. The local ophthalmologists in Oak Park, Illinois, Drs. GEORGINA THEOBALD and HAROLD KIRK, quickly recognized this competence and treated me more like a fellow rather than a mere intern. In surgery, I was first assistant to them. They took me to scientific meetings of the Chicago Ophthalmological Society. When I went to Colby College to attend the Lancaster course in basic ophthalmology, they lent me a binocular microscope and gave me an envelope with $100 inside! Dr. Theobald is the principal author of a textbook on ophthalmic pathology. What an honor it was for me to know and learn from her!

That trusty VW allowed Donna and me to visit all the interesting attractions in and around Chicago, visiting all the museums and even driving all the way to Tennessee to attend the wedding of my best friend, MARCELO MANIAGO, to JOANNE BAKER. The wedding was in the middle of winter. Heavy snow and freezing weather did not deter us from attending. The VW had excellent traction on snowy or even icy roads. Most times, we followed a snowplow. We were fearless.

The first summer in Chicago was brief for me. I had taken leave from West Suburban Hospital to take the Lancaster course at Colby College in Waterville, Maine. With our friend ELVIRA, we got on the road to Maine. One interesting occurrence remains forever embedded in my memory bank. As we left Chicago, driving along State Street, I spotted what appeared to be a dollar bill on the street. I drove up alongside it, opened the driver's side door, and picked it up without leaving my seat. Upon inspection, it turned out to be a $10 bill. What a bonanza! You see, $10 paid all the gasoline the VW needed to bring us to Waterville, Maine, about 1,200 miles! The car got an average of forty miles per gallon, and gas was twelve cents a gallon.

We did not spend on hotels because we called on friends and classmates along the way who let us share their hospital dorms. In Baltimore, Donna's brother Rady and my classmates Fe Palo and Mutya San Agustin were among those who each provided us with a room. In New York City, I remember staying with Medical School classmates BEN SISON, ARTHUR CONDE, LOPE SEMANA, and FORTING SUNIO. In Hartford, Connecticut, CLOD ORQUIZA was our host. All were interns in different hospitals.

Arriving in Waterville, Maine, I checked into a room I had previously arranged to rent. It was not far from the Colby campus. The address stuck in my mind, 13 Peyton Place, the name of a popular movie at that time. My landlords, Mr. and Mrs. RYAN, were both nice New Englanders of Irish descent. I found out later that Mr. Ryan was a fighter pilot during World War II when he flew a Corsair fighter plane.

Donna returned to Chicago with her friend Elvira, taking a Greyhound bus. The Lancaster course was everything that I needed to solidify my already extensive clinical and surgical experiences. The basic course delved into anatomy, optics, pharmacology, physiology, and other important subjects that I had neither insight nor opportunity to learn while at PGH. The subjects were taught by prominent ophthalmologists at that time: Drs. PETER KRONFELD, ARTHUR LINKZ, FREDERICK BLODI, MARSHALL PARKS, PAUL BODER, PAUL CHANDLER, and W. MORTON GRANT. Many came from HMS.

Some of them I would later come to know on a personal level. Dr. Walter Morton Grant was one of them. Two years after I took the course, he took me in as a research fellow at the GCS, Howe Laboratory, HMS, and MEEI in Boston. I named my only son after him, taking his first name, *Walter*, that he usually just listed as W. To his wife, family and colleagues at MEEI, he was *Morton*.

There were about one hundred budding ophthalmologists in my class of 1960. They came from all over the United States and a few other countries across the globe. MARCOS FOJAS and I were the only ones from the Philippines. In the following year, two more Filipino ophthalmologists took that same course: my classmate Felipe Tolentino, also in my UPCM class of 1957, and ELEAZER SUSON, UPCM class of 1955. The latter stayed in the same Waterville boarding house where I was.

During this two-month basic science course, Donna paid for the room at Peyton Place, all the meals, and fees for the course. To do this, she had to work two full-time jobs, at Cook County Hospital and at Mother Cabrini Hospital. We barely managed on the income she earned from these two jobs. At one time, our car was in danger of repossession!

However, opportunities for a better future started to emerge. While at Colby, I saw an advertisement for a senior resident in ophthalmology in Boston. Immediately, I applied for the position. To my surprise, I got the job! Dr. ROBERT ALPERT, the chief of BCH Department of Ophthalmology, sent me an acceptance letter. Apparently, his department needed a chief resident because the one holding that position had developed a serious health problem and could not continue. None of the junior residents were qualified to assume that position. With that good fortune, I drove back to Chicago, happy to be reunited with Donna and anticipating a golden opportunity to further sharpen my skills as an ophthalmologist. Marcos Fojas hitched a ride with me to Chicago, visiting some classmates along the way. Later he married a cardiologist from Greece, and they both settled in Athens. Our paths had not crossed again since that time in Colby and Chicago.

With Donna working two jobs, it was almost impossible for us to see each other as often as we desired. She did not have time to come to West Suburban Hospital. This we solved by renting a one-bedroom apartment near Mother Cabrini Hospital. It had a kitchen, but we had to share a bathroom with another tenant.

My appointment at BCH was to start in January 1961. The rest of 1960, Donna and I prepared for that trip back east. I had informed West Suburban Hospital about my plan to resign from my intern's job. The hospital administrator was surprised but supportive that my next job would be as a senior resident in a major Boston teaching hospital. He regretted that I would not get an internship certificate from the hospital because I did not complete the required twelve months. That was the least of my problems because I already had one from PGH, Philippines. This was enough when I applied for licensure to practice medicine in the New England states.

In January 1961, with the VW filled literally to the roof with our meager belongings, I drove alone to Boston. Donna waited behind until I could get an apartment there. This time our separation was short, only about two weeks. During the drive, I was listening to the inaugural speech of President JOHN F. KENNEDY while a fierce northeaster dumped several feet of snow in some parts of New England along the route I had to take. Again, each time I was given free use of a room, by some of my classmates. At least for a night, I also stayed in a motel.

I safely arrived at BCH with the whole city blanketed with two feet of snow. The room I was assigned to was in an old building that used to be a ward for patients with infectious diseases. The building was so old that electrical wiring was DC, and that was good only for lamps and radio. The radiators for heating were not working. That first night was the coldest in my life! There were *not* enough warm clothes and blankets to keep me from shivering from the cold. In the morning, I reported this to the building superintendent. Heat was restored immediately. When Donna arrived from Chicago, she stayed with me briefly at this old BCH building. Now the room did not feel cold anymore!

Among the residents, I was the shortest, not the oldest—and I was chief resident. Work at BCH was not as busy as the one I had gone through at PGH. Being chief resident was now a piece of cake. The consultants quickly noticed my expertise and surgical skills. I was the favored one as first assistant in the surgery of their private patients.

A consultant at PGH, Dr. GLORIA LIM helped me perform my very first cataract surgery. She was taking the same one-week course in ophthalmic pathology at Walter Reed Armed Forces Institute of Pathology in Bethesda, Maryland. Dr. Alpert had allowed me to take the seminar that augmented the basic subjects I had already taken at the Lancaster course in Colby and my two-week rotation in surgical pathology at PGH. The knowledge I gathered from this comprehensive course I shared with the other BCH residents, and that gesture raised my level of professionalism with them.

By this time, Donna had already arrived from Chicago via Greyhound bus. We rented an apartment at 13 Dixwell Street in Roxbury, a suburb of Boston that is *not* known for affluence. Donna got a job at New England Hospital for Women, which was conveniently just a few minutes' walk away from our apartment. In this apartment, which was in the poorer part of town, we gave temporary lodging to friends who were coming to Boston for training just like us—newly married ROMAN IBAY and his wife, NENA, FELIPE TOLENTINO and his wife, FLORA, together with their children LULU and PHILIP. Many classmates came to visit. RADY and CONNIE VILLAFLOR visited too.

In 1962, we moved to Dorchester, a step up from Roxbury. At first, we shared an apartment with ROLAND and LINDA NAVARRO, both resident physicians working in other area hospitals. In a few months, we rented our own apartment in a new building at 90 Wrentham Street. Donna got a job at Carney Hospital.

I was nearing the end of my contract as chief resident in Ophthalmology at BCH, but I was still yearning for more knowledge. Glaucoma was the subspecialty I wanted to pursue. GCS at MEEI was the only place for this. I requested an interview with Professor Grant, head of Howe Laboratory of Ophthalmology. I must have impressed him because he immediately accepted me as a clinical research fellow in the service. I was third in a long line of fellows who got their subspecialty in glaucoma training there.

Under the tutorship of Dr. Grant, I immersed myself in clinical research. This meant that, together with regular residents assigned to the service, I saw all the patients referred to this specialty clinic from the general clinic. Additionally, I was called numerous times by consultant surgeons to assist them in surgery. The calls came with welcome supplements to my income. Usually, I was paid in cash, $25 per case.

While doing this work, I interacted with almost all the staff at MEEI, the majority of whom were HMS graduates. I realized then I was equal to almost all of them, better than some, but could definitely learn more from a few at the top.

My guru, Dr. Grant, was one of the best. Dr. Paul Chandler was another. To them, I owe most of the confidence I gained for myself. Once Dr. Grant asked me to take his place in a class lecture for undergraduate students at HMS. I was nervous, but I did well.

Donna and I were not the only Filipinos in Boston. Other colleagues from UPCM came to this Mecca of medical training— ROMAN IBAY JR., FELIPE TOLENTINO, CLEMENTE GATMAITAN JR., VICENTE JOCSON, ANTONIO GARCIA, and FLORENCIO HIPONA. Newly married, Roman Ibay Jr. came with his wife, Nena, and briefly stayed with us at 13 Dixwell Street in Roxbury. Donna and I were godparents to their first child, THERESE. Fel became a fellow in MEEI Retina Service under the tutorship of world-renowned Dr. CHARLES SCHEPENS, who invented the indirect ophthalmoscope. Fel later became a partner in Retina Associates of Boston.

Clemente Gatmaitan Jr. got a fellowship at Massachusetts General Hospital (MGH) Cardiology Department. His excellent training there almost came to a tragic end when he got infected with chickenpox that landed him in the hospital because of cardiac complications. He was isolated in a room previously occupied by a graduate nurse who also got the viral infection and died from the same cardiac complication. I was the only one allowed to visit him because I had a strong immunity from chickenpox, which I had acquired while still a clinical clerk at PGH.

VICENTE JOCSON, who was one year ahead of me at UPCM, also came as a glaucoma research fellow under Dr. Grant. We worked in the same service, but he did more basic research in the laboratory. His main contribution was demonstrating the complex venous drainage of the anterior segment of the eye, using a colored plastic liquid that he injected into the tiny veins with his own miniature glass needles drawn from ordinary glass tubing. He later became full professor in ophthalmology at the University of Pittsburgh.

RONALD TABLANTE, a graduate of UST, was a resident in ophthalmology at BCH when I was chief resident there. His eldest daughter was brought to the clinic one day. I made a diagnosis of retinoblastoma, a common cancerous tumor of the eye among Filipinos but rare among Caucasians. I was the assistant during the enucleation of the eye performed by the department chief, Dr. ROBERT ALPERT.

While doing all this clinical work, I was reviewing for the American Board of Ophthalmology (ABO) examinations. A certificate from the ABO is considered a crowning glory for any ophthalmologist. During the Cuban Missile Crisis in October 1962, I took a Greyhound bus to St. Louis, Missouri, where the examinations were to be held. I said goodbye to Donna and asked her to wish me luck in the examinations, meanwhile thinking that this might be the last time we would see each other because of the Cuban Missile Crisis confrontation between President John F. Kennedy and Premier Nikita Khrushchev. The world was never closer to an all-out nuclear war that would have annihilated most of the world's population.

All that, however, did not stop me from concentrating on the ABO examinations. I passed the written part easily. The oral part was even more of a breeze because many of the examiners who asked me where I trained and whom I trained under were impressed with both Dr. W. Morton Grant and Dr. Paul A. Chandler, my mentors. Additionally, I was well prepared. I do not think I missed any question in the written and oral parts of the examinations. To celebrate this success, I was treated to dinner at Playboy Club in St. Louis by JOE SUBA, youngest brother of GLORIA DAVID, who married my mother's younger brother DELFIN and lived in St. Louis at that time. Gawking at the novelty of Playboy Bunnies, we enjoyed a good meal.

On November 1, 1962, I got my ABO certificate. I was the only one among all the residents and fellows at MEEI certified by this body while still in training. Some established full-time consultants at the infirmary had yet to take the ABO examinations.

I conducted several clinical research projects. My favorite was the one regarding the effect of alcoholic drinks on intraocular eye pressure. Below is the abstract with Dr. Grant as coauthor:

Glaucoma, Alcohol, and Intraocular Pressure
JOSE D. PECZON, MD; W. MORTON GRANT,
MD
Author Affiliations
Arch Ophthalmol. 1965;73(4):495-501.
doi:10.1001/archopht.1965.00970030497009

Abstract

Ophthalmologic literature relating to ethyl alcohol consists of many reports of influences on eye movements, nystagmus, visual physiology, and on so-called alcohol amblyopia, but little is to be found concerning influence on intraocular pressure. A systematic search of textbooks and the periodical literature has disclosed only one previous study on this subject in human beings and very little additional in animals. This is surprising when one considers how common is the drinking of alcohol, how many other effects of alcohol have been studied in great detail, and how often glaucomatous patients themselves raise questions about the possible influence of alcoholic beverages on their glaucoma. It seemed to us that one of the most frequent questions asked by patients whose condition had been diagnosed as glaucoma was whether it was safe for them to continue to take their customary alcoholic beverages.

My study showed that the answer is a resounding *yes!* This discovery I later used during my extensive cataract surgical practice. I routinely advised my patients to take a good shot of an alcoholic drink equivalent to two glasses of wine right after the patient got home from the surgicenter. That gave them an almost pain-free post-operative period because of lower intraocular pressure. Without the alcohol, that pressure was usually elevated, resulting in a lot of pain. That probably contributed a lot to my popularity among my cataract patients. They were both comfortable with and happy with the alcoholic drink. Getting 20/20 vision after surgery was a bonus!

It was not all work and no play for Donna and me. We visited interesting places around Boston, Cambridge, Cape Cod, Nantucket, Martha's Vineyard, New York City, Maine, and New Hampshire. We did not have much money, but we were confident and adventurous. AND WE LOVED EACH OTHER NO END!

One trip as leaf peepers in New Hampshire was particularly memorable because the small cottage we stayed in caught fire during the night. Donna and I barely got out unharmed. We did not lose anything, though, not especially the Canon camera I used to record this harrowing experience. Fellow BCH hospital resident Donald Cherr, his wife, Peggy, and their daughter, Elizabeth, were with us during that memorable trip.

On November 22, 1963, I was seeing the usual number of glaucoma patients when the news of President John F. Kennedy's assassination was somberly announced on TV by WALTER CRONKITE and other news outlets. Everyone in the hospital was stunned and saddened by this monstrous act. That night, Donna and I somberly watched TV for more coverage of the assassination. For me, it had a poignant meaning because I was listening to his inaugural address to the nation when he became the thirty-fifth US president while I was driving from Chicago to Boston. His frequent briefings with newsmen and women assigned to the White House were legendary for their clarity, truthfulness, and humor. He and his brother ROBERT, as attorney general, expertly handled the Cuban missile crisis with bravery and decisiveness. They were my heroes too!

While enjoying the unparalleled opportunities we had in accumulating professional knowledge and growing socially more mature, there was a nagging worry because Donna could not get pregnant. She often cried when receiving letters announcing the birth of a child from relatives and friends. It was not because she resented their fecundity but that she wanted a child of our own. So did I. She felt that she was approaching the age of becoming an old primipara at thirty. All of that changed when Donna missed her period in December 1963. Then she started to have nausea in the morning and complaining about funny smells and other odd things she never experienced before. Those were suspicious symptoms of a possible pregnancy that we had fervently wished for. To get a more definitive answer, a urine test for pregnancy was done. The report came out positive!

On August 15, WALTER MARTIN PECZON came to enrich our lives. Felipe and Flora Tolentino and Linda Tablante were the godparents at Walter's baptism in a Dorchester, Massachusetts, Catholic Church.

Soon our contract with the Student and Exchange Visitor Program (SEVP) was coming to an end. We could stay in this program only for five years. Preparations were made for our return home to the Philippines to start a new life in the land of our birth. We had no plans to stay in the USA permanently.

With the arrival of Walter, our original plan of returning to Manila via a leisurely trip to Europe was replaced by a more practical, shorter flight home to the Philippines. Late in October 1964, we bid goodbye to Dr. W. Morton Grant and our other Boston friends. We made the trip back home to Manila with stopovers in Houston to visit brother Ben; in Los Angeles to visit Disneyland that had recently just opened; and in San Francisco, Honolulu, Tokyo, and Hong Kong before setting foot on our homeland to start a new life.

Returning to Our Homeland

Walter was seven weeks old when Donna and I left Boston in early October 1964 to start a new life in the Philippines. For months before that, I was busy gathering items we needed to start a home and a private practice in Manila. I was full of enthusiasm and energy for the challenge. For the practice, I bought a brand-new Haag-Streit slit lamp biomicroscope, which was a mainstay in any modern ophthalmology practice. That Swiss-made instrument was the Rolls Royce of the genre, a status the manufacturer carries to this day. I also bought a surgical cataract set, various handheld diagnostic instruments, and other optical devices needed for a comprehensive ophthalmological practice. For the house, I bought a brand-new two-door GE refrigerator. We kept these items in our apartment along Wrentham Street, Dorchester. I got hold of several wooden crates and carefully packed all those things and had them shipped to Manila.

Important items we packed in our luggage. One treasure I hand-carried is a book given to Walter, our son, from my guru. The book is *Toxicology of the Eye*, authored by W. Morton Grant, MD. Inside the front cover is this dedication: *To Walter Martin Peczon from Walter Morton Grant, with best wishes for the future and with respect and admiration for his father, Jose.*

After saying goodbye to Dr. W. Morton Grant, we flew from Boston to Texas, where we met my brother Ben. He had just arrived to start his postgraduate studies at Texas A&M University. From there, we flew to Los Angeles and visited Disneyland. We then flew to San Francisco and, from there, to Hawaii. In each city, we stayed for two nights to enjoy the sights.

At the Hilton Hotel in Waikiki, we had a scare. Walter was in a baby crib provided by the hotel. Somehow, he got his head through the side rails, and to my horror, I discovered him with his head dangling out of the crib and not crying. For a moment, I thought he was dead. With so much adrenaline, I must have pulled the wooden slats quickly, and Donna got him out safely. It was with a huge sigh of relief for Donna and me to see that he was safe, unscathed from that scary ordeal.

On to Tokyo and, finally, to Hong Kong, where we met Tony and Lourdes Garcia, who were also returning to Manila. The two families arrived in Manila on October 14. Arlene Garcia, the eldest of the Garcia children, led the way to the arrival area. Those were exciting days. Both the Garcias and the Peczons wanted to plant their new roots permanently in the home country.

We stayed briefly in Grace Park, Caloocan, before renting an apartment along Dita Street in Makati, next door to Uncle Ruben's residence.

Donna's Daddy and Nanny were in Grace Park to welcome us back. During the first night back in our home country, Donna's father lost a pair of pants to intrepid burglars who apparently used a long pole through the wrought iron window grill to do the "fishing" feat. Similarly, one of my cousins also lost a pair of pants that same night. Welcome to the land of our birth!

After about a month, our household goods and all the ophthalmic instruments arrived at the port of Manila. Taking them out of the customs area was another traumatic experience, something we did not expect. Not only did we willingly pay all the legal taxes, but we were still forced to pay so many people with small bribes just to get our goods released from the customs area. The last person to sign his name on the release papers even had the audacity to take my Gold Cross ballpoint pen given me as a gift by Dr. Robert Alpert of BCH and put it in his shirt pocket after he signed the papers. Immediately, I took it back from him and returned it to my shirt pocket. Matter closed.

We got all the wooden crates loaded on a rented truck and drove to our Dita Street apartment, escorted by a pair of uniformed motorcycle cops, presumably to prevent other policemen from stopping us and demanding more bribes. After the crates were unloaded from the trucks, the contents were placed inside the apartment. During all this time, the motorcycle cops stayed around. After the crates were emptied, they asked if they could keep them. Without hesitation, I said yes. It was a giant relief to get all that unpleasantness behind. I then realized why those motorcycle cops escorted us out of the customs area to our apartment. They wanted those wooden crates probably to be used in their houses to make repairs or to add a cabinet or two. Without hesitation, I said yes, even asking the truck driver to deliver them to their houses. It was a giant relief to get all that unpleasantness behind.

Less than a month after returning home, both Donna and I decided that we did not want any part of this kind of life any longer. The very next day after our decision, we went to the US Embassy in Manila and applied for immigrant visas. At that time, only one hundred Filipinos were given immigrant visas to the US each year, and already there was a fifteen-year waiting period. I told the US consul that we did not mind waiting that long; we just wanted our names placed on the waiting list.

A year later, President LYNDON JOHNSON signed a new immigration law that was authored by Senator TED KENNEDY of Massachusetts, allowing twenty-five thousand Filipinos to enter the US every year, equal to the number of visas issued to Western European countries.

So to our surprise and delight, we did not have to wait fifteen years for that green card. Our application for immigrant visas was granted that year. However, we still had to wait two years before we could return to the US because of the SEVP requirement that all participants in that program had to return to their home country first and stay there for two years before returning to the US. Both Donna and I had participated in that program during our first visit to the US for postgraduate education.

That same day, we also went to the telephone company (PLDT) to apply for a telephone line. We were again placed on a waiting list. Unbelievably, we got a notice from them four years later when we were already living in Greenfield, Massachusetts, that a telephone number was now available to us. We gave it to our friend JEB ROSALES, who lived in Manila.

While waiting for our green cards to enable us to return to the US, I did my best to support my growing, young family. I had a small office in a medical office compound along Mabini Street in Manila. This suite of offices was owned by Dr. PABLITO CAMPOS. There were other young doctors in that compound: my friend and fraternity brod CLEMENTE GATMAITAN, a cardiologist, and AUGUSTO LITONJUA, another frat brod, who practiced endocrinology. I did not have as many patients as the others who started earlier, but I managed to get by. Many of my patients were not well-to-do. Some paid me with whatever they could afford, not in pesos but in goods—sacks of rice, fabrics for pants or barong Tagalog (a finely woven fabric made from pineapple fibers made into a shirt worn untucked and considered formal attire), cooked food (*relyenong bangus*, *chicken adobo*, etc.), and most noteworthy and almost unbelievably, a live goat! Both Donna and I thought that was comical. The goat was given to Imang Pacing for disposition. It ended up as *kaldereta*, meat cooked with tomato sauce.

In addition to that small start-up office along Mabini Street, I went back to work with Dr. Geminiano de Ocampo at his office and hospital along United Nations Avenue. I was also appointed as consultant in the Ophthalmology Department at PGH. Additionally, I visited the UP Infirmary once a week in Diliman, Quezon City, for any patient.

To be able to accomplish all that, I bought a new car, a VW, just like the one we had in Chicago and Boston. This was our second car ever. The first one was painted gold, and this second one was green. VW Beetles were popular because of their dependability; as a result, they were also a frequent target of thieves. During the first week out of the dealer's lot, I lost all four tire caps. That was a minor loss, but shortly afterward, the theft escalated. In a few weeks, all four hubcaps were gone, next the tools, then the spare tire. What more could be stolen!

I was totally flabbergasted by the next episode. That came a few months later when Donna and I had to leave our apartment early in the morning to be at a wedding. It was still dark. I switched on the headlights. Nothing happened. The headlights had been stolen! Unbelievable! To add to the absurdity, our car was parked in front of our apartment that had a 24/7 guard in the compound. Naturally, I complained to the apartment owner.

What happened next was even more absurd. The guard was made to come to our place to answer our complaint. He tearfully stated that he did not have any money to pay for replacing the headlights. He had many children to feed, and he recited a litany of so much economic misery. He was supposed to pay us for the stolen headlights. We could have been adamant and demanded compensation, but Donna and I ended up giving him a few pesos instead. The next day my cousin DAN, who lived next door, told me that I could buy a used pair of VW headlights from a local junk dealer. Sure enough, when I went there, I was able to find the two headlights I needed. Quickly I realized that those were the very ones stolen from our car! Reluctantly, I paid for them after haggling for the price. It was a mild form of carnapping; the VW headlights and other spare parts had been stolen for ransom. Disgusting episodes like this made Donna and me even more determined to escape Manila and return to Boston.

No, returning to the Philippines was not all a crown of thorns. There were numerous delightful events. We met many relatives whom we had not seen in five years.

On September 19, 1965, LISA came into our lives. She was born at Anita Ty Hospital along United Nations Avenue, almost next door to the office and hospital of Dr. De Ocampo, for whom I worked as an employee. The birth was complicated, with Lisa needing to be in an incubator for a week because of anoxia due to the umbilical cord having wound tightly around her neck. Donna almost died because of post-delivery bleeding due to a lax uterus. The first night when we got home, I spent my best effort to do uterine massage to control the bleeding. All went well after that. Lisa developed normally, except for some residual and minimal brain damage.

During that time, Taal Volcano was erupting. Was this another omen? Our two-bedroom apartment quickly became crowded. Help from Bacolod came in the form of a very dependable babysitter for

Walter, NENA. Lisa had BELLA, the daughter of my in-law's house-keeper. A third helper, FELIPA, helped Donna keep our little apartment neat and clean. My patients gradually increased in number, and I started to make some money to pay all expenses, but not enough to save for the future. We were not too worried about that because we knew this situation was temporary. Our dream for the future was rising on the horizon. We now had the much-desired green cards. Thieves who feasted on our green-colored VW could never lay hands on those precious green cards!

An opportunity to earn extra income came from an invitation by Dr. EMMANUEL ESTACIO, who had a hospital in Butuan, Agusan. Many of his patients needed cataract surgery. His hospital did not have an ophthalmologist, and most of those patients had to travel, either to Davao or to Manila, for their much-needed eye care. Butuan was where Fel Tolentino came from, and this was a welcome opportunity to give back to his hometown. Armed with my trusty cataract surgical set, Fel and I flew there. We stayed at Dr. Estacio's house and operated on several patients with mature cataracts right there in his hospital. We restored the sight of these patients and saved them the extra expense of traveling to distant cities. The incomes, although modest, were a welcome addition to the separate finances of Fel and me.

An interesting episode occurred during our mandatory two years of waiting in the Philippines to meet all the requirements needed to immigrate to America. Fel and his wife, Flora, Marcos Fojas and his wife, Helen, and Donna and I went to Vigan in Ilocos Sur at the invitation of MRS. CARMELING CRISOLOGO, the wife of Governor FLORO CRISOLOGO of that province, who knew Fel, to conduct a medical mission screening for cataracts and glaucoma. The latter is a particularly dangerous malady that can lead to permanent loss of vision if not discovered and treated in the early stages. It was sort of a goodwill gesture on the part of Governor Crisologo to provide free eye consultation, glaucoma screening, and treatment of minor eye conditions for his and his wife's constituents. All went well during the duration of the mission.

On driving back to Manila on Fel's Plymouth, I felt chest pain and palpitation. It was alarming enough that we stopped in San

Fernando, La Union, where classmates RUFINO and VICKY MACAGBA had the family-owned Lorma Hospital. Helen, a cardiologist by training, evaluated my symptoms and did an EKG. She then declared that I had angina pectoris, meaning that I had coronary artery disease, and ordered me complete bed rest. The rest of the way home, I was made to lie down in the back seat of the car, using Donna's lap as my pillow. That was nice, but the diagnosis was devastating for me to be able to relax.

Upon arrival in Manila, I immediately consulted with good friend Clemente Gatmaitan Jr., who was with me when he trained in cardiology at MGH in Boston. After a thorough physical examination of me and his review of the EKG tracings done at Lorma Hospital, he assured me I did *not* have coronary artery disease. Instead, I had a benign condition called *premature ventricular contractions* (PVC). That assuaged me of my anxiety, and I happily reverted to a normal lifestyle. He proved to be correct because at age eighty-seven years, as I write this, I have no evidence of coronary artery disease. I do have atrial fibrillation, which is under control under the care of my most capable cardiologist and electrophysiologist, Howard I. Frumin, MD, who implanted a cardiac pacemaker in 2012; a cryogenic ablation of the foci of the site of abnormal electrical signals two years ago; and my taking of antiarrhythmic medication.

After that unplanned stop at Lorma Hospital, Rufi called me with an invitation to return, this time with the idea that I might like to establish an ophthalmology practice there. The hospital provided general medical and surgical services but none in ophthalmology. I accepted his invitation and drove there in my VW with my cousin RENATO DAVID. I liked the place, but before deciding, I had to consult with Donna. She was steadfast in her determination that our fortune was in the US. That was that! No discussion was needed.

Looking back now, Donna was right. I probably would have made a fortune as the first ophthalmologist in that underserved area for eye care, but I do not think I could have achieved the high level of my professional career as I was able to do in Greenfield, Massachusetts.

An unexpected event happened on the drive back home. The windshield wipers of the VW, which was not even two years old, refused to function. On top of that, the clutch would not work. Luckily, I was still able to drive home, albeit with much-reduced speed and with a lot of anxiety. I was grateful Rene was with me. An omen?

While playing mahjong at the house of the Gianzons, which was directly across the street from our apartment, I met an interesting patient, FERNANDO LUZ. He had cataracts and decided to come to my office for a consultation. There was no doubt that he needed surgery. I advised him and he consented but not before I got a call and a grilling from her daughter NENITA. She wanted to know how many cataract operations had been under my wings and what was my success rate. Aside from PGH, where did I train in the US? She was married to an anesthesiologist, BENNY ADORABLE. Like Donna and me, they just returned to the Philippines after training in the US for five years. I performed the surgery at De Ocampo Eye Hospital. It was successful.

Soon I was recommended by FERNANDO LUZ to other family members, a brother and a sister. I will never forget his sister, PAZ LUZ DIMAYUGA. After a successful cataract surgery, she asked for the bill, and I presented it to her. Looking at it, she seemed surprised and asked me to change the amount. Anticipating that she would ask me to reduce the amount, as is the custom in the Philippines (bargaining is an art and is not considered an insult), I was so pleasantly surprised when she told me that I was charging her too little! She paid me, I think, double of what I had asked for payment. That was the first experience I encountered from *a thoroughly satisfied patient!*

As the two-year mandatory stay in the Philippines was ending, *we prepared ourselves for the great adventure ahead.* I sold all my ophthalmic equipment to classmate Fel Tolentino and his partner, RON TABLANTE. I also handed over all my meager records of private patients to them. They had started a joint practice specializing in retinal diseases.

To digress a bit, I want to mention that my brother Pons was the only person who was able to repair a laser surgical device that Fel

118

and Ron needed badly in treating certain retinal diseases. Pons did this remarkable repair by just studying the circuit diagram that came with the device. It was so unfortunate that my electronic genius of a brother did not achieve his acme in this new electronic world because he died of sleep apnea when not yet fifty years old.

Uncle Ruben's house along Dita Street in Makati had a notable significance in our lives. I lived there while in training at PGH as an intern and resident ophthalmologist. Donna was introduced there to the family at my graduation party. Our wedding reception was also at that house. As newlyweds, we rented a bedroom in the house of the Gianzons across the street. Five years after our advanced training in Chicago and Boston, our apartment was next door. Welcome and farewell parties were all held there.

With two pieces of luggage and a hundred dollars in my wallet, our young family left the Philippines for good on October 28, 1966. That was my thirty-third birthday. Land of the Free and the Home of the Brave, here we come!

Leaving behind the Pearl of the Orient Seas, we bade a sad farewell to our family and friends who came to the Manila international airport to see us depart for a foreign land where we sought to find our place in the sun.

Donna carried Lisa in her right arm. Walter tagged along, clutching at her left arm. I followed behind with all our carry-on luggage. There was no turning back now. It was just Donna, Walter, Lisa, and me, facing an uncertain future in a foreign land, but with confidence in our trainings and abilities. Also, we knew Dr. Walter Morton Grant and MEEI were waiting for us in Boston with open arms.

Longing for a Better Life

With green cards attached to the passports of Donna, Lisa, and me, together with a USA passport for Boston-born Wally, we left our homeland and headed out to the Land of the Free and the Home of the Brave on October 28, 1966, my thirty-third birthday.

Pan Am flew us to Guam, then to Honolulu. Here, we passed through customs and immigration. The friendly immigration officer welcomed us by saying, "Doctor, we need people like you here in the States." That was an unmistakably encouraging remark coming from a citizen of the country we chose to spend the rest of our lives in. San Francisco was the next stop, where we arrived very exhausted but extremely happy. After crossing the international dateline, I celebrated my birthday two days in a row! Was that another harbinger of good things to come?

At Logan Airport in Boston, we were met by my friend Marcelo Maniago and his wife, Joanne. They graciously allowed us to temporarily stay in their apartment in Brookline while I went hunting for an apartment of our own. Within a week, I found a suitable one in Arlington Heights, a suburb of Boston, accessible by train and an easy thirty-minute drive by car.

Dr. Grant, my old boss, rehired me to my old position at MEEI where I resumed my clinical research activities. This was an opportunity for me to prepare myself for private practice that I knew was our ticket to achieve our dreams. There was but a single pathway for me to achieve that. The key was to secure a license to practice medicine. This required my passing a state medical board examination in Massachusetts or any other state. To give myself the best chance to achieve this, I applied to all the New England states to take the examination. All I needed was to pass one, and I could practice in all these states by reciprocity. It was now nine years since I got my MD, and so my knowledge of general medicine was already quite a bit rusty. In ophthalmology, there was no problem, but I had to shore up my knowledge base in all the other aspects of medicine, especially the basic subjects of anatomy, physiology, embryology, neurology, pharmacology, and others, twelve subjects in all.

Our landlord at Arlington Heights, ALDO FIORVANTI, gave me free use of their own residence on the first floor of the apartment house while the entire family went on a vacation. For almost a month, I was able to study without interference while Donna took care of Walter and Lisa. With this ideal atmosphere, I was able to prepare myself for the exam. The first was in Burlington, Vermont; a week later, it was New Hampshire. The examination for Massachusetts was a month later. Within a week, I was informed by mail that I passed the tests in Vermont and New Hampshire. Using just the license from the Granite State (New Hampshire), I applied and got a medical license in Massachusetts by reciprocity. That made it unnecessary to take the exam I had applied for in my home state. By that time, I had rejoined my family upstairs in our own apartment to be a full-time husband and father. Spending a lot of time reviewing for examination was now in the rearview mirror, and I could devote all my time to having a normal life. That license to practice medicine was the key that would allow Donna and me to pursue our dreams.

Dr. Grant was particularly happy to hear this news. He immediately rewarded me with a higher position at GCS. I was now assistant director. I continued with clinical research and started a tiny private practice that my benevolent patron allowed me to do in the clinic. I was not a member of the medical staff at MEEI, but I had full private practice privileges at Boston University Hospital! My patients were not many, but for the first time, I started to earn money on my own, not solely dependent on a salary from a grant coming from the National Institutes of Health (NIH).

Donna diligently performed her part being wife and mother, taking care of our young children. Our apartment was on top of a hill about a mile from the shopping area near the train station. To go shopping while I was in the hospital, she would bundle up the two children and walk down easily to the center of town, buy whatever was needed, then walk up the hill carrying not only her purchases but also Lisa, who was still too small to walk on the snow and ice on her own. Walter was able to walk by himself, holding on to his mom's left hand. This was a repetition of the tableau when we left Manila Airport, but this one was in the snowy and cold winter of New England.

We only had one car at that time, and I used it for commuting to the office. In the spring, Donna got her own driver's license, and life became a lot easier for her. Never did she complain about anything. She drove the Ford Fairlane wagon, our first car outright purchase, to do errands. Our family was now too large for a VW. I took the train to go to work in Boston.

These halcyon days were exactly what we had only dreamed about when we left our country of birth and immigrated to the USA. All of this was initiated by the adventurous spirit of Donna, who made the courageous decision to go abroad, alone the first time, and waited eight months for me to follow.

My career in ophthalmology developed quickly. I was making enough to be able to afford a house of our own. I did not know it at that time, but I was apparently recognized by other Boston ophthalmologists as a desirable partner in their practices. Dr. IRVING PAVLOV, an MEEI consultant, made me an offer to join him in his practice with an initial yearly stipend of $50,000, at that time a princely amount I could not imagine possible for me even in my wildest dreams! I started to work in his office on a part-time basis.

Those were heady days. However, some dark clouds appeared. These were expected but not welcomed.

As soon as we got settled in Boston, I registered in the Military Draft Board as was required of all physicians, citizens, and green-card holders alike, below the age of thirty-five. I was two years from being exempted. At the time I registered, there were twenty-eight doctors already on the list. Some were older than me, many younger. Vietnam War was raging at that time, with over half a million US soldiers sent there by President Lyndon Johnson. I found it ironic that the same POTUS who signed an immigration reform bill that enabled us to immigrate into the country was also responsible for this massive war I was now facing, possibly getting involved in, albeit not directly as a combatant but as a physician ready to take care of any of the casualties. Many of the younger doctors in my draft board had already been drafted and sent to Vietnam. To avoid the draft, others left for Canada. Some returned to their home countries and gave up their green cards.

Donna and I decided that we would face whatever fate had in store for us by staying in our adopted country; I also tried legal ways to get a deferment, hoping after a medical and physical examination, I would get a deferment because of a partly paralyzed left foot from a gunshot wound in the left thigh in 1948. The physician who gave me the examination did not allow me an exemption for the foot drop. A second opinion was not an option.

Persistent in trying to get a legal deferment, I interviewed with a General of the Massachusetts National Guard. He wanted me to be a part of the unit, but orders from the Pentagon closed that possible safety net. Next, I tried to take advantage of the BERRY PLAN that allowed physicians to volunteer to any US Armed Forces branch of the military. If accepted, my strategy was to volunteer to the US Air Force and ask to be assigned to Clark Air Force Base in the Philippines, away from the shooting in Vietnam. This could have allowed me to return to the Philippines, out of danger in Vietnam, without losing my permanent immigrant status. That route got shut down too. I was now classified 1A, meaning that I could be drafted at any time. This was in the early spring of 1968. Donna and I were now resigned to whatever fate had in store for us.

One other option was a possibility, but neither one of us gave it serious thought. That was to accept a job offer from ARAMCO, in Saudi Arabia. The company was actively recruiting doctors at that time. Suddenly, out of nowhere came ROBERT E. GRAVES. He came to see me at MEEI and told me that he represented the town of Greenfield. To my disbelieving ears, he told me that if I set up a private practice in his hometown, I would be exempted from the draft.

I thought he was full of bull, pardon the language, but I played along with the idea. I had resigned myself to becoming a member of the US Armed Forces, and I knew that with my qualifications, I would at least be a captain with all the rank's privileges, whatever they were. Bob Graves told me that if I refused this offer, I could expect to be called shortly and be "measured for military fatigues," as he put it.

After discussing this situation with Donna, we decided to take up Bob Grave's invitation to visit Greenfield, which was in the western part of the Commonwealth of Massachusetts, about one hundred miles west from Boston. We rode in his car, and as we approached the town, I saw a lot of trees, beautiful snow-covered meadows, an uncountable number of cows, but very few humans. He laughed when I asked him if there were enough people there to keep me busy. He was more serious when answering my question on how people in the area will treat the first foreign-born and trained doctor like me in their midst. "Doctor, it all depends on how you present yourself to the public, but I know they would love you," he said.

We made the mandatory visit to the two local hospitals, Franklin County Public Hospital, later renamed Franklin Medical Center, in Greenfield, and Farren Memorial Hospital in the neighboring town of Turners Falls. He also bought us to Schaff's Opticians along Main Street, Greenfield, which he owned and operated. He introduced me to the local ophthalmologist in town, Dr. VICTOR ELMER KENNEALLY, who was just recovering from a recent heart attack.

With nothing to lose and everything to gain, we made the decision to accept the invitation to set up a private practice in that town starting in June 1968. Bob found a vacant doctor's office for me on 40 Church Street, a block from Main Street in town. Interestingly, this was the former house of the first EENT doctor in the area. Bob's secretary started taking appointments for me in his own office that was quickly filled for the first four weeks before I saw the first patient. I realized then why Bob was amused when I asked him if there were enough people in the area to keep me busy. The list of appointments kept getting longer even after I started practice, and it was not long before the appointment book got filled up for almost eight months. Talk about being busy from day one!

When I informed Dr. Grant about my plan to start a private practice in Greenfield, he not only approved it unequivocally but was delighted with my decision. I knew he was disappointed with the medical staff at MEEI for disapproving my application for membership among their ranks, but he was elated, as I was, that I found a place with a promise to get me out of harm's way in Vietnam.

For me personally, this was a perfect scenario because I really did not relish practicing in Boston, where there was so much competition and hospital politics. The competition I could have handled well, but the politics was something else.

The medical staff at MEEI was lily-white except for a lone Japanese ophthalmologist who was accepted ahead of me. I would have been the first and only Filipino. In a way, I was grateful to the chief of the medical staff, who informed me that my application to join the medical staff was denied. That made it easy for me to completely divorce myself from Boston ophthalmology politics and go completely on my own to develop professionally, guided by my own instincts.

Looking back now, I know I could not have chosen a better place than Greenfield to practice ophthalmology and to raise a family. Professionally, socially, and financially, we flourished beyond our wildest dreams. Life there left nothing more to be desired. Happy home is Greenfield!

Dodging the Bullet

Monday, June 17, 1968, was when I saw my first Greenfield patient, MARION DELANO. I will always fondly remember her because she was so nice and appreciative of what I did for her. (When I retired from practice thirty-two years later, June 25, 2000, she was on the final day's list of patients I saw in GEC.) That June, we were still living in Winchester.

Each Monday morning, Donna and I drove to Greenfield. Donna was my receptionist, secretary, and cashier all at the same time. Candlelight Motel and later Howard Johnson was our temporary house/abode after office hours. At night every Friday, we drove back to Winchester. Ima took care of Wally and Lisa in our absence.

It was not long before our presence in the area became known. SIMON COHN, the local Realtor, came to visit us in the office, not as a patient, but as a businessman who knew that we will be staying in Greenfield permanently and will be needing a house of our own soon. I did not realize it at the time, but the first several houses that he showed us were not only unattractive, but they were not in the best neighborhoods in town. He probably reasoned that because we were so young and new to the area, we did not have enough financial resources to get a house in a better neighborhood. Was this a sign of discrimination? I do not know. While driving around town, we noticed a beautiful English Tudor brick house along High Street, within walking distance to the hospital. Donna casually remarked how beautiful the house looked. Unfortunately, the owner of the house, Dr. STEVE WOLANSKE, a general practitioner, and his wife, PEGGY, did not have their house on the market. That did not deter

Mr. Cohn from making a U-turn, drive up to the front of the house, knock on the door, and introduced us to Dr. and Mrs. Steve Wolanske, and we saw a house that we liked enormously, and it was in the right neighborhood.

The next day, Si Cohn called us with a surprise to say that we could make an offer for the house if it was what we had wanted. Bingo! We offered $37K, and the Wolanskes accepted it. No haggling! We immediately put our Winchester house for sale at $35K and got that settled promptly too. A local Greenfield bank approved our loan without checking our financial background that was next to nothing!

The bank was banking (no pun intended) on my future earnings! The loan was approved. Our monthly mortgage payment was $67, taxes included.

Sometime in July, we moved the entire contents of our Winchester house to our new house at 210 High Street, Greenfield, MA 01301. Mayflower movers did all the heavy stuff while we did most of the small and delicate items. We did not have much furniture, and the move really was quite simple. Ima was a great help to us, taking care of the kids while we concentrated on nurturing the budding ophthalmology practice.

In nursery school, Wally, when asked by the teacher how he came into town, in all seriousness, he said, "I came on the Mayflower."

Our first office at 40 Church Street was formerly the house of the first EENT doctor in the area who had been deceased for several years. By July, less than a month after I saw my first Greenfield patient, the practice got busier each passing day. I now hired a full-time receptionist, Susan Rose, who later was replaced by Peggy Wolanske. Yes, she was the wife of Dr. Wolanske, from whom we purchased our first house. Meantime, Donna returned to being a full-time housewife.

A couple of months into the practice, Donna called me one afternoon to say that a piece of mail from the Massachusetts Military Draft Board was delivered to our house. She had opened the letter and already knew that my 1A designation had been changed to 5A, which meant that I was no longer subject to being drafted into the military service, but she did *not* tell me that important detail. That was pure loving mischief on her part. When I arrived home, she showed me the letter with a big smile on her face. The promise of Bob Graves had now been fulfilled beyond any doubt!

About ten years into our lives in Greenfield, my best friend Bob invited me to dinner at the house of a recently retired EENT doctor in town by the name of Dr. Lawrence Dame. Mrs. Dame had been one of my patients, and I thought it was her idea to invite us to their home for dinner. In fact, it was Dr. Dame himself who wanted to have us as guests because now, he was free to tell me how I got that deferment from the military draft. He revealed that he was chairman of the Massachusetts Military Draft Board during that unpopular Vietnam War and was the man responsible for deciding who the doctors in the state were to be drafted and who were not. I thanked him profusely.

My performance at the GCS at MEEI made me well known to consultants, residents, and fellows at the hospital. I also became noticed by many drug and ophthalmic device representatives. Bob knew many of the latter, through his business as an optician, and my name came up when he asked them for leads trying to recruit an ophthalmologist for his hometown. For his business to prosper, he knew he had to have a full-time ophthalmologist in town. He did not want the local optometrists to dominate the field. It was Bob who talked to Dr. Dame about me, and without a second thought, he gave Bob the authority to recruit me with the promise to get me a military draft deferment.

That was the reason why Bob was so sure of himself when he dangled that juicy bait before my disbelieving eyes and ears. The decisions that Donna and I made to take chances on Bob and Greenfield were two of the best choices we made together in life!

Donna and I were so grateful to these two gentlemen, Dr. Lawrence Dame and Robert E. Graves, not only for getting me out of harm's way in Vietnam but also for giving me the opportunity to practice in a beautiful part of the Commonwealth of Massachusetts. If the sword of Damocles that was Vietnam was not hanging over my head, and I had diligently, on my own, tried to locate a suitable place for me to establish a private practice and to raise a family, I could not have done a much better job.

At my retirement party from practice on June 25, 2000, Bob was among the many guests who attended. In my parting speech, I publicly thanked him for all that he did for me. Foremost was his choice on betting on me rather than any other young ophthalmologist on that draft board list to come to Greenfield. Bob and I had become very good friends during all those years and remain so up to the present.

Meeting the Challenge

In Greenfield, from the very first day, my ophthalmology practice was busy. I saw as many patients as I could see in one examination room available to me in that first office located along Church Street. It did not take long before I admitted numerous patients in both hospitals, in Greenfield and in Turners Falls, mostly for cataract surgery.

Before I could do surgery on my own patients at my own time and pace, Greenfield Hospital required that an older member of the surgical staff be my assistant. In my case, this was Dr. Victor Elmer Kenneally, the only ophthalmologist in town who recently had a heart condition and was forced to cut back on his practice. This was the main reason why I was recruited to go to Greenfield. After observing me operate on an eyelid tumor, he immediately informed the chief of surgery that I was ready to go on my own. He had not even witnessed me doing cataract surgery.

The emergency rooms of both hospitals kept me busy at night after my office had closed. Almost every night, I got a call from the emergency room of Greenfield Hospital to take care of dozens of patients with foreign metal bodies embedded in the corneas of their eyes. These men were building a tunnel in the Northfield Mountain that was being prepared for use as an electric power storage system. Jackhammers and other power tools were primarily the tools used. Although the men were required to use safety eyeglasses, some probably did not comply with the safety rules, and they ended up with tiny pieces of metal that got stuck in their corneas. They came to the emergency room at night because it was at this time that the eye symptoms became acute. Taking care of all these patients cost me hours of sleep deprivation most nights, but at the same time, insurance payments for the services made our bank account grow at a healthy rate. A national debate on Medicare was going on.

In addition to this unusual circumstance, the usual ophthalmological needs of the community became more apparent. It did not take long for me to realize that I had to have additional help to meet this need. Dr. Kenneally had fully recovered from his heart condition and had resumed his practice, yet there were still more patients who needed care and had to wait for a long time. My appointment book stretched into months. Dr. Kenneally and I met to address this issue. We decided to recruit another ophthalmologist to form a group practice. At that point, DR. JANE A. WINCHESTER came into the picture.

We built a new office building on a vacant lot, the Med-Optic Building, in Turners Falls. There were six examining rooms for the three of us. Unexpectedly, Dr. Kenneally quit practice, and we recruited Dr. Robert Bousquet to replace him. Even this new office became too small for the rapidly expanding practice, requiring a move to larger quarters after a few years.

We added two more ophthalmologists to the group. We were the only show in town, and we became a model for other physicians/surgeons to form their own group practices. I did not consider a few optometrists in the area, who referred to themselves as eye doctors, as competition, because their training limited them to perform only refractions for corrective eyeglasses. They were neither licensed nor trained to do any medical or surgical treatment of eye diseases. However, there was one optometrist who called Dr. JANE WINCHESTER and me the Broad and the Chink Pair. Misogyny and racism, at least, but jealousy front and foremost.

The more spacious office on 33 Riddell Street in Greenfield had 12 examination rooms and additional rooms for minor surgeries, visual field examinations, and other specialized procedures. There were twenty-six employees. A satellite office was opened in a nearby town, Athol. We were the largest practice in Franklin County, larger than any other, including the Boston area. Originally, we called ourselves the Greenfield Area Ophthalmologists Inc. In the new office, we renamed ourselves Greenfield Eye Center (GEC). With more patients waiting for a long time to be seen and given adequate care, the practice added more ophthalmologists. Retinologists FELIPE TOLENTINO and HAL FREEMAN came from Boston to give their expert care. Due to the large number of employees, we created the position of office manager, who did all the administrative business while the doctors concentrated on giving the best patient care possible.

Personally, I introduced several surgical procedures never done in the area before. Most important among my innovations was the introduction of INTRAOCULAR LENS IMPLANTATION IN THE EYE DURING CATARACT SURGERY. In chapter 17, "My Role in the Evolution of Cataract Surgery," I will describe it in some detail. I am proudest of this achievement because with it, the visual rehabilitation of patients with cataracts is near-perfect.

The procedure became safer and more effective with more innovations. It became the standard procedure all over the world. I started this in 1975 and presented my first fifty cases to the members of NEOS on January 19, 1977. This placed my Greenfield patients eight years ahead of those in the Boston area.

In 1975, ROBERT BOUSQUET (my partner in the practice), CHRISTINA (his wife), Donna, and I went to Groningen in Holland to learn how to implant intraocular lenses from Dr. IAN WORST. We bought a few dozen lenses from his laboratory that I initially used in my surgical practice in Greenfield. No lenses for implantation were being made in the US.

Some colleagues in Boston were supportive of my initiative, but I believe they had neither the resolve nor the independence to follow their instincts. I did not have that limitation, which was a unique advantage for me and my patients; I was able to interact with ophthalmologists from all over the world, enabling me to pick and choose which innovations I considered the safest and most effective. I was shielded from conservative critics in Boston.

Following the success of this new procedure, I became aware of the benefits of removing cataracts through smaller surgical openings made on the corneoscleral area. I started using a simple IRRIGATION-ASPIRATION (IA) DEVICE that was made of two needles fused together, one needle to irrigate fluids and another to remove bits of cataract tissue in the eye. This was effective only on soft cataracts.

Prior to the use of the Kelman phacoemulsification machine, this was the instrument of choice for me. The first prototype of this needle combination was made by a local jeweler.

In a few more years, Dr. CHARLES KELMAN of New York City introduced a much better instrument than my simple device. His machine worked on the same principle as my primitive IA needle. I regret *not* patenting my invention.

The phacoemulsification machine can be described roughly as a miniaturized version of a jackhammer mated to a vacuum cleaner and a garden hose. Cataracts of different densities are broken into small pieces with the vibrating cannula and are removed by suction. With this new device, the cataract can be removed through a tiny incision of 2 to 3 mm, in contrast to the 10 to 12 mm incision used in the traditional way that was in vogue at that time. This phacoemulsification machine revolutionized cataract surgery all over the world. Initially, it was met with skepticism, especially in the conservative ophthalmological realm in Boston. I was an early adopter because I knew from experience with my primitive IA that it made a lot of sense.

I was among the first to use an early model of this new surgical device. It was introduced to me by ANDREW MORRISON, who became one of my best friends. He represented Optical Micro Systems, an early manufacturer of this machine, at one NEOS monthly meeting in Boston. He offered to bring one unit to Greenfield for me to try. He even brought a fresh pig's eye to practice on before I used it on a patient. Immediately, I saw the immense advantage of this new surgical technology, and I quickly integrated it into my own surgical armamentarium.

Boston again was late in adopting this. Patients operated in Boston had to wait for about ten more years to benefit from this more efficient and safer surgical procedure. Once again, my independence from the mecca of ophthalmology that was Boston became a huge advantage for my patients. It was for me too. The use of sutures became a thing of the past. Patients were able to resume normal activities immediately after the surgery. I even went to the extent of allowing some of my patients to play golf the day after surgery if they so desired. This procedure is now universally done all over the world, including Boston.

I invited Andy to visit the Philippines, where he helped me introduce phacoemulsification in the home country. He also donated a unit that was used in Mobile Eye Clinic, a facility for the indigent that Fel Tolentino and I helped to build in the Meralco compound in Manila with the financial backing of the Lopez Family. There, I performed the first cataract extraction with intraocular-lens implantation done on an ambulatory basis in the Philippines.

Although my subspecialty was glaucoma, the majority of my surgical cases were cataracts. This is because cataracts affect everybody if one lives long enough. Glaucoma is present in only 4 percent of the population. As a result, I concentrated on refining the surgical treatment of cataracts, although I did not neglect glaucoma.

When I first started cataract surgery, even as early as my residency days at PGH, the surgery was done under general anesthesia. Why not local anesthesia? I asked myself. That led me to use a retrobulbar injection of an anesthetic to block pain and movement of the eye during surgery. There was more improvement in the efficacy and safety of the anesthesia. By the time I was doing the greatest number of cataract surgery, anesthesia had been made safer and simpler with the use of anesthetic eye drops alone. No needles! No sutures! This was appropriately named "Stitchless Cataract Surgery," which became widely practiced all over the world.

I even eliminated the use of the traditional bridle suture on the superior rectus muscle when I discovered that a temporal approach was much more desirable. Another needle was eliminated. Now the procedure is totally without any needle except for the IV infusion, which is needed to deliver a mild sedative to relieve a patient's anxiety, through an arm vein.

Aside from the obvious rapid visual rehabilitation after a cataract procedure, this stitchless surgical technique eliminates a dreaded complication. With a large incision, there is always a danger that bleeding from inside the eye can occur. When this happens, it cannot be stopped. It is a catastrophic event that results in complete blindness.

Once during the early days of my career, I experienced this dreadful event. That was the time when cataract surgery was done under general anesthesia, and the incision was almost the entire 180 degrees of the corneal circumference. The anesthesia was not deep enough, and the patient started coughing. That triggered the bleeding. It is something that an eye surgeon never forgets. It happened a few more times during the period when I was already doing the "stitchless" technique. In these few cases, there was no panic and no stress. The surgery was just stopped and postponed for twenty-four hours. This was a minor inconvenience for the patient but a great relief for me, the surgeon. No other complications were encountered.

At the height of my surgical practice, I used a lot of intraocular lenses made by a company called Mentor Optical Radiation Corporation, based in Azusa, California. I must have been the top user of their intraocular lenses because they invited me to visit their factory, sending two first-class round-trip airline tickets for Donna and me. We were ensconced at Century Plaza Hotel in downtown Los Angeles, given a VIP tour of the factory, and brought to dinner at Chasen's in Beverly Hills. Paparazzi surrounded our limo as we arrived but quickly dispersed when they found out that we were not Hollywood celebrities. Emerging from the limo, Donna and I, together with Walter, were completely ignored. Later we were told that FRANK SINATRA and RONALD REAGAN had reserved tables there that night. We saw neither.

To be allowed to do these new procedures, especially the implantation of intraocular lenses, Franklin Medical Center required me to have prior approval from an experimental review committee. It must have been suggested by the legal counsel of the hospital to protect itself in case of a malpractice suit. As committee chairman, I was given total freedom to select the committee members from the prominent people in the area and at least one member of the surgical staff. It was not a difficult job to get the required number of members. All of them were my patients, including the surgeon. The committee was just a formality, and it never disapproved any of my innovations.

I must have done all things well. Not a single case of malpractice was leveled against me.

Another pioneering surgical procedure I undertook was the same cataract technique with intraocular-lens implantation, this time in children. Never was this done before in Massachusetts. It was not covered by health insurers. With no support from the establishment, I went ahead and did it anyway. I figured that there should be no difference between adult and children's eyes with cataracts. The established procedure for congenital cataracts was plain removal of the cloudy lens and rehabilitation of vision with either thick distorting eyeglasses or contact lenses. That was not acceptable to me. Eventually, I was again proven right.

Surgical correction of refractive errors was another field that I enthusiastically adopted after discovering how it was done by other pioneers. As performed in our office operating room, it was initially rather crude. It involved making six to eight radial incisions on the clear cornea, using a thin, ultra-sharp diamond blade under topical anesthesia. To make an incision on a clear cornea to change its contour was a bold procedure. It was effective in almost all selected cases, but the results were not permanent in some. It was also stressful for the surgeon. Accurate measurements of the thickness of the cornea and assessment of the depth of the incision were paramount. There was always a danger of perforation or infection.

In due time, lasers replaced diamond blades. Photorefractive keratectomy (PRK) was born. It was a much safer, more effective, and permanent solution to the problem. A drawback was that postoperative pain was considerable. When laser-assisted in situ keratomileusis (LASIK) came into use, it was both effective and painless. Many of my patients were happy with good vision without eyeglasses when I used PRK. I did not have a chance to do any LASIK procedure because it came toward the end of my practice.

GEC provided the best ophthalmologic care for all the people in the area. We conducted free glaucoma screening tests and opened our offices on some nights to accommodate patients who cannot come during regular office hours because of the nature of their jobs. We also offered our practice to indigent patients on certain days when

they can just come in with no appointments, insurance requirements, or cash. It was an expression that our practice was to offer the
best ophthalmologic care available without a hint of financial gains.
Financially, we did quite well. This enabled the practice to hire the
best staff and to acquire the latest diagnostic and surgical tools to
serve our customers best and keep our practice at the forefront, that
I consider the golden age of medical practice for me.

My contribution to health care was not limited to ophthalmology. As a member of Franklin District Medical Society in Western
Massachusetts, I was able to contribute something to the well-being
of the general population. For decades, there were two competing
hospitals in the county, Franklin Medical Center in Greenfield and
Farren Memorial Hospital in Turners Falls. The two hospitals were
no more than a mile apart, serving a community of approximately
forty thousand. Both had fully equipped emergency rooms, operating rooms, pediatrics, obstetrics, and medical and surgical wards.
The two, however, were different in their management philoso-
phy: Franklin Medical Center was a secular hospital, while Farren
Memorial Hospital was run by Sisters of Providence, a religious community of nuns based in Holyoke.

For many years, even before I came into the area, there were
many civic leaders, including physicians, who advocated merging the
two health facilities for the purpose of reducing redundancy in the
services and costly equipment needed to provide the best possible
health care. When I became firmly established in the area, and as
my reputation grew, I was elected to be chief of the Farren Memorial
Hospital (FMH) medical staff. In this capacity, I attended all the
monthly meetings of the FMH board of trustees. It became clear to
me that the hospital was always struggling financially to make both
ends meet. This was also true with the other hospital. Despite all
this difficulty, each hospital was obligated to spend more to keep up
with the other. In some ways, I contributed to this anomaly. For me
to provide the best care for my patients, I asked each hospital to buy
expensive equipment necessary for my practice. Operating micro-
scopes, phacoemulsification machines, a large inventory of intraocular lenses, and specially trained OR technicians were needed.

During one meeting with the board of trustees at FMH, my opinion was solicited about this talk of merger with the other hospital. I told them what I and other physicians before me had seen, that a merger was the only way to go forward considering the increasingly difficult reimbursement from Medicare and other insurance companies. I suggested converting the Catholic-run hospital from an acute care provider to a specialty care facility for the growing population of patients suffering from Alzheimer's disease. To my surprise and satisfaction, the Sisters of Providence followed my advice.

Patients in the Philippines directly benefited from this streamlining of health care in Franklin County. FMH had to get rid of all its expensive equipment that were not necessary to take care of the kinds of patients they now catered to. Coincidentally, at that time, Felipe Tolentino and I had a half-a-million-dollar worth of donation from the Miyake family from Nagoya, Japan. With this cash, we purchased the entire collection of FMH OR surgical instruments and supplies. The hospital was just too happy to sell those to us. The almost-new ophthalmic equipment was donated to the Miyake Eye Operating Room at PGH. The other surgical instruments and equipment were donated to the other PGH departments.

I CONTINUED TO FIND WAYS TO DELIVER THE BEST OPHTHALMIC CARE TO THE GREATEST NUMBER OF PEOPLE WITH THE LOWEST COST POSSIBLE. Following this principle, I came to realize that cataract surgery had to be done away from the hospitals that were not able to adapt to the increasing number of cases that I and the other ophthalmologists in the surrounding communities faced. Dr. Jane Winchester and I had a meeting with the Greenfield Hospital Director about forming a partnership with them to build a free-standing surgicenter, but they declined our initiative.

Together with the other ophthalmologists who shared our views, we built the first stand-alone surgicenter in Massachusetts. This led to a more efficient and less expensive way of doing cataract surgery. Our patients were happy, the ophthalmologists equally so. I surmise that health insurers were happy too. But the hospitals were not because of the loss of income from cataract surgeries.

The years from 1968 to 2000 were the happiest and most ful-filling period in my professional life. If I were to start all over again, I would choose the same path. The nine years of educational prepa-ration that led to that nirvana of private practice, blessed with luck in being at the right place and at the right time, made it all possible. Those were the golden years for me and my family.

I must emphasize that my professional career could not have been as successful without the enormous contribution of Donna. As a homemaker, she expertly took care of our home for our chil-dren and me. In a direct way to help me in the practice, she was the perfect hostess for the many patients, relatives, friends, and many VIPs, some who came all the way from the Philippines, seeking my professional care. She was responsible for providing them not only comfortable accommodations in our spacious house, but she also made them feel completely at home with delicious and attractively prepared meals. Some staff members at GEC called our home "The Greenfield Peczon Hilton."

Living the Good Life

Greenfield Follies is a yearly event that is the main fundraiser to benefit the Greenfield Hospital. Donna and I gladly first joined the troupe upon invitation by our neighbors, JANET and HERBERT HODOS. That was how we met the upper crust of society in town. With introductions to those folks, we developed many friendships that have lasted throughout the years and extended beyond retirement.

We were a happy family, enjoying life in a new and foreign town that welcomed us with open arms. I recall with wonder how friendly the local folks were. One incident, still fresh in my mind, I will now recount:

> *Donna sent me to buy some food items from the local grocery store, Fosters. Going to the cashier with my purchases, I discovered to my embarrassment that I had forgotten my wallet at home. "Not to worry," the cashier said. She called the store manager, who came in to resolve the issue.*
>
> *Without asking any questions, he got his wallet out, paid the total bill in cash, and told me just to send him a check at my convenience.*

Where else can you find trust and friendliness like that? Certainly not in Boston.

The store manager had known me only from the newspaper publicity that preceded our coming to town, but I never met him until this pleasant encounter. Naturally, Fosters became our favorite grocery store and not just because of the friendly staff but also because they carried the freshest seafood, especially lobsters.

In summer, we did not do much shopping for fresh vegetables. Many of my patients were farmers who brought us almost endless supplies of tomatoes, corn, and other comestibles. A maple-sugar producer supplied me with gallons of freshly boiled syrup every spring. I had treated him for a penetrating injury in one eye. I did not charge him for the services because he did not have any insurance. The gratitude of this farmer and others was priceless.

Once, a farmer drove his pickup truck onto our driveway and unloaded an unbelievable amount of fresh produce, which I shared with friends. The fresh tomatoes, potatoes, corn, and so on were better than those in local grocery stores.

The local police force was quite friendly too. Once, while driving home from the Athol office, I was stopped by a police officer for overspeeding. After I rolled down the car window, he asked rather cheekily, "Why the hurry, sir?"

Lying with a straight face, I said, "There is a patient waiting for me at the emergency room in Greenfield."

Instantly, he recognized me and even apologized. "Doctor Peczon," he said. "You operated on my mom's eyes. Sorry I did not recognize you earlier. Would you like me to escort you to Greenfield?"

Again, with a straight face warmly smiling, I told him it was not necessary. No ticket, not even a warning. He even gave me an apology.

The only time we got a ticket for a traffic violation was for Donna. An officer came knocking at the door bearing a citation for Donna. It was for making a right turn on a red stop sign without making a full stop in the Quincy area of Boston. There was justification for the traffic citation, but had that happened in Greenfield, the violation would have been completely ignored. A state trooper, not a local officer, made the delivery. Well, that was Boston.

Years ago, before immigrating to the US, one of my early worries was whether there would be any discrimination against us. I was the first foreign-trained physician in town with brown skin. Happily, there was but one incident of racism, which I would never forget, and it occurred in Keene, New Hampshire. Donna and I were having lunch in a nice restaurant. A white woman, out of nowhere, came to our table and suddenly said, "Why don't you go back where you came from?" Both Donna and I were stunned but said nothing.

Cats, a popular Broadway show, had the longest-running performances on Broadway and on a national tour. When it was shown in Hartford, Connecticut, Donna and I got tickets. Just before the curtains opened, a well-groomed lady came to sit on the empty seat to my left. She was reeking with perfume to that which I was highly allergic. Anticipating that I would be embarrassingly sneezing during the entire show, I asked Donna to change seats with me. Obligingly, she did, of course. I whispered to the lady sitting to my right that we did the exchange of seats because of my allergy to perfumes. She smiled and whispered back to me. "Don't worry. I go to my ophthalmologist in Greenfield who has a large sign in his waiting room office, requesting patients to refrain from using perfume when coming for consultation because he is very allergic to it." When I told her that I was that ophthalmologist, she turned, looked at me, and exclaimed, "Yes, of course, Dr. Peczon!" Even from Connecticut, I had many patients.

Indulging in sports was an enjoyment in this new environment. Since the early years in medical school in Manila, I had always enjoyed tennis. To a limited extent, I was able to play with fellow doctors at MEEI who invited me to their private clubs. In Greenfield, there were a lot of public as well as private courts that were available to us.

Every weekend, during summer and fall, I usually did not have to make calls to form a foursome for doubles play. Many tennis enthusiasts in town just went to the beautiful tennis courts at Deerfield Academy, which was about two miles from our house. There we drew cards to form teams. It was a wonderful way to meet with players of different skills and athleticism. In the winter, I had a core group that allowed us to easily form a foursome to play doubles in an indoor tennis facility in Sunderland: Dr. WILLIAM MCCLELLAND, HERBERT HODOS (an attorney and later a judge), JACK KIRKWOOD (a local businessman), VIC MROZ (an electrician), and I would take turns on the court on Monday evenings. Occasionally, we encountered BILL COSBY in the next court. He had a winter house in Shelburne Falls. He was also a patient at GEC.

Skiing became our number one sport in the winter. Bob Graves introduced us to this popular New England winter recreation. He took us to Maple Valley Ski Resort just north of the border of Massachusetts in Dummerston, Vermont. This was a small ski area catering to novice skiers. The trails were not too challenging, and they had a well-run children's ski school where Walter and Lisa learned the winter sport with us. As we became better skiers, we visited more challenging ski resorts within easy driving distance from Greenfield, such as Bromley, Killington, and Mt. Snow. Donna and I even spent a week of skiing in Vail, Colorado.

Walter became an expert and a graceful skier, qualifying him to join the ski patrol in Berkshire East, located a few miles from home. After his graduation from high school from Deerfield Academy, I treated him to a week of skiing in Sun Valley in Idaho. Lisa was not as graceful but equally skillful and most daring. She just skied down the hill, a la a downhill ski racer, fearless and making turns only to stay on the trail. I do not remember her involved in a crash.

In summer, Donna was even more involved in sports. A triathlete is not an inappropriate description of her. Most mornings, she would walk to the local YMCA to swim a mile, twenty-five laps in the Olympic size indoor pool, play two sets of tennis with her buddies in the afternoon, then join me for a five-kilometer jog when I returned home from work. During the jog, she would always challenge me on the last half-kilometer sprint to home. Trying as hard as I could, I barely kept pace with her.

On many weekends, we played doubles matches with other couples in town, primarily with BETTY and BILL MCCLELLAND. These were highly competitive matches. We won some. In swimming, I could not join Donna. I just could not learn, even after taking lessons from a swimming instructor at the Y. Whenever the ocean was part of our vacations, like snorkeling in Maui, I always held on to her for dear life! My phobia was barely assuaged even when wearing a bright yellow buoyancy device.

To Donna, swimming was as natural as a fish at home in the water. During the war, she learned how to swim on her own in the river near their house. She might have overdone this sort of activity, though. In her sixties, she required a major repair of a torn rotator cuff on the right shoulder.

Gathering firewood became a new passion for me. I started with buying a 15-acre woodlot in Northfield, then a two-hundred-acre one in Bernardston. On many weekends I asked Walter to help me with cutting dead trees for firewood. He seemed to enjoy spending time with me there in the woods with a chainsaw and a four-wheel-drive Toyota Land Cruiser to haul the cut wood back home. After I retired and had moved to California, I heard him tell his friends, with me in short hearing range, that he did not enjoy those firewood gathering forays at all. He said he would have preferred to have spent more time with his friends, doing what most boys would do. So I learned that back then, he was simply being a good son, keeping me company in the woods.

I finally gave up on this activity after I barely escaped doing serious injury to myself. If not for the helmet I wore diligently while using a chain saw, I could have caused horrendous harm to myself. The darn saw hit something hard and kicked back at my face. Without that helmet, I would have been the only surgeon in the USA to have done a do-it-yourself craniotomy on his own skull!

Donna made a lot of hand-stitched quilts. Not a single stitch was done with a sewing machine. With precision, she cut all the small pieces and joined them together with thread and a needle. She had the pattern all in her head, but I believe that she also made a rough pencil drawing on how the finished product would look like.

Her first attempt at making a quilt took two years to finish. It was a classic. The pattern represented the Four Seasons in New England. After it was finished, her quilting instructor was so impressed that she asked Donna's permission to display it in the Old Indian House in Historic Deerfield. It stayed there for over a year. Today, we lovingly use it daily in our bedroom in Dove Canyon, California.

"The Old Indian house is in the center of Main Street in Old Deerfield, an 18th and 19th century collection of houses of the village center, many on their original sites and filled with antique furnishings, reveal the lifestyles of Deerfielders from the time of the first English settlement to the Arts and Crafts Movement in the early 20th century. The village has been on the National Register of Historic Landmarks since 1962" (Wikipedia).

Four years after settling down in Greenfield, Donna, Lisa, and I became naturalized citizens. Walter was born in Boston, which gave him automatic citizenship.

Donna. I was enormously proud of the mother of my children, my personal Florence Nightingale, my office secretary and cashier, my tennis partner in mixed doubles, my jogging mate, my ski buddy, my gourmet chef for home-cooked dinners, my seamstress, my impeccable hostess for VIP patients coming from the Philippines for cataract surgery, my traveling companion, my dancing partner, my lover, and my most loving wife. No man could be any happier!

Donna was just as happy, but to make her happier, we decided to move to a larger house. The house on 210 High Street was becoming too crowded. Both her parents and Ima lived with us intermittently but for increasingly longer periods of time. Both of us wanted them to stay with us for as long as they wished, and we wanted to give them more space as an inducement. Besides, we also did not want to live with the annual flooding of the basement at 210 High Street. Each spring, as the ice and snow melted, water invaded that foundation of the house, in spite of two powerful sump pumps.

In the summer of 1980, 11 Crescent Street became our new house. It was a huge structure, with six bedrooms and four bathrooms in the main house. There was a carriage house behind the two-car garage with its own small but complete kitchen and bathroom. Behind it was an in-ground swimming pool. Located on an acre lot, it was at the end of Main Street downtown, but it still had a lot of privacy because of a thick hedge shielding it from the street.

We added a sunroom at the back to enjoy a feeling of the outdoors, even in the cold, ice, and snow of winter.

Donna's parents stayed with us in Greenfield for at least a year after my mother left for Manila. On the third week of September 1985, our beloved Nanny succumbed to a massive cerebrovascular accident (CVA). Her remains were interred in one of two burials plots we bought at Green River Cemetery in Greenfield. The other plot next to her, we reserved for our own final resting places. Greenfield is home.

Death inevitably comes to all creatures on earth, and we mourn the passing of our loved ones. As a counterbalance, births inevitably occur, and we rejoice.

Our first grandchild, Patrick, grew up almost entirely under the watchful and loving care of Lola Donna during these early formative years. Both his parents were employed at GEC. My sister Alma remarked that Donna had raised a remarkably gentle pair of males in our family, Walter and Patrick. I cannot claim much credit for that because I was too busy in my professional life. Let me give you specific examples. Donna was the one who introduced them to music. She was the one who showed them how to fly kites. Most of all, she showed them how to be perfect gentlemen!

On September 6, 1984, Donna and I celebrated our twenty-sixth wedding anniversary and her fiftieth birthday at Newfane Inn in Vermont. During that romantic candlelight dinner, I presented her with an engagement ring! Twenty-six years late, but as the popular saying goes, it is better late than never, and diamonds are a woman's best friend that lasts forever.

Our daily short runs gradually extended to longer distances until we felt we could do a five-kilometer run easily. There was an annual Greenfield race of this length each year. We entered and finished the race. Donna finished third in her age group. I finished in second place—from the bottom of the list of finishers, regardless of age!

Asia's Queen of Songs, Filipina PILITA CORRALES, had a concert in NYC on May 25, 1980. We met her in her hotel room. RYAN CAYABYAB, Pilita's musical director, visited us in Greenfield and accompanied Donna to belt out a song. Ryan's brother, BERT, lives in Greenfield and is a friend of the family.

Walter got his high school diploma from Deerfield Academy on May 30, 1982. DAVID ROCKEFELLER was the commencement speaker. A younger Rockefeller was in the same graduating class. The present-day king of Jordan, ABDULLAH II AL-HUSSEIN, graduated from the same academy, one year ahead of Walter. Lisa got her high school diploma from Pine Ridge School in Williston, Vermont, one year later.

Greenfield Business Association celebrated persons and events that made Greenfield SPECIAL. I was one among a few Greenfield residents who were considered to have contributed to this image. The newspaper reporter mentioned one Dr. Jose Peczon, "the inventor of a microsurgical device used to treat cataracts worldwide." He must have been referring to the irrigation/aspiration device I invented to remove cataracts. Ima, my mother, was proud of that.

For my family, the grass is no greener anywhere than what we found in Greenfield.

Brush with History

When we look back, we can see our lives as part of the stream of world history, not simply personal experiences. Anyone growing up in the Philippines in the 1940s surely has stories of pain and privation during the Japanese invasion and occupation. As a seven-year-old boy, I remember my father, listening to the radio, very much alarmed by the bombing of Pearl Harbor. A few hours later, we saw and heard the bombing of Clark Air Force Base, a few kilometers away. Soon our small town of Mexico, Pampanga, was occupied by a company of Japanese cavalrymen. The unit commander, a Captain SAKUMA, and his second-in-command, Lieutenant KAMATSO, took over the upper floor of our house that was right next to the municipio. My parents became part-time servants of these officers.

The first year of the occupation was not too oppressive, thanks in part to the lack of opposition to the occupation and to the benevolence of the Japanese captain. A West Point graduate, he was fluent in English. He read to my sisters and me books and showed us pictures of his family and children. The lieutenant was stricter, more militaristic.

I did not realize it at the time, but the Bataan Death March passed near our town, five kilometers away in the provincial capital of San Fernando. Several soldiers were clandestinely saved from the marching ranks of prisoners. One of them was my godfather, a UPCM graduate, a medical officer in the Philippine Army.

The second and third years of the occupation became more oppressive when the Japanese cavalry unit was replaced by occupation forces. By this time, guerrillas were active in the countryside, and the Japanese became cruel as they tried to neutralize the threat. Our house was returned completely to our family when the Japanese unit garrisoned themselves entirely at the nearby town hall.

As a young boy, I was terrified to hear of the cries and groans of Filipino prisoners, tortured as guerrilla suspects. My best friend's father was one of these unfortunate men. After days of torture, he was forced to stand in front of the town hall, and all adult men in town were paraded one by one in front of him. He was ordered to point out who the guerrillas and sympathizers were. The few men he pointed out were promptly led to execution at the local cemetery that was near my school. The entire town was, in fact, sympathetic to the guerrillas, and I suspect now that the people he fingered were probably men he held a grudge against.

Food was rationed, medicine almost nonexistent, but life went on while waiting for General Douglas MacArthur to return as he had promised on clandestine radio. Schooling did not stop for my siblings and me. I learned to speak a little Japanese and read *katakana*. When the general finally returned to liberate the Philippines, in our town, it was the happiest occasion to greet a single US Army jeep manned by a couple of US Rangers with a fifty-caliber machine gun.

Somehow, the Japanese simply melted away without firing a single shot. Peace came slowly as the Japanese occupation ended but was followed by a threat of communism. Our family survived the Japanese occupation, but my father became a victim of the lawlessness that followed. In 1948, during a town fiesta, he was gunned down by an extortionist. He later died of his wounds in the hospital at Clark Air Force Base. A younger sister and I both were wounded in the same attack.

Despite all this, I followed my dream to get an education and graduated in 1957 with the degree of doctor of medicine from the UPCM in Manila. I started my career in ophthalmology with a residency at PGH in Manila and a second residency at BCH in the US. Then I completed four more years of fellowship and clinical research at MEEI and HMS in Boston. With this background, I returned to the Philippines to start a private practice, but after a couple of years,

I decided to immigrate to the United States to pursue and fulfill my dreams.

Today, decades later, a world away from the Philippines, having retired in my practice of ophthalmology in Greenfield, Massachusetts, I enjoy reading history, especially accounts of the war in the Pacific and its aftermath. Recently, as I read about the founding of the Japanese Constitution in DAVID BERGAMINI's *Japan's Imperial Conspiracy*, a name leaped off the page: Colonel CHARLES L. KADES. General MacArthur had entrusted General COURTNEY WHITNEY and his government section in Japan with the task of drafting an acceptable constitution. Whitney delegated the task to his right-hand man, Colonel Charles L. Kades.

Following the war, Colonel Kades practiced law in New York City. After retiring, he moved to my neighboring town of Heath. Colonel Kades was my patient for several years. Unfortunately, he died before I realized his historic role narrated above. His widow became my patient too, and I enjoyed discussing his wartime activities with her.

The coincidence of a Filipino boy, witness to the cruelty of the Pacific War, eventually caring for the rewriter of the Japanese Constitution founded on peace, represents my own merger of personal and world histories.

Note: This chapter was published as a stand-alone essay in Filipinas, The Magazine for All Filipinos, November 2003.

My Role in the Evolution of Cataract Surgery

Now that intraocular lenses are part and parcel of cataract surgery, it is difficult to imagine the time when they were looked upon with scorn. As a cataract surgeon, I participated in a remarkable revolution in ophthalmic surgery. I challenged the establishment by pioneering the use of intraocular lenses in New England.

To explain why intraocular lenses were/are a major advance, I will recount the state of cataract surgery prior to their acceptance. In the 1960s, cataract surgeons had developed reasonably safe and reliable methods for removing cataracts. Controversy surrounded the number and type of sutures needed to close wounds and whether to remove the cataract in one piece, that is, intracapsular (piecemeal) or extracapsular. In most cases, the result was restoration of vision with appropriate lenses.

The catch was that the power of the spectacle lens needed to replace the human lens removed at surgery was usually somewhere between ten and fourteen diopters. A lens of this power placed in a pair of eyeglasses magnifies the image in the operated, aphakic eye three to four times greater than the size of the image of the eye with a natural lens. In addition, aphakic spectacles created a scotoma, a blind spot, in the peripheral vision. Also, while postoperative cataract patients frequently attained 20/20 vision, their activities were often significantly limited by the distorted images created by glasses. In addition, if surgery were necessary for only one eye, they were unable to fuse the larger image with the normal size image of the unoperated eye. They remained monocular until the second eye also had parallel surgery. Contact lenses eliminated most of the undesired magnification, but most elderly patients were unable to handle or tolerate wearing them. We cataract surgeons had many grateful but unhappy patients.

Meanwhile, an English eye surgeon, HAROLD RIDLEY, noticed that bits of Plexiglas embedded on the eyes of Royal Air Force (RAF) pilots, sustained in penetrating injuries from shattered windshields of fighter planes, were inert. Reasoning that a lens could be manufactured from this material to replace the lens removed at cataract surgery, he began to design and implant lenses in patients. His initial results were frequently disastrous, leading to extreme prejudice against the procedure in England and the United States.

The few successes, however, prompted other pioneering surgeons like Dr. JAN WORST of Holland to follow through with improvements in manufacture and design. He developed a phenomenally successful procedure with a lens of his own design.

My personal odyssey in ophthalmology eventually brought me to Holland to learn the procedure from Dr. Worst himself. First, in 1959, after completing my ophthalmology residency at PGH in Manila, I journeyed to the United States. I completed an internship in Chicago, took the Lancaster course in ophthalmology in Maine, and moved to Boston to complete a two-year residency at BCH. Then Dr. W. Morton Grant, a renowned glaucoma researcher in Boston, chose me as a clinical research fellow in glaucoma at MEEI. During those years, I came to know the leading physicians in that mecca of eye care. Subsequently, I opened my own practice in Greenfield, Massachusetts, a small rural town ninety miles west of Boston.

There I was close enough to maintain my collegial ties with the ophthalmologic hierarchy of Boston, but far enough to do and implement my thinking independent of entrenched ideas, based on my own experiences.

In the early 1970s, I became aware of Dr. Worst's work during a talk given by a visiting Florida ophthalmologist. I learned that Dr. Worst was willing to train physicians in his technique. In 1974, I flew to his clinic in Groningen, Holland, to observe his surgery and his patients. I saw that the technique of implanting Dr. Worst's early lenses was obviously within my capability to implement. I was struck by the subjective response of his patients. They were immediately visually and generally incredibly happy with their vision from day one. I went back to Greenfield highly motivated.

Within six weeks, I began implanting the lenses obtained from Dr. Worst. I vividly recall my first implant surgery. The technique called for an intracapsular extraction under general anesthesia, a routine procedure at the time. After the lens was removed, a suture was passed through the two holes in the intraocular lens. The lens was then carefully inserted into the anterior chamber. Two plastic loops attached to the back of the intraocular lens were placed behind the iris. The suture was then passed through the iris and tied. The corneoscleral wound was secured with from six to ten sutures. The manipulations were very delicate. Great care was required to avoid injuring the cornea during insertion of the intraocular lens or tangling the intraocular-lens suture in the plastic loops, and great luck was needed to avoid losing vitreous during placement. However, my enthusiasm for the procedure only increased as I did more. The patients were indeed genuinely grateful for their "bionic" eyes.

In 1975, I presented my first fifty cases to NEOS at a monthly scientific meeting in Boston. To the best of my knowledge, only a handful of similar procedures had been performed in the region and none in Boston. Mine was the first report or series to be formally presented in that city. As happened to British eye surgeon Harold Ridley, I was denounced by the establishment. Dr. TAYLOR SMITH, chief pathologist at MEEI, declared, "There is no place for artificial implants in the human eye." His assertion was followed by loud applause from the NEOS membership.

I was undeterred. My experiences had already proven him wrong. I continued to perfect my technique and adopted improved lenses as they became available. In 1978, I performed the first intraocular-lens implantation in the Philippines on a Dutch expat patient of Dr. ROLAND TABLANTE at Manila Doctors Hospital. My confidence in the procedure persuaded me to implant these lenses on my mother's eyes in 1979. Happily, for patients, intraocular lenses later became standard in cataract surgery, even in Boston. Today, I derive immense satisfaction from knowing that my efforts helped advance the intraocular-lens evolution in cataract surgery.

Note: This chapter was published in a book entitled *The Healing Cut*.

Filipino surgeons write about the human drama, humor, and controversy surrounding actual cases. Compiled by the Audiovisual Communications and Publications Committee, Department of Surgery, UPCM-PGH, UP Manila. Edited by MARIA SOCORRO G. NUGUIT. Printed in the Philippines, 1999.

Notable Patients

Reflecting on my long career in ophthalmology from the time I started residency training in the Philippines at the Department of Ophthalmology, PGH, from June 1957 to retirement in June 2000, I look fondly at all the patients who were under my care. Most of them gave me a lot of joy and a sense of fulfillment. A few gave me sadness and a lot of stress because of circumstances beyond my control or perhaps inexperience, especially during the early years of my career. Some stand out because of their status in society.

I will start with my very first private patient after finishing residency training at PGH in Manila. She is the mother of our family physician from Mexico, Pampanga, Dr. Canda. Her first name escapes me now. She was almost totally blind from cataracts, and I did an intracapsular cataract extraction in one eye at Marian General Hospital along UN Avenue, next to De Ocampo Eye Hospital. A trusted and experienced OR nurse from PGH, CARMEN QUIDAY, assisted me. The operation went very well. The following day, to my horror, I found unmistakable signs of infection, endophthalmitis. This is a dreaded complication of cataract surgery that any ophthalmologist fears most. She had pain, swelling, redness, and suppuration, pus in the wound and inside the eye, hypopyon. It must have been a pseudomonas infection, that up to this time, is an ever-present danger in spite of all careful preparations before, during, and after surgery.

At that time, there were no effective antibiotics, and all we had were sulfa drugs, chloromycetin, and penicillin, all ineffective against this highly virulent bacterium. I was helpless in saving the eye that went on to complete blindness. At that moment, I felt so terrible for the patient, and I was fearful of my future as an ophthalmic surgeon. Fortunately, the patient and her family were very understanding and did not put any blame on me, but I bore that heavy burden on my shoulders for many years. It was fortunate for me that Donna had already left for Chicago, and I was just waiting to process my travel papers to join her there. I did not do any more intraocular surgery on any patient from that time on until, almost two years later, when I started as a senior resident in ophthalmology at BCH.

Later in my practice, as I gained more experience and became more confident of my skills, I applied all that to all my patients. Sadly, one other patient lost vision during my entire career, and it was not from infection but from expulsive hemorrhage.

UPCM classmate Fel Tolentino referred many of his patients to me for cataract surgery. Fel attracted the rich and famous because of his pioneering work in vitreous disorders. Together with Drs. CHARLES L. SCHEPENS and H. MACKENZIE FREEMAN, he authored the seminal textbook *Vitreoretinal Disorders: Diagnosis and Management*. This was published by WB Saunders Company in 1976. Some of these patients who had cataracts were graciously referred to me.

Among the first was a retired general from Turkey who had one eye blind from an unsuccessful cataract surgery in his country. He flew to Boston to consult with Fel. He, in turn, sent the general to Greenfield, where I did the cataract surgery on his remaining eye at Farren Memorial Hospital in Turners Falls. You can just imagine the weight of responsibility and stress that I went through to make sure this general could see again. At that time phacoemulsification was not yet invented, but intraocular lenses were already available, although not yet totally accepted, especially by the conservative Boston ophthalmology circle. The surgery went very well without complications, and the patient returned to Turkey a very happy man. As compensation, he gave me a beautiful handmade oriental rug, five feet by eight feet, that we shipped to our house in Ayala Heights, Quezon City, Philippines.

JESUS TANCHANGCO was the minister of food under President Ferdinand E. Marcos of the Philippines. He came to Greenfield in 1983 for cataract surgery and intraocular lens implantation, accompanied by his wife, a secretary, valet, and driver. Surgery was done at

Farren Hospital, where he stayed postoperatively for a week with a private duty nurse, JACKIE CHOATE. During that week, all the flowers were depleted from local florists' shelves because there were so many requests for get-well cards with flowers from the Philippines. Our house at 11 Crescent Street looked like a funeral house filled with all those flowers. This was just the overflow from his hospital room at Farren Hospital.

That same year when we visited the Philippines during our annual December visit, Mr. Tanchangco sent a couple of his agents to meet us inside the plane. They took care of everything. We did not even need to stop by customs and immigration. From the plane, Donna and I were transferred directly to our hotel suite at Regency of Manila. The Tolentinos, who were with us, were whisked to the presidential suite of the same hotel. We stayed there for two weeks, and not a single peso was spent out of our pockets. Mr. Tanchangco took care of all hotel charges. He also feted us to a sumptuous dinner at Manila Hotel.

Senator SOTERO LAUREL JR. came a few years later. I did one cataract surgery on him at Franklin Medical Center. His other eye I did in Manila at Eye Referral Center. Senator Laurel was a very good golfer, but I never had a chance to play with him.

Banana King of the Philippines, ANTONIO FLOIRENDO, came to Greenfield twice to have his cataracts treated. Each time he came with a valet-secretary who kept in touch with his myriad business enterprises throughout the world with a portable radiotelephone that connected anywhere in the universe. That was a forerunner of present-day cell phones. In 1984, he invited us to his family retreat in Mindanao. This was the famous Pearl Farm Beach Resort on the southeastern coast of Samal Island, not too far from Davao City in Mindanao.

The Tolentinos, Fel, Flora, Phillip, and Mike, together with Donna and Walter, flew ahead to Butuan and were taken to the banana plantation. I flew alone a day later because of patients I had to take care of first at Eye Referral Center. Upon my arrival at Butuan Airport, my bags were transferred to a waiting helicopter that brought me to join the rest of the party.

We flew over hectares of banana trees. No wonder Mr. Floirendo was dubbed Banana King of the Philippines. He certainly deserved it. The secret of his success was in the employment of the state-of-the-art method of farming using the best of Israeli technology. He had his workers well-taken care of, not only providing them food and shelter but also free medical care and education for their children. Certainly, the Philippines needs more progressive businesspeople like him. Aside from the banana plantation, he also had a swine farm where pigs were fattened by unmarketable bananas. No items were wasted.

He also bred Arabian racehorses that were sold all over the world, including Ascot in England. He told me about a recent plane-load of purebred racehorses he delivered to somewhere in the world. The chartered plane was a huge Boeing 707 jet with a veterinarian onboard.

We played a round of golf at Apo Country Club, arriving there by helicopter. I do not remember how I scored but I had a very good time. Walter enjoyed it too. From there, we transferred to a swift boat that took us to the Pearl Farm, staying in two of four houses built for the Floirendo children and grandchildren. Separate units on different locations in the islands were for tourists.

The houses were built on stilts over water. Well-admired architect FRANCISCO MIÑOSA of the Philippines had designed the houses like the traditional *salacot* hats with bamboo walls and shingles and *ipil* wood for decking. Inside was a Ritz Carlton kind of luxury. In each suite was a well-stocked small refrigerator with a bottle of Dom Pérignon, chilled together with local San Miguel beer, with California, Italian, and French wines, as well as mundane Coke and 7-Up soft drinks. Each morning, Mr. Floirendo himself knocked on each door to tell us that breakfast was ready at the main house that was perched on an elevated coral rock overlooking the entire resort. Mr. Floirendo and his wife, NENITA, were the most hospitable host and hostess one could imagine, and we considered ourselves to be so lucky to enjoy this unparalleled lap of luxury. (Pearl Farm Resort was featured in the January 1997 issue of *Architectural Digest*.)

RON VELASCO was another patient referred by Fel. I only saw him a couple of times in consultation, but I did not perform any surgery on him. I saw him at Eye Referral Center in Manila. This must have been in the early 1990s. I mention him because he invited Donna and me to play a round of golf in "his grandchildren's little golf course." I thought he meant a par-3 executive-type golf course. It turned out to be TAT FILIPINAS, an eighteen-hole par-71 golf course leased to a group of Japanese business people and located in San Pedro in far-off Batangas. Mr. Velasco told me the golf course was indeed in the name of his grandchildren and was leased for twenty-five years to a Japanese group.

Everything in the golf course was authentic Japanese, including kimono-clad hostesses in the clubhouse, Japanese menus, no English or Filipino translation, and air-conditioned teahouses scattered in strategic areas on the course. It was not a particularly difficult course, but it was very interesting. Most players were Japanese. At the time we played there, we were the only Filipinos. I played that course again after several years with my classmate CENON CRUZ because his son knew a Japanese businessman who was a member there.

Speaking about golf, I was invited by Philippine ambassador BIENVENIDO TANTOCO to attend the Ryder Cup Tournament in Spain. I think this was in 1998. I had successfully performed cataract surgery on both of his eyes. He must have been much pleased, and so he invited me to his vacation house in Spain, which was on one of the fairways in the golf course where the Ryder Cup was to be held that year. Due to a very heavy schedule in my surgical practice, I was unable to find time to join him. Looking back now, I wish I had accepted the invitation because I now know that *that* was my one and only chance to see a Ryder Cup in the flesh rather than just on TV. On top of that, I would have been in the company of Ambassador Tantoco, who was a member of that Valderrama Golf Club. Incidentally, the US lost that match to the European team despite the presence of TIGER WOODS.

The ambassador also invited me to a New Year's celebration in his Forbes Park house later that year while I was in the Philippines. Again, I declined simply because I did not have a tuxedo that was the dress code printed on the invitation. That one I did not regret much because Donna was not with me on that trip and I would have been left alone with a whole bunch of society figures and politicians.

Fel became friendly with the Lopez (Meralco owners) family through his deep involvement with the Ophthalmologic Foundation of the Philippines (OFPHIL). The Lopezes donated a whole mobile eye clinic that I helped to equip. My friend ANDY MORRISON donated a used phaco machine for this clinic that was parked in one area of Rockwell Center before it was transformed into Rockwell Shopping Mall and high-rise condominiums that are seen today. I performed the first phaco cataract removal and lens implantation in that mobile eye clinic of OFPHIL in December 1994.

The following year Fel introduced me to EUGENIO LOPEZ Jr., the patriarch of the family Lopez. He had cataracts in both eyes that needed surgery. I had this scheduled and performed at Franklin Medical Center in Greenfield. Geny Lopez, as he wished to be called, stayed at our house at 11 Crescent Street accompanied by the love of his life, SUSAN REYES, a former Miss Philippines. A few days after the successful surgery, we drove them to Cambridge, where Donna and I were treated to a fabulous dinner at the Harvard Club where Geny was a lifetime member. From him, I learned a few pointers on how to better enjoy red wine.

Genie's other eye I operated on at Eye Referral Center in Manila one year later. When he left the clinic, he gave everyone on the staff an envelope with some cash inside. I did not know what the amount was, but it must have been substantial because I saw all of them were very happy. I charged him my usual fee that he thought was too low; he doubled the amount!

Further, he invited Donna and me to a cruise in his private yacht, *Miss Iloilo*. This was in December 1995. We started at the Manila Yacht Club, where we met the other passengers, Mr. and Mrs. GERALD EGGLESTON of Lexington, Virginia. Gerald was in the same class as Geny at Virginia Military Academy. The three couples, Geny and Susan, Anna and Gerry Eggleston, and Donna and I, were served by a crew of seven, including the captain.

We toured Corregidor and Subic. Wearing hard hats, we inspected a national tollway being built by the Lopezes for the Philippine government, linking Subic with the North Superhighway. Later in the week, we were invited to a dinner at the BenPres Building, where Geny introduced me as his cataract surgeon. The following days, I got swamped by calls for appointments to see me for their eye problems. Among them was the son of Geny himself, on whom I did a laser refractive surgery PRK.

This was before pain-free LASIK was in vogue. On the same day, a TV personality, CHARO SANTOS, underwent the same procedure. Both were near-sighted and had successful outcomes, though each one complained of a lot of postoperative pain that was common with PRK.

The president of United Drug, Dr. DELFIN SAMSON, was referred to me by my brother Ben. Dr. Samson was credited with United Drug's most profitable drug, the analgesic and anti-inflammatory medication PARACETAMOL. Dr. Samson came to Greenfield to have cataract surgery. I think he came again to have the other eye done. My first digital camera came from him as a gift. During one of my annual visits to the Philippines, I saw him for follow-up care at Eye Referral Center, which is located along TM Kalaw Street, just across Luneta Park (now Rizal Park). During one of my visits there, he treated me, together with Walter and his friend JOEY SUNICO, with a helicopter ride to and from Puerto Azul Golf Club in Batangas. It was in July 1997, and the second time Wally and I flew together in a helicopter, both times to play golf.

My sister Alma referred Senator HELENA BENITEZ to me for consultation. The senator had had a cataract operation in one eye done by a well-known society ophthalmologist at Makati Medical Center. Unfortunately, it ended up in a disastrous infection that eventually led to the removal of the eye. That ophthalmologist had my sympathy. Fortunately, the other eye was done by another ophthalmologist at a different facility, and the result was very good. She consulted me for a glaucoma that affected her only remaining eye. Had I been asked to do that cataract surgery originally, I would not have refused, but the stress would have been considerable because I know an infection cannot be ruled out 100 percent of the time, no matter where it was done or who did it.

The senator came to Greenfield several times, and I also saw her more than once at Eye Referral Center. She was a very lovely person, very unassuming despite her high stature in academic and political circles. Once, she invited Alma, Ben, and me to dinner at her house. She was a gracious hostess and made us completely comfortable as her guests. Dinner was at her house, located just behind the campus of Philippine Women's University on Taft Avenue in Manila, where she was president at one time.

Col. CHARLES KADES was a retired lawyer from Manhattan when I first saw him at GEC sometime in the late 1980s to early 1990s. He was wearing very thick eyeglasses as a result of bilateral cataract surgery done in a New York City hospital. I offered to implant intra-ocular lenses in both his eyes, but he refused, probably because he was aware that a leading ophthalmologist in NYC warned that "arti-ficial lenses inside the eye are intraocular time-bombs." At a second visit a year later for a routine annual examination, I again broached the idea of implanting those intraocular lenses, telling him that his quality of life would be much better after the implantation. This time he took my advice. After one eye was done, he could not wait to have the other undergo the same procedure. He was so happy with the restoration of normal vision without the need for those thick eye spectacle eyeglasses that gave him a narrow and distorted view of the world in front of him. Unfortunately, he died about three years later, but those last three years of his life were much more enjoyable with the normalized vision.

When I read his obituary in the newspapers, *Greenfield Recorder* and *New York Times*, I read with surprise and wonder that he was the one person responsible for the new Japanese Constitution of Peace. He was the lawyer and officer entrusted by General Douglas MacArthur to change the militaristic prewar Japanese Constitution to the one that the entire world now knows prohibits war as a means of settling disputes with other nations. I learned more about him and his work during the post-war years of rebuilding Japan from his widow, who also became my patient and who gave me a lot of papers and a book written about him. With Dr. Jane Winchester, I wrote an article about him, linking him to my wartime experience as a young boy in the Philippines. This essay was later published in *Filipinas* magazine November 2003 titled, "Merging Streams: The War, The Japanese Occupation, and My Practice."

JOE GUEVARA was the writer of the *Manila Bulletin*'s very popular column "Point of Order." Geny Lopez had recommended me to him. I performed cataract operations on both his eyes, after which he wrote a nice laudatory item in his column of December 19, 1994, about me and Dr. Felipe Tolentino. More patients came to me for surgery after that.

MARCIAL PUNZALAN was a congressman from the Philippines who represented the province of Quezon. He was the husband of LYNNETTE, a sister of Donna's best friend from kindergarten, NELIE ARAO ANTIGUA. I believe it was the latter who referred him to me. I saw Congressman Punzalan in Greenfield, remembering him as an ardent golfer. We played a round of golf at the Country Club of Greenfield. He also bought a new set of golf clubs from a custom golf club maker who made my own golf clubs.

During one of our regular visits to Manila, he invited me to play a round of golf at Ayala Alabang Country Club. There were a couple of bodyguards with him, who I assumed were armed and were discretely behind us in a separate golf cart. As a politician, he was aware of the danger of assassination by political rivals at any time. Indeed, this tragic event happened to him in May 2001 during a campaign for reelection.

SOSTHENES CAMPILLO SR., another patient from the Philippines, was also referred by Fel to me. He was the founder of one of the largest housing developments in Metro Manila, and his family owned a factory supplying disposable shaving blades to Gillette. He was aphakic bilaterally from previous cataract surgeries in Manila. He wanted better vision, and he came to me for the implantation of intraocular lenses that made the quality of his life that much more enjoyable. His son, JUN, became my golfing buddy whenever Donna and I visited the Philippines. He made it possible for us and our Japanese guests to play golf at Wack Wack, the premier club in Metro Manila. His wife,

Tess, is a Lazatin descendant from my hometown, Mexico. While he was Undersecretary of Tourism under the Cory Aquino administration, he helped me in arranging venues for my medical class reunions.

My *ninong*, godfather in the dialect, Manuel Panlilio, MD, UPCM class of 1938. was the inspiration for my parents to point me to a medical career. He was a member of the US-Filipino army captured after Bataan and Corregidor surrendered to the Japanese Imperial Army. Both of his eyes had cataract removal and were replaced with artificial lenses in my Greenfield clinic. His wife, Herminia Basa, MD, a classmate in the same UPCM class, was a famous obstetrician who coauthored *Philippine Textbook of Obstetrics* with Fe Palo-Garcia, MD, my own medical school classmate. *Inning* Herminia's cataracts I removed and replaced with intraocular lenses at Eye Referral Center in Manila.

Dr. Jose Vergel De Dios was a patient who had moderately severe glaucoma and whose remaining vision I preserved with timely operations. He was so grateful that he and his wife invited Donna and me and our mutual friends, Remy and Rey Reyes, to a one-week tour of Ho Chi Minh City, formerly named Saigon. Dr. De Dios had a pharmaceutical factory in that Vietnamese city in partnership with a former Viet Cong senior officer. The medical products produced by Filipino chemists in that facility were used in veterinary medicine. You can imagine the red-carpet treatment we received. It was the first taste of the famous Vietnamese staple *pho* for Donna and me. We explored the famous tunnels under the city and the suburbs that were a huge factor in the successful Viet Cong's fight against a superiorly armed US Army. Stealth was the secret.

Traditional medicine frowns on performing surgery on one's own family. In the Philippines, this was first articulated by Dr. Jose Rizal, who was the second trained ophthalmologist in the country. Philippine national hero Rizal wrote about his experience operating on his own mother for cataracts, lamenting poor results. This failure he partly attributed to less than complete cooperation from his mother to follow his instructions, but I think the problem was really a lack of adequate training and also the dearth of knowledge regarding cataract surgery in general at that earlier time.

With this background, you can surmise that I took a lot of chances to operate on the eyes of three generations of mothers in my own family, starting with my grandmother Apung Taqui. I did both of her eyes at PGH while I was chief resident in ophthalmology. Both eyes were successfully done, although she had to wear thick eyeglasses after the surgery for the rest of her life until she died at age ninety-eight. Intraocular lenses were not yet available at that time. I had a bit of a scare with one eye that developed a mild infection, but that responded very well with antibiotic medications given every hour around the clock, dutifully administered by Ima, her daughter, and my mother.

Ima's turn for eye surgery came in 1977. Intraocular lenses were just being introduced then, and she was among my first fifty patients with the new controversial procedure of artificial lens implantation that I presented in a monthly meeting of NEOS in Boston in 1978. I did her first eye at Farren Memorial Hospital in Turners Falls, Massachusetts, the other eye a few years later at Eye Referral Center in Manila. When my mother died at age 102 in 2004, she still had 20/20 vision in both eyes.

Imang Guring, the wife of Uncle Delfin David, had helped me a great deal by partly paying for my medical school expenses. In a small way, I had the privilege of repaying her for this by improving her vision with cataract extraction and implantation of intraocular lenses.

Four generations of firstborn mothers I wanted to remove the cataracts of. I did implant intraocular lenses on my sisters Zon, both eyes, and Alma, one eye. Jokingly, I offered to do the same surgery to Zon's eldest daughter, GRACE, just so I could claim to have done four generations of mothers, all firstborn, probably worthy of inclusion in *The Guinness Book of World Records*, but she refused. Instead, she had me perform PRK to correct her nearsightedness, myopia. Her sister NANIQUE had this procedure too. Opportunity exists no longer to extend this three-generation of surgery on firstborn mothers in my family because of my retirement from practice in 2000, but princi-pally because Grace did not need cataract surgery, anyway.

Serendipity and Philanthropy

Between 1970 and 2000, my colleague Felipe Tolentino and I made frequent trips from the USA to the Philippines and back in order to see some private patients and help train ophthalmology residents at PGH. In 1988, we visited the hospital just after President FERDINAND E. MARCOS was driven out of office by the People Power of Cory Aquino. Escorted by the director of PGH, Dr. FELIPE ESTRELLA, we were given a tour of Central Core, a new multistory building in the center of the hospital, built with funds released by then FIRST LADY IMELDA ROMUALDEZ MARCOS. An entire floor was dedicated to ophthalmology. Dr. Estrella showed us the numerous operating rooms, recovery rooms, supply rooms, and so on.

However, all rooms were completely empty. The usual limited hospital budget did not provide funds to buy any equipment, and so he asked us if we could help. With a promise to do our best, we returned to Massachusetts and made a list of what a modern, state-of-the-art eye operating room would need. We planned to seek donations for used equipment from supply houses, as well as manufacturers like Bausch & Lomb and Stortz. Dr. Tolentino then told me about the Miyake family, whom he had previously visited in Nagoya, Japan. In Nagoya, he and his wife, Flora, were invited to the Miyake home, where they met CHIYO MIYAKE, the matriarch of the family. She told them the following story:

> Chiyo's husband, Dr. TORAZU MIYAKE, was a medical officer in the segment of the Japanese Imperial Army that was occupying Leyte during the latter

166

part of the Pacific War. When General MacArthur invaded the islands, in the first stage of the liberation of the entire Philippines, the entire Japanese force was killed, almost to the last man, some with self-inflicted wounds. The latter was an example of bushido, *a samurai code of ethics in that a warrior never surrendered in battle. News of this catastrophic battle was reported in the Japanese homeland, and the Miyake family accepted this tragedy with dignity and sorrow. Proper ceremonies for the dear departed were made, and they went on with their lives.*

However, unbeknownst to them, Dr. Miyake had not died. He had been found by two Filipino boys on the battlefield, still alive but wounded. Instead of reporting him to Filipino guerrillas who were operating on that battlefield and who surely would have killed him on the spot, those two boys reported him to American soldiers. By his uniform, they recognized that he was a medical officer. Consequently, Dr. Miyake was taken to the rear, his wounds were treated, and he was sent to a prison camp in Australia. At the end of the war, he was sent home.

His arrival in Nagoya was a complete surprise to his family. The first time they saw this thin, pale ex-prisoner of war, the family thought he was a ghost. Of course, there was rejoicing when reality sank in. In due time he regained his health, restarted his practice of ophthalmology, and had two more sons. The oldest son, KENSAKU, was just a baby when the war started. His second son, YOZO, went to Boston to train under Fel. A third son also became an ophthalmologist. All three sons married medical doctors who were all trained ophthalmologists. With seven ophthalmologists in the family, it is easy to see how they were able to establish the largest eye hospital in Nagoya.

All this success would not have been possible were it not for the kind-heartedness of those two Filipino boys who saved the life of the elder Dr. Miyake. He never told these circumstances to his family because of shame that he survived while all other members of his battalion perished. However, at his deathbed, he finally told the story to his wife and family. He asked them to look for those two boys who saved his life, intending not only to thank them but to reward them for their kindness. Twice the family went to Leyte but could not get any leads in locating those boys. The family had not given up, hoping that someday they could find ways to show their appreciation to the Filipino people.

With this knowledge, Fel and I decided to write to the Miyakes. We sent them a wish list, hoping to get one or two major items. Within days of sending the letter, we received an enthusiastic response: they wished to *buy all* the items we had on the list! The amount was almost $500,000.

At that time, Farren Memorial Hospital in Turners Falls, Massachusetts, where I was a staff member, decided to change its mission from an acute to a chronic care facility, following my previous advice, thereby closing their operating rooms. They had an excellent Wilde operating microscope, which we bought for a fraction of the cost of a new one. We also bought all their eye surgical instruments. In addition, we purchased a brand-new phacoemulsification machine from Stortz. All that equipment was shipped to PGH.

On November 9, 1989, the Department of Ophthalmology of PGH, in association with the Association of Philippine Ophthalmologists in America and Ophthalmologic Foundation of the Philippines Inc., inaugurated the MIYAKE OPERATING ROOM. Chiyo Miyake, accompanied by her son Kensaku and his wife, flew from Nagoya to be at the inauguration.

At its inauguration, the Miyake Operating Room was the best in the whole Philippines and became a model for other hospitals to emulate. It boasted of having the first phacoemulsification machine for cataract surgery in the country. Two years later, in 1991, ELEAZER SUSON, Fel, and I taught the first phacoemulsification practical course in the Philippines at PGH. With that course, Fel and I introduced phacoemulsification techniques to the Philippines. We demonstrated that cataract surgery can be done safely on an outpatient basis.

This beautiful story came out of the brutality of the Pacific War. It is an illustration of how human kindness can survive, indeed, overshadow the destructive forces of war.

A Memorable Gold Watch

The year was 1982 when Rev. HENRY BARTLETT handed a gold Omega pocket watch, which had been given to the first UP president, MURRAY S. BARTLETT (1911–1915), by the UP faculty upon his retirement, to Jose D. Peczon, MD, UPCM class of 1957, in the presence of Rev. FEDERICO AGNIR, AB, UP 1959. This event occurred in the house of Rev. Henry Bartlett in Old Deerfield, Massachusetts. Both were ministers of the United Church of Christ, and both were patients in my private ophthalmology practice in Greenfield, Massachusetts.

Aside from being my patients, they were also my good friends. The first time I saw Rev. Henry Bartlett as a patient, he remarked that he noticed and read my UPCM diploma that was displayed in the waiting room of my office and told me that he had a close affinity with the university. Indeed, he had, as he informed me that he was a nephew of Murray S. Bartlett, who was the first president of UP when the main university campus was still along Padre Faura Street. Murray Bartlett was married but did not have any children, and when he and his wife died, their estate was inherited by Henry, who was their closest relative. Henry found the gold Omega watch, with the UP logo and dedication on the inside of the pocket watch, when sorting out the papers and other mementos of his uncle Murray. Since that time, he had been wondering how he could somehow return the watch to the university. When he met both UP alumni Frederico Agnir and me, he knew that the gold watch would now be able to "return home." That was the exact phrase he used to indicate his plan for the watch.

I enthusiastically encouraged him and his wife to fly to the Philippines themselves to deliver the watch to the then UP president EDGARDO J. ANGARA in Diliman, Quezon City. With his consent, I offered to buy airline tickets for them to make this sentimental journey, with the watch, back home to UP. Alas, this did not happen. Shortly after he showed Rev. Agnir and me the watch for the first time, his wife died, and he himself became seriously ill, from which he never recovered. Knowing that he will never be able to make that long plane ride to the Philippines and back, he entrusted the watch to my care with my solemn promise that his intention will be carried out.

The watch stayed in my home safe while waiting for the proper time for me to deliver it to UP just as Rev. Henry Bartlett wanted. That opportunity came during the Annual UPMAS Reunion in 1995 held at the Fiesta Pavilion, Manila Hotel. At that event, I announced that I had a special surprise gift for the college. Earlier, I told the UP Manila chancellor PERLA SANTOS-OCAMPO and the UPCM dean AMELIA REYES-FERNANDEZ, who graduated in the same class of 1957 as I did, of this plan, and both enthusiastically embraced it. That night the historically significant watch came home.

Sometime after that event, another special celebration was arranged by the UPCM chancellor at PGH Science Hall. In addition to UPCM chancellor Perla Santos-Ocampo, current UP president Emil Javier and former UP president Edgardo J. Angara were also present. I made a short speech describing how that watch came to my possession. I told those in attendance that I was just fulfilling the wishes of the first UP president Murray Bartlett's nephew, Rev. Henry Bartlett, and that it was an honor for me to be entrusted with that watch. It became possible only because of the MD degree I earned from UPCM.

Subsequently, the watch was displayed inside a Plexiglass box in the University Library at the UPCM campus. It was placed there during the eighty-eighth UP Manila Foundation celebration in 1996. I took great pride in showing it to my classmates, relatives, and friends whenever I made my annual visit to that campus until 1998 when I was shocked to discover that it was no longer there. Until someone told me that it had been transferred to some other place in the campus, I had dreaded the possibility that it had been stolen.

This artifact is now located at the recently inaugurated UP Manila Museum of a History of Ideas, formerly the College of Dentistry Building.

Life Well-Lived

My Greenfield ophthalmology practice started in June 1968 and ended in the same month, thirty-two years later, in 2000. Those thirty-two years were the most productive and enjoyable time for not only Donna and me but also for our children, Walter and Lisa. The practice started modestly with one examination room in a three-room rented office space. In the reception area, Donna greeted all the patients, took all the relevant bits of information, and collected the fees. There was a waiting room for patients. This was strictly a family affair.

The practice ended thirty-two years later in an office that I owned with two partners, Dr. Jane Winchester and Dr. Robert Bousquet. It was one of the largest, if not the largest, ophthalmology practice in Massachusetts, featuring twelve fully equipped examination rooms. In this large office were numerous other rooms: reception, cashier, optical shop, business office, laser surgery, fluorescein angiography, minor surgery, restroom, dining room for the twenty-six employees, and office manager. Our group practice provided eye care to residents of Franklin County and parts of Vermont and New Hampshire. There was also a satellite office with two examination rooms in Athol, fifteen miles east of Greenfield, and part ownership in a stand-alone surgicenter in Gardner, twenty-five miles east on Massachusetts Route 2, the main route to Boston.

We had a twelve-passenger Ford van to give free rides to our cataract patients from their houses to the surgicenter and back to their houses. Donna became a full-time housekeeper, a role she resumed with full pleasure. She raised our son, Walter, and grandson, Patrick, to be perfect gentlemen as adults! Lisa needed special care that her mom lovingly provided.

Although I tremendously enjoyed the practice, we started to make plans for an inevitable and anticipated retirement. Donna and I thought that Greenfield was where we will retire for life. Our house along 11 Crescent Street would remain our permanent retirement nest. We owned a two-bedroom condominium in Greenfield that Lisa occupied while she was still single. Upon her wedding to OMAR TIONGSON and the birth of first our grandchild, JOSE PATRICK, we bought a house for them along Lillian Street, a lovely quiet place, barely a mile away. Income from two good rental properties in Boston provided more reason to make Massachusetts our permanent home state. One was a one-bedroom condominium on the thirty-second floor of Boston Tower in the highly desirable waterfront area of Boston. Another was a two-bedroom unit at Longfellow Place, next door to MGH. Those two rental properties greatly augmented our social security benefits and proceeds from our private retirement funds.

During the last ten to twelve years of medical practice, both Donna and I gave up tennis and devoted most of our recreation time to golf, that ancient game that originated in fifteenth-century Scotland and had been popularized in modern times by the likes of JACK NICKLAUS and TIGER WOODS. Membership in the Country Club of Greenfield opened a new world to both Donna and me—to make new and lasting friendships.

Our love for the game was the reason why we chose to buy a winter house in a golfing community in Homosassa Springs, Florida. But this well-thought-out plan shattered when Omar and Lisa announced to us that they wanted to move to Southern California. The harsh New England winters, which often lasted as much as half of the year, were becoming unbearable to Omar. Obviously, our only grandchild will be going with them. That would have left us woefully lonely. We also knew that other grandchildren were inevitably arriving to join Patrick. Walter informed us that he was getting married to RINA CONCEPCION, and so we decided to make a rapid change in plans for our retirement. After graduating from college, Walter had left Greenfield for Los Angeles, California. The choice to retire in California was not difficult to make.

Walter acquired a house at Hermosa Beach in the desirable South Bay area of Los Angeles. We visited there often. During one visit, he made a tee time for us to play golf at Tijeras Creek Golf Club in Rancho Margarita, situated halfway between Los Angeles and San Diego. It was love at first sight for us. The golf course and housing community built around it was everything we had dreamt about for our retirement years. The year was 1999.

During that visit, we happened to lunch with our long-time friends who had been settled in Los Angeles for as long as we had been settled in Greenfield, Massachusetts. Lourdes and Tony Garcia, upon learning of our desire to find a house in a golfing community in Orange County, pointed to fellow *cabalens*, SYLVIA and LU GAMBOA, who lived in exactly the kind of community we desired. Tony offered to call Lu to make an introduction. We met the Gamboas at their house in Dove Canyon that was located on the left side of the fairway of the first hole on this famous Jack Nicklaus signature-designed golf course. As their guests, we played the entire eighteen holes, had lunch at the clubhouse, and met the manager. Lu told Donna and me that he did extensive research about golfing communities in California before he and Sylvia decided to settle in this place. We were impressed with his knowledge of golf courses and never doubted his choice. There was no need to reinvent the wheel, and so, based on what we saw and heard about Dove Canyon Country Club, we decided to look for our retirement house in this alluring golf community of 1,400 houses. We immediately contacted a Realtor to help us in our search.

The first Realtor took us on a tour of available houses inside Dove Canyon as well as houses in other golfing communities in the area. Of the houses that she showed us, we liked one. We made an offer to buy the property, but the owner decided not to sell after all. Undaunted and impatient, we asked another real estate broker to show us more homes in Dove Canyon.

The first house this second real estate broker showed us was on Foxtail Lane. We were smitten on the first visit. We were happy that our offer on the first house was rejected! The dwelling we fell in love with was at the end of a cul-de-sac. It had the largest lot and longest driveway along the whole street. Behind the house along the street was the second hole of the golf course. From the kitchen window, it had a perfect view of the putting green just over the fence. To the right of the house was a hill separating the other homes by several hundred yards. The front view was a continuation of the hill on the right side. To the left was a typical house along the whole street with small lots. There was no other house along the street on Foxtail Lane that offered more privacy.

Immediately we made an offer that was promptly accepted by the owner. The house was occupied by a tenant whose lease was not going to be renewed. Our choice for this house did not waver as we were shown a few more houses in the area just for comparative purposes. The more houses we saw, the deeper our love for Foxtail Lane grew!

Foxtail Lane, Dove Canyon, CA 92679, officially became ours on June 7, 1999. Upon returning to Greenfield, I immediately sold stocks, which had appreciated much in value and sent the whole amount to the escrow company to buy the property—cash. There was no need to apply for a loan, and I believe this was the reason why the seller immediately accepted our offer. After acquiring the title to the property, we immediately started renovations to the house and the large yard by a contractor to make the house conform to our specific desires and needs.

For two more years, I had to stay in the practice after GEC was sold to fulfill a signed agreement of sale to the new owners before Donna and I were free to start a new phase of our odyssey to become California dreamers. Our Dove Canyon house was made ready for occupancy a year before I saw my last patient at GEC. Donna again was the pioneer in our westward quest for a new life. As soon as the new house was ready, she moved there.

I remained in Greenfield, living alone in a nearly empty house for a total of five months before I could join her. However, those months were neither as long nor as lonely as the seven months we had to endure in the first year of our married life.

The telephones and computers with Internet connections helped to bridge the physical separation. Donna had the rest of the family with her as support in California. The busy practice served me as a partial shield from loneliness.

Finally, on June 25, 2000, I saw my last patient, said goodbye to relatives and friends, and enjoyed a retirement party given by the medical and supporting staff of GEC. Donna and Patrick flew over from California to be with me in enjoying my farewell party and on the final trek to the Golden State, taking eight days to complete the journey by car.

Not surprisingly, GREENFIELD RECORDER ran a small article about me on that last day of practice. However, the newspaper erred in saying I was in Greenfield for forty years. It was only thirty-two years. The "extra" eight years were in Boston.

On June 26, Donna, Patrick, and I drove westward to the Golden State to savor the fruits of our labor in retirement. As a retired but still physically active couple, we soon settled into daily activities centered on golf.

On October 15, 2000, club pro DAVE CANTRELL handed me the trophy for winning the Senior Match Play Club Championship. That was just eight months after joining the club. To win that coveted championship was totally unexpected, and I was enormously proud of it. I did not think that a relatively new member like me could rise to the occasion. My golfing partner did her part: Donna won first net among women in the same tournament. Not bad for a couple who were only in the first year of membership in the golf club. Winning the club championship was most exciting and unexpected. Even more so was making a hole-in-one on the fourth hole, 148 yards, par 3, using a 4-wood on June 8, 2006.

Golf took the greatest share of our time, yet we were busy with other social activities too. Family came first. There were numerous times spent with our children and grandchildren. During the first few years after we settled at Dove Canyon, Walter and his family lived at Hermosa Beach. Lisa and her family had a house at neighboring Redondo Beach. Both houses were within one hour of driving from our Dove Canyon house. Most weekends, we spent time with them either at Dove Canyon or their houses at the beach area that was teeming with good dining places. Onami, a Japanese seafood buffet restaurant, was a favorite for all of us. These family-oriented activities stimulated and strengthened our already close family relationship. After all, to be with our grandchildren was the primary reason why we left Greenfield.

I did not completely retreat from ophthalmology in the first few years of retirement. During our yearly visit to Ima in the Philippines, the knowledge that I had accumulated in Greenfield I continued to share with my colleagues in my old hunting ground—the Eye Department at PGH that recently relocated from the old main PGH building to a new one. The new building was called SENTRO OFTALMOLOGICO JOSE RIZAL, in honor of the Philippine national hero. With $15 million donated by the Spanish government, a modern five-story building was constructed. Here, I examined, diagnosed, and managed PGH patients side by side with residents and fellows.

ILDEFONSO PECZON (Don), the youngest son of my brother Pons, was a resident in that department. Here is an email he sent me on February 9, 2003, after one of those trips: "I introduced topical anesthesia for cataract surgery, local instead of general anesthesia for dacryocystorhinostomy (DCR), and elimination of expensive preoperative examinations to get cataract patients ready for surgery." Don and his fellow residents were appreciative of the innovations I introduced in that department. There is no doubt that patients benefited much more.

My activities were not limited to PGH. I also tried to spread the gospel of doing small incision cataract surgery to the provinces. To members of the Northwestern Luzon Chapter of the Philippine Academy of Ophthalmology, I gave a seminar. It was held in the conference room of Lorma Medical Center. When I first returned from my five-year residency and fellowship training in Boston back to Manila, I was tempted to practice in this hospital with an invitation from the hospital director, Dr. RUFINO MACAGBA, a classmate in UPCM. But Donna had other plans for us, and I was a willing accomplice.

Travels

Travels to domestic and international destinations were activities that Donna and I enjoyed even before retirement. We started when we were still in Greenfield, and my practice had started to prosper. At first, we traveled to cities in North America, then to international destinations, where ophthalmological meetings were held. Not only did I learn many new developments in my field, but Donna and I also enjoyed the travels themselves—fabulous destinations with luxury hotels and restaurants. Also, all expenses were legitimate business tax deductions!

Retirement allowed us to explore more and fortunately visit most of the popular tourist destinations throughout the world. Some trips were more memorable than the others because of the special circumstances surrounding them.

There was a negative side to our constant travels. Two of these almost ended in tragedy, either one of them would have been unspeakable, both happened in the Philippines. The first was a trip to Kabankalan and Bacolod. We were with Donna's parents, together with her brothers Rady and Edward and their children. Donna and I, with Walter and Lisa, were in a convoy of three cars with the other families driving back to Bacolod after an enjoyable day-long reunion with close Villaflor-Ibañez relatives in Kabankalan, where Donna was born. Along the road in the middle of a sugarcane field, we encountered thick smoke from fires deliberately set by sugarcane farmers to get rid of the leaves prior to their harvesting the tall stalks. This was done to make it easier and safer for the farmers to cut and load cane stalks onto trucks. The choking smoke was so thick that visibility was reduced to a few feet in front of us. I do not remember who, but a relative got out of the lead car, and with his handkerchief covering his nose, he led the caravan of three cars to safety. Those few minutes were harrowing. I thought that was the end of the entire Villaflor-Ibañez and Peczon-Villaflor clans!

Another, even more harrowing experience happened in the same island of Panay where Bacolod and Kabankalan are located. This time it was in a resort outside Dumaguete, Negros Oriental.

To give a little background, let me explain that when visiting Ima, almost always during the Christmas season, Donna and I naturally stayed in Ayala Heights, Quezon City. Many homes in Ayala Heights were owned by the Chinese who, by tradition, ignited a lot of fireworks during these festive days of the season to drive away evil spirits. On New Year's Eve, the noise and smoke from the fireworks became so intense that we had to place wet towels under the doors to minimize smoke sneaking through the narrow spaces under the doors. It was like a war zone.

Aware of this cultural habit of the Chinese and Filipinos alike, Donna and I decided to avoid it by going to isolated resorts where few fireworks were ignited. We tried this in Tagaytay and in Olongapo. Those places gave us some respite from the noise and smoke that we started to dread. One year, we decided to go to a recommended resort outside the city of Dumaguete that was one hour by plane from Manila. Arriving at the airport, there we met by chance ALLAN PECZON, the third son of my brother Pons, accompanied by his wife, RIZZA, and son MIGGY, who were visiting Rizza's parents to welcome the New Year. They invited us to a traditional New Year's Eve dinner at their house. Reluctantly, we accepted, with the stipulation that we did not like to be outside if there were fireworks in the area.

As we had feared, just before the passing of the old and coming of the New Year, fireworks outside the house became intense. Donna and I stayed in the safety of the house. We emerged only when Rizza's mother told us that it was safe for us to come out of our shelter. We did unknowingly, just as Rizza's older brother lighted the fuses of a couple of celebratory rockets. Donna and I were standing safely far away, or so we thought, holding hands as we usually did, and watched from this "safe" distance of about one hundred meters. To our horror, one of those rockets flew horizontally directly at us and *exploded between us!* It happened so quickly and was terrifying. It could have hit one of us directly that almost certainly would have resulted in a serious injury, even death. Donna suffered some minor burns on the legs because she was not wearing pants like I was. Both of us suffered hearing loss that lasted for several days. Ringing in my ears continued for more than a month.

If I believe in karma, I could say that *that* was payback time for what I did as a young boy in Mexico, Pampanga, exploding firecrackers in wrong places, like inside a church, or embedded in a freshly laid cake of carabao dung on the road, waiting for a crowd of townspeople trying to enjoy the town fiesta. But I do not believe in that. Like all things in life, it is a matter of being in the wrong place at the wrong time.

Due to our belief in science, we are keenly aware of the role of human activity as a significant factor in global warming. We want to do our part in mitigating this dangerous threat to the planet. To reduce our carbon footprint, we installed solar panels on the roof of our house. We got rid of our internal combustion-powered cars for a purely electric Tesla S. Storage batteries, Power Walls, were installed in the garage. At this writing, our carbon footprint is near zero. I enjoy driving the most desirable car in the world today—fast, no exhaust, no fluids except for windshield washing, no annual maintenance except to replace the tires, and free electricity for life to charge the batteries.

Foxtail Lane provides all the comforts in life that we desire. In addition, we are blessed with sincerely friendly neighbors.

Anniversaries

Enjoying life to the fullest as retirees, Donna and I had been savoring the celebration of important anniversaries in our lives.

Our grandchildren and their parents helped us celebrate our fiftieth wedding anniversary on September 6, 2008.

September 2018 was a special year of celebration. Patrick and Sami got married on September 3 in Oakland, California. Donna and I celebrated our sixtieth wedding anniversary and her eighty-fifth birthday on September 6. Relatives and friends from the Philippines, Australia, and several states in the US came to celebrate this doubly significant day in our lives. The Dove Canyon Country Club house was the venue.

How did we manage to have such a long happy marriage? I told relatives and friends that for the past sixty years, we have not gotten tired of holding hands. I also revealed to them that Donna rated men in her life with numbers; Walter is always number 1 as the only son, and Patrick is also number 1 as the only male grandchild. I do not have a number because she said God does not need one. How can you not adore a loving wife like that?

Grandchildren

Success in life we do not measure in tangible things alone. It is not just how healthy our financial resources are. It is not just how comfortable our lifestyle is. It is intangibles, like the high regard we earned from our colleagues, friends, and relatives, which our children and grandchildren have taken notice of. All have followed our emphasis on the value of hard work, especially in education, to get where they want to be. We have shown them the basic values on how to be humane in all aspects of life, how to be kind, respectful, and understanding of others.

The three oldest grandchildren, Patrick, Michaela, and Haley, all have earned inclusion on the dean's list in the colleges they are enrolled in. Patrick and Michaela are seeking degrees in nursing like their Lola. Haley is enrolled in robotic engineering, probably a reflection of my inquisitiveness about how things work. Brianna inherited her Lola's artistic leanings and creativeness in card-making, flower arranging, and good taste in fashion. Charlie, the youngest, shows a lot of interest in her Lola's recipes of favorite family dishes. We cannot be happier and more satisfied than that.

Health

As expected with all living creatures on earth, aging, and all that comes with it, started to intrude into the picture. We had been extremely fortunate to enjoy healthy lives from our youth to adulthood and beyond. A permanent foot drop on my left lower extremity, resulting from that gunshot wound in the leg when I was fifteen, had caused only minor difficulty. Since medical school days, I had premature ventricular beats. They grew increasingly more frequent starting from the sixth and seventh decade of my life. Finally, the irregularity became atrial fibrillation, a serious cardiac arrhythmia. This necessitated an implantation of a cardiac pacemaker in 2011 and cryoablation aimed at the foci of abnormal electrical signals in one heart chamber in 2018. Both procedures improved the quality of my life beyond my expectations. (*Thank you, Dr. Howard Frumin.*)

Donna started to have more consequential health issues with her spine. Despite excellent medical advice and treatment, the degenerative process slowly progressed. In the first year of our retirement, she was diagnosed with scleroderma, an autoimmune disease. This complicated the underlying issue of narrowing of the spinal canal. Most of the time, she stoically lived with constant lower back pain. Early in 2018, she started showing symptoms of more spinal cord compression, this time involving the cervical vertebrae. Thorough neurologic evaluations that included extensive imaging diagnostic procedures (MRI) led to a conclusion that she would either have to have surgery on her cervical spine at some point or face inevitable quadriplegia.

About two months before she went to the hospital for the surgery, there was an episode that alarmed both of us. Holding hands, as usual, we were standing at the end of our driveway while chatting with the foreman of a work crew who were resurfacing our street. Donna suddenly collapsed to the ground. She was not turning or doing anything. She was just standing there on my left when she fell.

The foreman and I immediately helped her get on her feet again. There were no injuries. Fortunately, she did not hit her head on the pavement. I interpreted this to mean that paralysis of her legs was starting to show.

We mulled over this serious condition carefully, asking the opinions of two neurologists and two neurosurgeons. After careful deliberation, we both felt that doing nothing was not an option. Both of us could not face the prospect of her becoming a quadriplegic. Despite the obvious possibility of serious postoperative complications, which could be made worse by her weakened immune system from the treatment she received for scleroderma, she had a 6-hour operation on four cervical spines on September 5, 2019. The surgery went well, according to the surgeon. I was happily optimistic.

The following day, September 6, was her eighty-sixth birthday and our sixty-first wedding anniversary. She had survived the ordeal of the surgery. In the post-surgery intensive care unit, she was fully awake, speaking to all of us who were by her bedside. Balloons were inside the room, but the birthday cake was not permitted to be brought in. Happy with her condition in the immediate postoperative period, I went home that night to get some rest.

In the middle of the night, I received a call from the hospital. The attending doctor wanted my permission to do an intubation to assist her breathing. This had an ominous meaning that I instantly recognized. I do not want to go into the details of what happened in the next few days because they were the most difficult days for me, and I could not live through them again. On September 9, my beloved Donna passed on to the great beyond with all members of the family by her bedside.

We left our home country in 1966 in search of a better future in a foreign land, but we did not seek to be in this small New England town of Greenfield, in Western Massachusetts. Instead, the town sought me out and invited us to come. In the process, I was saved from the danger of actively being involved in the fog of war in Vietnam in the 1960s and 1970s.

In June 1968, Donna, Walter, Lisa, and I came to plant our roots in this unfamiliar place in North America. Here, as the first Filipino immigrants, we immersed ourselves to be fully integrated into the community, in part contributing to the well-being of the entire population by providing the best ophthalmological care available at that time. In exchange, we found complete satisfaction that life could offer, the fulfillment of our dreams.

For the past twenty years, we had been temporarily away from this welcoming place. A year ago, Donna returned to stay for good.

Here I, too, will surely return sometime in the future to lie beside her for eternity.

10-10-2020
Foxtail Lane
Dove Canyon, CA 92679

Autobiographical and Historical Notes

This autobiography essentially covers the period from May 1948 to October 2020 and necessarily includes such places as Clark Air Force Base in the Philippines, Osaka in Japan, and Groningen in Holland, among others. Names of world leaders such as President John F. Kennedy and Premier Nikita Khrushchev are also mentioned. To help the reader appreciate events of world history necessarily mentioned in this personal story spanning seventy-two years, this part of the book has been prepared. The entries include names of people, places, and happenings.

Atomic Bombs

To force the Japanese to surrender, atomic bombs were dropped on Japan in 1945: Little Boy on Hiroshima on August 6 and Fat Man on Nagasaki on August 9. Less than a month later, on September 2, on the USS battleship *Missouri*, General Douglas MacArthur accepted the formal surrender of Japan to the Allies.
https://en.wikipedia.org/wiki/Atomic_bombings_of_Hiroshima_and_Nagasaki

Bataan Death March

The Bataan Death March passed near my hometown of Mexico, Pampanga, some five kilometers away. It began in Bataan and ended in San Fernando, Pampanga, a distance of forty kilometers. Several

Filipino soldiers were clandestinely saved from the ranks, such as when the guard was not looking. One of them was my godfather, a medical officer in the Philippine Army.

Benevolent Japanese Captain Sakuma

After the Fall of Bataan and Corregidor, our town of Mexico was completely occupied by a company of Japanese cavalry. Our house next door was where the commander of the unit, with his aide, was billeted. Captain Sakuma and his second-in-command, Lieutenant Kamatso, took over the upper floor of our house. The first year of the Japanese occupation was not too oppressive, thanks in part to the lack of opposition to the occupation and to the benevolence of the captain. A West Point graduate, he was fluent in English. He read books to Zon, Alma, and me. He showed us pictures of his family and children. I had the impression that he was against the war with America but had no choice except to obey his emperor.

Central Core

This was a multistory building in the center of the campus of PGH, built with funds released by then First Lady Imelda Romualdez Marcos. An entire floor was dedicated to ophthalmology. We helped raise funds to equip a state-of-the-art operating room. (See also Miyake Eye Operating Room.)

Charles Kelman

A few years after I invented my IA device, Dr. Kelman of New York City introduced a phacoemulsification machine that worked on the same principle as my device. It is a sophisticated, computer-controlled device that can emulsify any type of cataract through a tiny incision. It is now used universally all over the globe. By all ophthalmologists, it is considered the best technological advancement in cataract surgery. I regret not having patented my invention. (See also Irrigation-Aspiration Device.)

Charles L. Kades

At the end of the war, based on instructions of General Courtney Whitney coming from General Douglas MacArthur, Colonel Kades steered his committee to draft the Japanese Constitution that renounced war as an instrument of national policy. This restored the Japanese's normal vision from the blindness of war. In later years, I operated successfully on both eyes of Col Kades—this restored his own normal vision.

Clark Air Force Base

Clark Air Force Base (CAFB) was America's largest overseas military facility. The base was located in the town of Angeles, now a city, in Pampanga. It was first established as a US military camp for the Fifth Cavalry after the Spanish-American War (1898). The base was named Clark Field in 1918 after Major Harold M. Clark, a pre-World War I pilot. On December 8, 1941, at the outset of the Pacific phase of World War II, the installation was the principal target of raids by Taiwan-based Japanese bombers that destroyed more than half of the US Army's aircraft in east Asia. After the Japanese occupied the Philippines (1941–1942), the airfield became a major Japanese base of operations during the war. The first Japanese kamikaze (suicide) flight was made from Clark in 1944 as US forces began the process of recapturing the Philippines.

https://sites.google.com/site/majorharoldmclark/ https://www.britannica.com/topic/Clark-Air-Base

https://www.stripes.com/explore-the-storied-history-of-a-former-american-military-base-at-clark-museum-1.552596

Clark Air Force Base Hospital

Located in the town of Angeles near our own Mexico, Pampanga, Clark Air Force Base (CAFB) was reputed to be the best-equipped medical facility outside the USA. It had to be: CAFB was where sick and wounded American military from all over Asia were sent to receive all kinds of surgical/medical help.

Cocoa, Cocaine

My grandmother Apung Taqui prepared a concoction of *samat* (betel leaves), lime, and betel nut—the resulting product is called *maman*. The women in town chewed on this betel nut-*samat*-lime combo, turning their saliva almost bloodred in color. I believe that cocaine is present in small amounts in the betel leaves and nuts. Peruvian Indians living high up the Andes chewed on cocoa leaves for the same reason. Cocoa leaves contain a powerful alkaloid that acts as a stimulant, its effects including raised heart rate, increased energy, and suppression of hunger and thirst. https://www.nationalgeographic.com/history/magazine/2016/11-12/daily-life-coca-inca-andes-south-america/.

Cuban Missile Crisis

Also known as the October Crisis of 1962, this lasted from October 16 to November 20, one month and four days. First, the US deployed missiles in Italy and Turkey; subsequently, these were matched by Soviet deployments of similar ballistic missiles in Cuba. This is considered the closest the Cold War came to escalating into a full-scale nuclear war. https://en.wikipedia.org/wiki/Cuban_Missile_Crisis

Dormitory, UP-PGH Campus

Some members of my fraternity, Phi Kappa Mu, donated each $5,000 to build a Phi House dormitory, the only existing dormitory on the UP-PGH campus.

Dr. Geminiano de Ocampo

Chief of EENT at UP-PGH, I moonlighted as his assistant in his office and his own hospital. I learned a lot of medical science from him. He was a pioneer in corneal transplantation and encouraged all residents to engage in research for new or improved knowledge.

Dr. Walter Morton Grant, MD

Author of a textbook, *Toxicology of the Eye*, which provided authoritative, ready answers to questions about the manner in which chemicals, drugs, household, and industrial substances of all sorts injure the eyes or disturb vision.

Coauthor of the seminal *t*extbook on the subject of glaucoma, with Dr. Paul A, Chandler, *Lectures on Glaucoma.* He was the director of the GCS, Howe Laboratory of Ophthalmology, HMS, and MEEI, Boston, Massachusetts.

Dr. Jose Rizal

The national hero of the Philippines was the second trained ophthalmologist of his country. He operated on the eyes of his mother with less than satisfactory results. While Rizal attributed the failure to the patient's lack of cooperation, I attribute it to lack of available knowledge at that time regarding cataract surgery. He lived from 1861 to 1896, when he was martyred by the Spanish colonizers.

Dr. Lawrence Dame

He was the chairman of the Massachusetts Military Draft Board who decided to keep me in Massachusetts and not be drafted to the US Army to fight in the American Vietnam War of the 1960s–'70s. It was Robert E. Graves who interceded with Dr. Dame, on my behalf, in exchange for continued ophthalmological services in Greenfield, Massachusetts.

Dr. Manuel Panlilio

He was saved surreptitiously during the Bataan Death March. He was my godfather, an alumnus of UPCM (class of 1938). He was the inspiration for my parents to point me to a medical career.

Dr. Vergel De Dios

He was a patient who had moderately severe glaucoma and whose remaining vision I preserved with timely operations. He was so grateful that he invited me and Donna and our mutual friends REMY and REY REYES, to a one-week tour of Ho Chi Minh City, where he had a pharmaceutical factory in partnership with a former Viet Cong senior office. The medical products produced by Filipino chemists in that facility were used in veterinary medicine.

Dr. Vidal Tan

He was President of FEU when I graduated from FEU High School in 1950. And he was president of UP when I graduated from UP Medical School in 1957. He was one of the sponsors in my wedding with Donna I. Villaflor in 1958.

Errol Flynn

At St. Joseph's Academy in Mexico, as young ones we played "pirates" following the example of popular swashbuckler Errol Flynn that we watched in pirate movies—there were movie houses next town, in San Fernando City.

Fall of Bataan and Corregidor

After the Fall, it was accepted that the Japanese Imperial Forces had the upper hand at this point, and the family elders of the Peczon-David clan thought that we might as well make the most of it. By that time, the town was completely occupied by a company of Japanese cavalry. The municipio (municipal hall) was occupied by the troops as their headquarters, and our house next door was where the commander of the unit, along with his aide, was billeted. Captain Sakuma and his second-in-command, Lieutenant Kamatso, took over the upper floor of our house while my parents and our maids became part-time servants for these officers.

Galleon Trade

A galleon was a large three-mast sailing ship with a square rig and usually two or three decks (TheFreeDictionary.com). The Galleon Trade was actually a Spanish government monopoly. Only two galleons were used: One sailed from Acapulco to Manila with some 500,000 pesos worth of goods, spending 120 days at sea; the other sailed from Manila to Acapulco with some 250,000 pesos worth of goods spending 90 days at sea.

https://www.philippine-history.org/galleon-trade.htm#:~:text=The%20Galleon%20Trade%20was%20a,spending%2090%20days%20at%20sea

General Douglas MacArthur

He promised "I shall return" after the Fall of Bataan and Corregidor. And he did, triumphantly. Upon the surrender of Japan, he caused the rewriting of the Japanese Constitution into one that sought peace and not war as a national policy in dealing with other nations. Under the new constitution, the military was placed under civilian control and established new rights for women.

https://www.cfr.org/japan-constitution/japans-postwar-constitution

Gold Omega Pocket Watch

When MURRAY S. BARTLETT retired as the first UP president in 1915, he was given by the UP faculty a gold Omega pocket watch as a souvenir. The watch was handed over by his nephew Henry Bartlett to me in 1982 at the house of United Church of Christ minister Rev. Bartlett at Old Deerfield, Massachusetts. At the 1995 UPMAS Reunion at the Manila Hotel, I handed over the watch to UPCM, where it belonged.

Insufficient Supervision of Medical Students

Up to now, I am still campaigning for sufficient supervision of medical students by full-time, more experienced, and older physicians at PGH as well as other hospitals in the Philippines. This is to protect both the patients and the attending medical doctor in training.

Intraocular Lens Implantation

I introduced intraocular lens implantation in the eye during cataract surgery in Greenfield, Massachusetts. I started doing this in 1975. With success, the visual rehabilitation of patients with cataracts is near-perfect. It became the standard procedure all over the world.

Irrigation-Aspiration Device

IN 1975, I invented this tool for removing cataracts in preparation to implanting intraocular lenses into patients with sight problems to recover vision. The IA device was made of two needles fused together, one needle to irrigate fluids and another to remove bits of cataract tissue in the eye. This was effective on soft cataracts only.

"I Shall Return"

These have been the most famous three words in the world ever since World War II. General Douglas MacArthur uttered it as a promise to the combined US-Filipino forces fighting the Japanese army in the Philippines, at the point when the Japanese forces had defeated them. MacArthur fulfilled that firm promise and liberated the country from the invaders.

https://en.wikipedia.org/wiki/Douglas_MacArthur%27s_ escape_from_the_Philippines

Japanese Bathing Custom

The Japanese soldiers took turns bathing themselves in a large empty metal barrel filled almost to the brim with hot water. Led by Captain Sakuma, this was a cavalry with horses larger than the local ponies that took over the upper floor of the Peczon-David house in front of the municipal building in Mexico, Pampanga. Many years later, Donna and I enjoyed this same exquisite Japanese bathing custom in several traditional Japanese onsen ryokan hot spring inns, along the base of Mt Fuji, in the company of friends TAISUKE and KAZUMI KUBOYAMA

Mexico, Pampanga

My hometown, sixty-eight kilometers north of Manila. It got its name from Spanish settlers from Acapulco, Mexico, who were involved in the galleon trade that lasted for 250 years, between 1565 and 1815. Originally called Nuevo Mexico ("New Mexico"). The Spaniards made Mexico the capital of Pampanga. April 24 is Mexico Day, the date when the town and parish were established in 1581 by Spanish missionaries. The town was founded as a river trading port. It was the first capital of Pampanga.

https://en.wikipedia.org/wiki/Mexico,_Pampanga

Miyake Eye Operating Room

Dr. Torazu Miyake, a Japanese eye surgeon, survived World War II in the Philippines because two Filipino boys brought him to American soldiers when they saw he was wounded. In their utmost gratefulness, when classmate Felipe Tolentino and I wrote for medical equipment assistance for PGH, the Miyakes donated $500,000!

From that donation, we arranged for the Miyake Eye Operating Room to be equipped with used but still excellent equipment and a brand-new phacoemulsification machine from Stoltz. At its inauguration, it was the best in the Philippines and became the model for other hospitals to emulate. The Miyakes attended its inauguration.

Notable Patients

Over the years, the list of my notable eye patients has included the following:

ANTONIO FLOIRENDO, the Banana King, cataract surgery for both eyes

CHARLES KADES, World War II hero, cataract surgery on both eyes

DELFIN SAMSON, president of United Drug, cataract surgery on both eyes

EUGENIO LOPEZ JR., Lopez family patriarch, cataract surgery on both eyes

HELENA BENITEZ, senator of the Philippines, for glaucoma

JESUS TANCHANGCO, minister of food under President Ferdinand Marcos, cataract surgery

JOE GUEVARA, popular Manila Bulletin columnist, cataract surgery on both eyes

MARCIAL PUNZALAN, congressman, removal of corneal scars

SOTERO LAUREL JR., senator, cataract surgery at Franklin Medical Center in the US and Eye Referral Center in Manila

Pearl Harbor

Pearl Harbor, a US naval base near Honolulu, Hawaii, was the scene of a devastating surprise attack by Japanese forces on December 7, 1941. Just before eight o'clock on that Sunday morning, hundreds of Japanese fighter planes descended on the base, where they managed to destroy or damage nearly twenty American naval vessels, including eight battleships and over three hundred airplanes. More than 2,400 Americans died in the attack, including civilians, and another 1,000 people were wounded. The day after the assault, President Franklin D. Roosevelt asked Congress to declare war on Japan. The war lasted up to 1945.

https://www.history.com/topics/world-war-ii/pearl-harbor

Pilita Garrido Corrales

A Filipina pop singer and songwriter, actress, comedian and television presenter. She is dubbed as Asia's Queen of Songs and is widely known for her rendition of "Kapantay Ay Langit," which eventually became her signature song. Donna and I met her when she had a concert in New York City on May 25, 1980.

https://en.wikipedia.org/wiki/Pilita_Corrales

Sentro Oftalmologico Jose Rizal

This now houses the Eye Department of PGH; it was constructed with a $15 million donation by the Spanish government. The offices and equipment are housed in a modern 5-story building. The name is in honor of the Philippine national hero, Jose Rizal.

Treaty of Paris (1898)

Signed between Spain and the United States on December 10, 1898, ending the Spanish-American War, whereby Spain surrendered sovereignty over Cuba, Guam, Puerto Rico, and the Philippines. It marked the end of the Spanish Empire and the beginning of the American. In the 1900 US election, Democrat WILLIAM JENNINGS BRYAN opposed the treaty (imperialism), while Republican president WILLIAM MCKINLEY supported it and easily won reelection. Empowered by the Spanish Constitution, Queen Regent MARIA CHRISTINA signed the treaty, "moved by lofty reasons of patriotism and humanity."

https://en.wikipedia.org/wiki/Treaty_of_Paris_(1898)

UP BS Pharmacy

The UP BS Pharmacy program was first offered as a four-year course in 1913. In 1935, the School of Pharmacy became an autonomous college. In 1951, the five-year BS Industrial Pharmacy program was created by the university in response to the need for graduates for the growing pharmaceutical industry.
http://cp.upm.edu.ph

UP College of Medicine

UPCM is considered the best Medical School in the country, and the best way to get accepted there is through the UP premed course in UP Diliman. The Philippine Medical School, which later became the College of Medicine of the University of the Philippines, opened its doors to the first medical students on June 10, 1907.

UP President Vidal Tan

He was president of FEU when I graduated from FEU High School in 1950. The same man was president of UP when I graduated from UPCM in 1957.

Viet Cong Underground Tunnels

Courtesy of Dr. VERGEL DE DIOS, who owned a veterinary drug manufacturing company in Vietnam in partnership with a former Viet Cong officer, Donna and I toured the famous Viet Cong tunnels under Ho Chi Minh City. This was a huge factor in the successful fight against a more superiorly armed US Army. Stealth was the secret.

Vietnam War

I would have been drafted into the US Army to fight in the Vietnam War in the 1960s–1970s of the Americans had it not for the intercession of Dr. LAWRENCE DAME, who was then chairman of the Massachusetts Military Draft Board. Knowing Dr. Dame, it was Robert Graves who convinced me to set up practice in Greenfield, Massachusetts, and I thereby earned the privilege of being exempted from the draft, although I did not believe it at first.

World War II: September 1, 1939–September 2, 1945

President Harry S. Truman announced Japan's surrender and the end of World War II. The news spread quickly and celebrations erupted across the United States. On September 2, 1945, formal surrender documents were signed aboard the USS *Missouri*, designating the day as the official Victory over Japan Day (V-J Day).
https://www.google.com/search?client–opera&q–end+of+world+war+2&sourceid–opera&ie–UTF-8&oe– UTF-8

X-ray Examination

San Fernando Provincial Hospital in Pampanga did not yet have an x-ray machine at that time, 1948, so my gunshot wounds were not x-rayed until I was brought to Clark Air Force Base Hospital in San Fernando, the capital town. I sustained the wounds during the broad-day shooting of my father JOSE PECZON, who died; I was also shot at but not fatally.

My hometown is sixty-eight kilometers (forty-two miles) north of Manila. It got its name from Spanish settlers from Acapulco, Mexico, involved in the galleon trade sometime between 1565 and 1815. Spain ruled the Philippine Islands via Mexico, not Madrid, because of a shorter route across the Pacific Ocean versus a longer one from the Atlantic Ocean, then around the Cape of Good Hope.

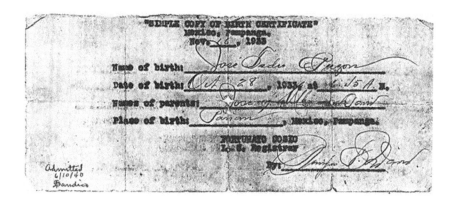

This is a copy of my original birth certificate signed by my maternal grandfather, Benigno Flores David. Note that my second name is Tadeo on the certificate. It was when I started to go to the school when my name became officially Jose David Peczon, dropping Tadeo altogether.

Paternal family portrait

Maternal family portrait

This is the second house for our family in Mexico, Pampanga. It is located on leased land to the right of the municipio (municipal hall). The front of the house is FARMACIA A. DAVID, popularly known as BOTICA DAVID by the townsfolk. My younger siblings, ALMA, PONS, and BEN were born in this house. PINING, LUVY, ZON, and I were born in the first house in front of the Catholic church, less than half a kilometer away to the left of the municipio. My earliest recollections of childhood started here.

This was the historic municipio built with Spanish architecture during the eighth century. Our second house was to the right of this building. Tragically, this building was demolished sometime in the 1980s by town officials who had no appreciation for history. The site, together with our house, was converted to a public marketplace. In my youth, the only telephone in the entire town was in this building.

To honor our parents, my siblings and I built the David-Peczon Family Library donated to the Mexico Elementary School. The first floor is a classroom equipped with donated computers. The top floor is the library. The original iron handrails on the stairs rusted and were replaced by ceramic and cement material. Maintaining the library is a continuing responsibility of the David-Peczon clan. The architect is Ariel Orlina, the youngest son of my sister Zon.

On January 2, 1929, my parents tied the knot.

The address 23 Jose Abad Santos Street, Ayala Heights, Quezon City, is the home Donna and I built for my widowed mother, Ima. Here, she was lovingly well taken cared for my family who lived close by and by hired caregivers who came from Mexico, Pampanga.

Directly across the plaza from our house fronted by Farmacia A. David is the St. Joseph's Academy where I started my formal education starting in kindergarten class. To the left of the building is the bell tower, a remnant of an old Spanish church in the 1880s, which was subsequently destroyed by an earthquake. The statue in front is that of a favorite town hero, Gen. MAXIMINO HIZON, who led the local militia against the Spaniards during the rebellion against the colonizers. Not shown, a similar statue about fifty meters to the right is that of the national hero Dr. Jose Rizal, who was also an ophthalmologist. He was the second eye surgeon in the entire country.

With many of my friends, countless hours I spent at the tower top just looking at the town plaza below. We earned a few centavos ringing the bells for baptisms, weddings, and funeral rites. Occasionally, I took my turn to ring the largest bell to announce the Angelus; that is the time at sundown when all young kids were supposed to be at home.

As a five-year-old, I was enrolled in kindergarten class with a Filipina teacher. There were several nuns belonging to a Benedictine order coming mostly from Germany and Belgium teaching the higher elementary grades. That is me in the front row, second from the right.

After kindergarten, I transferred to the public-run Mexico Elementary School, where TATANG, my father, was a teacher and later principal. Sitting in the second row in a dark shirt is I, who graduated as salutatorian. To my left is ADORACION COSIO, the valedictorian. She was my first puppy love.

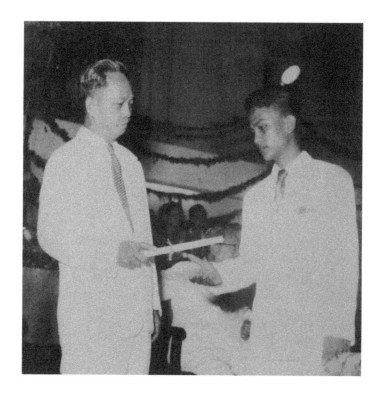

Dr. VIDAL TAN handed me my high school diploma when I graduated from FEU High School in Manila. He also handed me my doctor's diploma when I graduated from UP Medical School. After I met and eventually married DONNA, my lifetime partner, and he played more significant parts in our lives.

April 1948. A bus trip to Baguio. JDP is peering out of the bus window, second from the left. Tatang is kneeling in front, third from left. Brothers Jaime and Rogelio de la Rosa, popular movie actors, are the two tall men standing in the middle. They were shooting a movie in that area. They were Tatang's friends. Less than two months after this photo, Tatang was killed by extortionists.

Among the ranks of these forlorn Filipino and American soldiers who surrendered in Bataan and Corregidor is my *ninong*, godfather, Dr. MANUEL PANLILIO. As the bedraggled long column of men was about to end their journey at a train station in San Fernando, Pampanga, to be brought in railroad boxcars to the prison camp at Capas, Tarlac, some fifty kilometers up north, fearless members of the clan snatched him away when the guards were not watching. It was a dangerous and bold action that saved the life of *Ninong Maning*.

I was named after my father, JOSE PECZON, whom we fondly called Tatang (father). I signed my UP student I.D. in UP Diliman, two ways—one with a middle initial D and the other without. Both signatures had Jr. in the end. While in medical school, I decided to drop it altogether, reasoning that there was no confusion about my name since Tatang had already passed on.

The circular Chapel of the Risen Lord in Diliman. A few times, I was an altar boy when Fr. JOHN DELANEY offered Mass in this first ecumenical church in the Philippines. I was not yet an atheist then.

COLLEGE OF MEDICINE, U.P.
FIRST YEAR CLASS 1952-53.

One hundred aspiring medical doctors were admitted to the UPCM in 1952. Eighty-six graduated in 1957. Of the fourteen, two dropped to the class of 1958 the following year. The rest either enrolled in other medical colleges, University of Santo Tomas or Manila Central University, or went on to other universities to pursue alternate careers. I am in the second row, fourth from the left.

Villaflor family portrait. Dolores Ylaguison Ibanez and Ramon Magong Villaflor, standing in the back. Edward, Donna and Rady, sitting in front.

BOB HENDRICKS, the lone *Americano* in the class, thrived among the rest of the classmates who all spoke grammatically correct English, with a Filipino accent, of course. With the patients in the hospital out-patient clinics and wards at PGH, who spoke little or no English, he likewise managed to do what had to be done. He also did not hesitate to eat local delicacies, including *balut*. Unfortunately, we never saw him after graduation because after a few years when he returned to America, he died prematurely from a heart attack.

This tennis court is adjacent to the main building in the UP Medical School campus. Here I spent some spare time playing with other classmates who enjoyed the game. There were more tennis courts on the PGH campus behind Nurses Home reserved mostly for residents and consultants. As a resident, I played there most of the time, where the special student nurse I dated sometimes watched from a window of her room at the dorm. My tennis shoes were used to the utmost. Holes in the soles were patched with rubber taken from inner tubes of used automobile tires. This was done at a nearby vulcanizing shop. When Donna arrived in Chicago, the first package she sent to me was a pair of brand-new Chuck Taylor sneakers; we simply call them *rubber shoes*. There was a bowling alley too, but I did not play there that much because of the money involved, and I was never good at it anyway.

Here is a peacock-proud clinical clerk with all the trappings of a budding physician—a name tag over the left shirt pocket and a stethoscope. Riding in public transportation with this look elicited a lot of flirtatious stares from nubile young females. It would have been easy-to-pick-up dates, but this medical student had only eyes for a special **student nurse**.

Internship in PGH was a hectic part of medical school life. For instance, when assigned to the Emergency Room, it was twenty-four hours of relentless wakefulness taking care of endless emergency cases, some involving life and death situations. Note that none of the interns in the picture are overweight. However, there was still some time to relax and play pranks on each other.

Here is the newly minted physician who took up the Hippocratic oath.

A few months after earning MD after my name on April 9, 1957, I successfully passed the National Medical Board Examination to become a full-fledged physician. Every one of the eighty-six passers of my class passed the examination. Some landed on the top ten list. I landed somewhere at the bottom of the upper third. At the banquet, sitting in the front, to my left, is Dr. Pura Torres, who was first to spot DIV, that beautiful student nurse in Ward 5. Seventeen months after this banquet, that student nurse became Donna V. Peczon, my lifetime partner in our odyssey to find our place in the sun.

Phi Kappa Mu Fraternity brothers of UPCM class of 1957. Front row, left to right: S. Padilla, N. Nolasco, A. Cruz, faculty adviser, a cofounder of the fraternity, and PGH Director Dr. Jose Barcelona, R. Tongco, V. Velasco, J. Florendo. Second row: C. Cruz, N. Velarde, R. Casino, J. Suero, E. Rivera, G. Dacumos. Back row: J. Peczon, E. Regala, and T. Collantes. Not in the picture is W. Yutuc, who helped me pass the PE class by swimming on my behalf (the PE teacher did *not* notice) during premed in UP Diliman.

Diplomas were handed out at a ceremony on the UP Diliman Campus, Quezon City, by UP president VIDAL TAN, the same distinguished academician who handed me my high school diplomas when he was president of FEU in 1950. When Donna and I became one, he was one of two principal sponsors, the other one being my classmate Dr. PURA TORRES.

This is the entire PGH EENT staff before it was split into two separate sections, the Eye and ENT. Extreme right is JDP.

Brod GIL VELASCO and his wife, MUTYA SAN AGUSTIN. I was introduced to my future wife by Gil. He was a brilliant surgeon who unfortunately succumbed to a rare form of liver cancer early in life, at age 31, before he could reach the acme of his profession. Mutya and I remain life-long friends.

Picnicking on the beach along Manila Bay, courtesy of the United Drug. This is the first-ever picture of just the two of us. Shortly after this photo was taken, she unexpectedly told me that we should *not* see each other anymore. It was a bombshell that exploded inside my chest and made me depressed for a few days. What scared her was a casual remark I made mentioning that the woman I marry will have to be a Roman Catholic. She was raised in a devout Protestant Baptist family. Eventually, I was able to persuade her to overcome this conflict. She converted to Catholicism just so we can have a traditional church wedding, but in the end, we both ended up not belonging to any religious group. She retained her belief in a supreme being, while I became an atheist.

Donna was introduced to the entire DAVID-PECZON clan at a small celebration party, following my graduation from medical school, at the house of Uncle RUBEN, kneeling in front with a striped shirt and black pants. Donna and I are standing in the back row, fifth and sixth from the left. In front of Donna is my father's half-sister, IMANG CHARING. APUNG TAQUI and IMA (my mother) flank Imang Charing. That little girl sitting on Uncle Ruben's knee is my cousin NONIE, who was the flower girl at our wedding.

Bacolod is a city on the northwest coast of Negros Island in the Visayas region of the Philippine archipelago. It is 705 kilometers south of Manila. Ilonggo is the dialect spoken on this island. It is aptly described as *malambing*, meaning affectionate, and Ilonggas are known for that trait too. Often, I referred to Donna as my Visayan Beauty Rose.

Dr. and Mrs. JOSE D. PECZON
SEPTEMBER 06, 1958

Six months after our wedding, Donna flew to Chicago follow-ing our prenuptial plans. I followed her eight months later.

November 19, 1958, was the date I first ventured outside the Philippines on my way to Chicago to rejoin my bride. At the airport, I said goodbye to relatives. Kneeling in front from left to right are Cousin RENE and my brother PONS. Standing, Uncle RUBEN with Cousin NONIE in front of him, IMANG PACING, APUNG TAQUI, my sister ALMA, me (men wore a coat and a tie to board planes at that time), brother-in-law PEPE FERNANDEZ, husband of ALMA, IMA, my sister ZON, and husband ARTHUR.

Our first car is this model 1958 VW Beetle that cost $1,500. Monthly payment was $15 a month. At one point, our beloved first car was in danger of bank repossession because we were late in a monthly payment. That was when I had no income while attending the ophthalmology Lancaster course in Maine. Donna had to work two shifts in two different hospitals to pay all the bills. Never did I hear her complain about this.

There were approximately one hundred budding ophthalmologists from across the US and other areas of the world who took the Lancaster course. In the second row, third and fourth from the left are MARCOS FOJAS and me, the only ones from the Philippines. The specialty of ophthalmology was dominated by males. Notice that only two females, middle, fourth row, were in this class. At the present time, females make up more than a third of active ophthalmologists. There was only one African American in the group, fifth from the right, fourth row.

This trusty VW, filled to the gills with all our earthly belongings, took me to Boston from Chicago in the middle of winter in January 1961. Along the way, I listened to the inaugural address of JFK on the radio on January 20. A fierce northeaster (severe winter storm on the East Coast) raged as I drove along the highways. I made the usual stops along the way with free accommodations, courtesy of my friends. I stayed in a motel on only one occasion. Upon arrival in Boston, the entire city was covered with about a foot of snow and ice.

This is the entire ophthalmology resident staff of BCH headed by Dr. ROBERT ALPERT in the dark suit. I was the shortest but not the oldest in the group, and I was chief resident.

Only two other ophthalmologists preceded me as a clinical research fellow at the GCS, Howe Laboratory of Ophthalmology, HMS, and MEEI. After me came a long list of other fellows who themselves contributed enormously to more understanding of glaucoma.

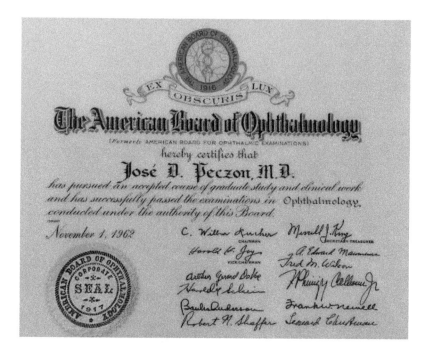

Even before I passed a medical state licensing board examination, I earned myself the title of DIPLOMATE of the American Board of Ophthalmology. I was the only resident or fellow at MEEI who took the examinations to get this certificate. There were several full-fledged consultants on the MEEI hospital medical staff who were still not certified by this board. The two and a half years of residency training at PGH, one and a half years at BCH, and the two years as a clinical research fellow at the GCS, coupled with glowing recommendations from my mentors, Dr. Paul A. Chandler and Prof. W. Morton Grant, made this possible. The examinations took place in St. Louis, Missouri, in October 1962 in the midst of the Cuban Missile Crisis. When I bade goodbye to Donna to board a Greyhound bus to that city, I was telling myself that our goodbyes may be the last time we will see each other if a full-fledged nuclear war was started. Fortunately, because of the skill of JFK and his AG RFK, who handled the situation expertly, Nikita Khrushchev blinked. It was a small step for me but a giant leap for mankind, immodestly using a statement by the first man on the moon.

I will never forget the near disaster that occurred that night we stayed in a tiny cabin in the woods. The oil burner used to warm the cabin malfunctioned and caused a fire to engulf the entire wooden structure, giving us little time to gather all our belongings, especially my treasured Canon camera, to get out unharmed and record this fiery near-disaster for both Donna and me. What a night to remember!

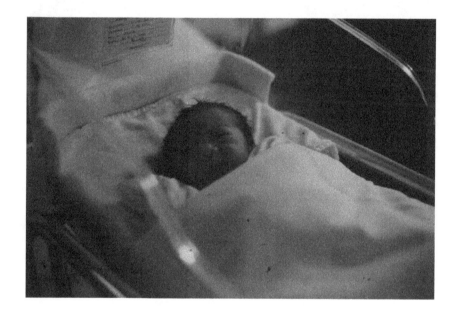

Ultrasonography was not yet available at that time, so we did not know the sex of the unborn child Donna carried. Whosit was the unisex name we called the occupant of Donna's womb. On August 15, 1964, WALTER MARTIN PECZON officially became a citizen of the USA.

A few days before boarding a plane at Logan Airport in Boston to start our journey back to the homeland, we showed our Walter to his namesake, Dr. WALTER MORTON GRANT. We said our goodbye to Dr. Grant, and he wished us bon voyage. He was fascinated with our travel itinerary.

First stop was in Houston to visit Ben, who just recently arrived from Manila, to start his quest for a PhD in his chosen field of physical chemistry.

In WAIKIKI BEACH, we had a scare in the hotel room when I found Walter with his head hanging out of the baby crib. How he got his head through the baby crib slats was a mystery to me. He just lay there without making a sound. For a moment, I thought Donna and I had a major tragedy. With adrenaline spiking in my blood, I quickly spread the crib slats wide enough for Donna to gently pull him out unharmed. Whew! That was close.

From then on, Donna stayed more focused watching Walter, making sure he was always safe.

EYE EXPERT RETURNS

Dr. and Mrs. Jose D. Peczon and their one-month old boy, Walter Martin, arrived recently after a 5-year stay in Boston, USA. Dr. Peczon is a diplomate in opthalmology and has done extensive research work on glaucoma at the Massachusetts eye and ear infirmary in Boston.

DR. AND MRS. JOSE D. PECZON (she is the former Donna Villaflor) and their one-month old boy, Walter Martin, arrived the other day after a 5-year stay in Boston, U.S.A. Dr. Peczon is a diplomate in Opthalmology and has done extensive research work on glaucoma at the Massachusetts eye and ear infirmary in Boston.

Uncle Ruben announced our return to the Philippines in the local papers.

We set foot on our home turf on October 14, 1964, five years after we left earlier to pursue more training as we sought for a better tomorrow. ARLENE, the little girl leading us in front, is the oldest daughter of our friends, the GARCIAS.

Upon arrival, we stayed for a few days in the house of my sister ZON and her husband, ARTHUR, with their children. Donna's parents flew from Bacolod to welcome us there.

Uncle Ruben and beloved Apung Taqui were happy to see us again after an absence of five years.

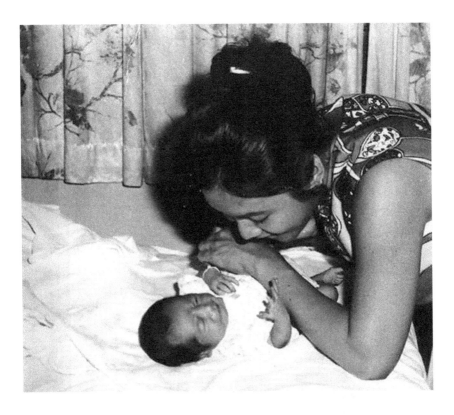

DONNA LISA came to join our family on September 19, 1965. At that same time, Taal Volcano was having a turbulent eruption. Lisa arrived in the same fashion. Precipitate labor is the medical term obstetricians use to describe ultra-short labor. Walter took over eight hours to traverse Donna's birth canal. Lisa did the same route in less than an hour.

Relatives and friends saw us off at the Manila airport.

The Dita Street home of Uncle Ruben was the venue for a small celebration of my thirty-third birthday and a *despedida* party for all of us, Donna, Walter, and Lisa. That same day we left Manila to seek a better life in a foreign land.

Donna carried Lisa in her right arm. Walter tagged along, clutching at her left arm, and I followed behind with all our carry-on luggage. It was now or never as we left the Pearl of the Orient Seas and headed to the Land of the Free and Home of the Brave.

DEPARTURES

Dr. Jose D. Peczon, consultant ophthalmologist of the Philippine Eye Research Institute of the PGH and the De Ocampo Eye Hospital, left recently via Pan-Am with his family for the United States to do further study on glaucoma at the Howe Laboratory of Ophthalmology of Harvard Medical School and Massachusetts Eye and Ear Infirmary in Boston. Diego S. Garrido Jr., manager—Philippines, for Trans World Airlines, departed on Philippine Air Lines flight to Hongkong to attend a sales meeting scheduled Nov. 3 and 4 in the Crow Colony; Najeeb B. Halaby, senior vice president of Pan American Airways, enplaned by PAL for Hongkong after attending the 30th anniversary celebration here of PAA's first trans-Pacific passenger-flight to Manila.

Uncle Ruben, as expected, announced our departure on the "Coming and Going" page of the *Manila Bulletin*.

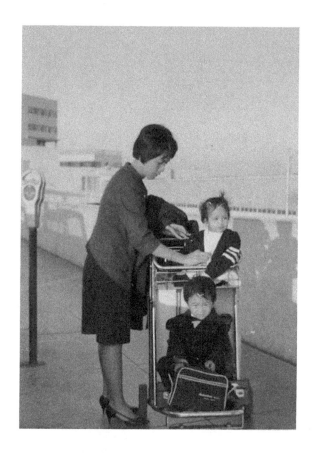

We were exhausted upon arrival at the San Francisco airport as permanent immigrants to the USA. Before that, in Honolulu, where we had our immigration papers checked, the immigration officer told me, "Doctor, we need people like you here in the States." That made us feel so welcome.

In November 1967, I was earning enough to afford to buy our first home in Winchester, the same suburb of Boston where my mentor Dr. Grant lived.

Having taken and successfully passed an examination to secure a license to practice medicine, we were on our way to forge ahead toward that pot of gold at the end of the rainbow.

The address 210 High Street, Greenfield, Massachusetts, purchased on July 8, 1968, was our first house in Greenfield. It had only been two years since leaving that crowded apartment back in the Philippines to now own a dream house built with English Tudor architecture, complete with ivy-covered brick walls and a large front and back yard.

My US private practice started modestly in a rented office at the rear of this house on 40 Church Street, Greenfield. It contained only one examination room. Due to a high demand for my ophthalmological skills, the practice grew rapidly, resulting in the recruitment of the third ophthalmologist, Dr. JANE A. WINCHESTER, to join Dr. VICTOR E. KENNEALLY and me to form an incorporated practice. We built our own office building with six examination rooms. When Dr. Kenneally retired, he was replaced by Dr. ROBERT BOUSQUET.

Ophthalmologist To Open Practice

Dr. Jose D. Peczon, teacher at Boston University Medical School and Tufts University, will establish an office for the practice of ophthalmology (care of the eye) at 40 Church St. next month.

Dr. Peczon will conclude in June his work as assistant clinical professor of ophthalmology at Boston University Medical School, as assistant director of Glaucome Consultation Service at Massachusetts Eye & Ear Infirmary and as instructor in ophthalmology at Tufts University.

He and his wife and two children, three and two years, will move from their present home at 17 Wellington Rd., Winchester, Mass., to Greenfield. He has scheduled his office opening for the third week in June.

Dr. Peczon received his MD degree from the University of the Philippines in 1957 and after two years as resident in ophthalmology at Philippine General Hospital took a postgraduate course in ophthalmology.

He served as chief resident at Boston City Hospital for a year, was certified by the American Board of Ophthalmology in 1962 and became a fellow of the American Academy of Ophthalmologists and Otologists in 1963. He was clinical reserach fellow in glaucoma at Howe Laboratory, Harvard and Massachusetts Eye and Ear from 1962 to 1964 before returning to the Philippines.

During his two years in the Philippines he was clinical instructor in ophthalmology at the University there and consultant in ophthalmology at the Philippine General Hospital in Manila.

He is the author of a number of articles on the eye that have appeared in medical magazines.

DR. JOSE D. PECZON

I was introduced to the citizens of Franklin County via this newspaper article in the town newspaper, *The Greenfield Recorder*.

ROBERT E. GRAVES is this gentleman, an optician, who picked me out of a long line-up of qualified ophthalmologists on the Massachusetts Selective Board list for the military draft. To him, I owe my not being drafted into the US military to serve in Vietnam. We became lifelong friends and remain so up to the present time. He attended my retirement party in June 2000, thirty-two years after I first settled in the town we both love and call home.

ELMER V. KENNEALLY, M.D.
JOSÉ D. PECZON, M.D.
ROBERT N. SPETH, M.D.
JANE A. WINCHESTER, M.D.
SCHAFF OPTICIANS, INC.

The Med-Optic is the first professional office building in the entire county of Franklin in Western Massachusetts. The six examination rooms in this first building soon became inadequate for the volume of patients we had to take care of, and we started to look for a larger office.

The address 33 Riddell Street was the answer. This vacant building was once a car dealership, then a tofu factory. It was unoccupied for a number of years before it was converted to multiple offices for multidisciplinary medical practices. Greenfield Eye Center (GEC), the group practice we now called ourselves, had the largest space complete with a dozen examination rooms and others for specific functions, like a reception area, cashier, billing office, operating room, photography room, record room, restroom, and a basement used as a dining room for twenty-six employees. At that time, it was the largest ophthalmology office in the entire state of Massachusetts.

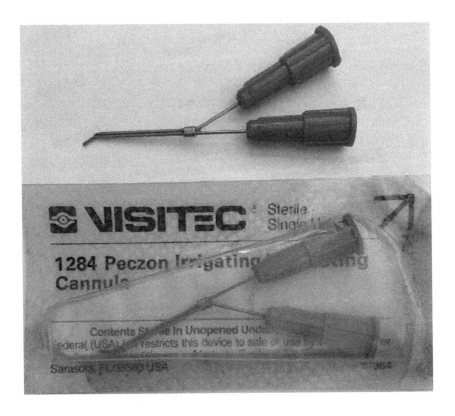

VISITEC, a commercial manufacturer of sterile, disposable ophthalmic surgical devices, manufactured my original design of an irrigating-aspirating cannula. It was a simple device that was effective in removing soft cataracts through a tiny incision. A couple of years later, Dr. CHARLES KELMAN, a visionary ophthalmologist in NYC, invented a better device that could be used to remove any cataract regardless of the hardness or maturity, as we say in ophthalmology parlance. The Kelman phacoemulsifier can be compared to a miniature jackhammer mated to a vacuum cleaner and a garden hose fluid irrigator. It was based on a similar idea as the simple device I invented. It is too bad I did not apply for a patent. The Kelman phacoemulsifier is completely automated and is used worldwide, including Boston.

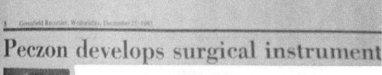

Peczon develops surgical instrument

JOSE PECZON

DR. JOSE PECZON, a Greenfield physician, has developed a surgical instrument that is currently being manufactured for worldwide distribution.

Peczon, an eye specialist at Franklin Medical Center, has developed an irrigating and aspirating cannula, a specialized needle used during surgery to remove cataracts.

A cataract is a clouding of the lens of the eye. During treatment, the clouded lens is first removed, using the cannula, and then replaced by a synthetic lens.

Peczon developed the needle locally with the help of Justin Moore, a Greenfield jeweler, who performed the welding of the needle's tiny components.

The device serves to streamline cataract surgery and to eliminate the need for more costly equipment. Peczon describes the 400 trials of the device as "very successful."

The manufacturer, Vitec, produces a disposable model to reduce the risk of contamination.

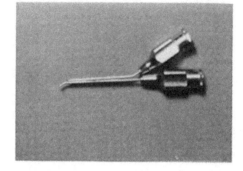

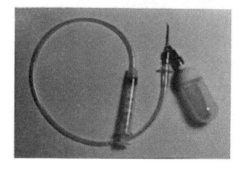

My original invention was a simple device consisting of two conventional needles welded together and connected to an irrigating bulb made of silicon and a tube connected to an aspirating needle. It was effective on soft cataracts only. Its main advantage was that types of cataracts found in children and younger adults could be removed through a tiny incision.

Greenfield Opthalmologist Invents Surgical Instrument

A Greenfield physician has developed a surgical instrument that is currently being manufactured for world-wide distribution.

Dr. Jose Peczon, an eye specialist at Franklin Medical Center, has developed an irrigating and aspirating cannula, a specialized needle used during surgery to remove cateracts.

A cateract is a clouding of the lens of the eye. During treatment, the clouded lens is first removed, using the cannula, and then replaced by a synthetic lens.

Dr. Peczon developed the needle locally with the help of Justin Moore, a Greenfield jeweler, who performed the welding of the needle's tiny components.

The device serves to streamline cateract surgery and to eliminate the need for more costly equipment. Dr. Peczon describes the 400 trials of the device as "very successful."

The manufacturer, Visitec, produces a disposable model to reduce the risk of contamination.

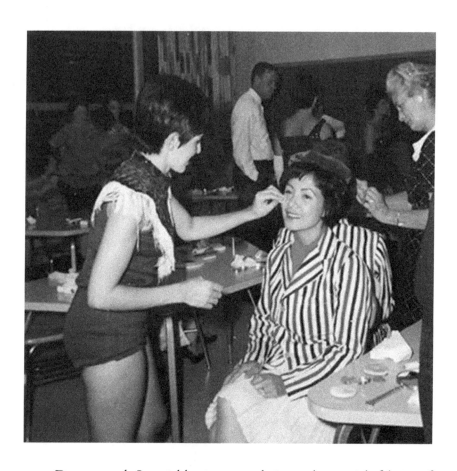

Donna and I quickly integrated into the social fabric of Greenfield. JANET HODOS, our lovely next-door neighbor, introduced us to Greenfield society via an annual fundraiser show to benefit the local hospital—THE GREENFIELD FOLLIES.

Our dream brick English Tudor house on High Street provided us with warmth. With the same degree of warmth from the populace, we enjoyed all the comforts of life.

We lived within a few hours from major ski resorts, and we enthusiastically adopted this winter sport. Like the other seasons, we enjoyed winter. Walter became an expert and graceful skier who joined a ski patrol at the Berkshire East Ski resort. Lisa was not as graceful, but she was fearless, and like a downhill racer, she barreled down even the most difficult trails without once suffering a wipe-out. Donna and I managed to handle all but the most difficult trails, albeit at a much slower and more controlled pace.

This 100 percent hand-stitched quilt, now a family heirloom, covers the bed in our master bedroom in Dove Canyon. It took Donna two years to create this masterpiece.

Greenfield (Mass.) Recorder, Friday, May 19, 1972—17

Six From Area Swear Citizenship

Six new citizens were naturalized at the opening of the Superior Court session this morning by Judge Paul A. Tamburello.

They are: Dr. Jose David Peczon and Mrs. Donna Ibanez Peczon, both of 2. High St., Greenfield, born in the Republic of Philippines; Frederick Korenewsky, 35 King Philip Ave., South Deerfield, stateless; Carlo Pederzini and Mrs. Meri Pederzini, both of 2 Water St., Greenfield, born in Italy; Mrs. Bertha Anna James, 31 Haywood St., Greenfield, born in Canada.

Following the naturalization ceremonies, a coffee hour for the new citizens took place at the Greenfield Public Library, planned by the First Methodist Church, under the direction of Mrs. Harry Douvadjian.

Assisting were Mrs. Edna Gregory, Mrs. Rosalie Bellany, Mrs. Joan Hume and Mrs. Elsie Prescott.

Four years after settling down in Greenfield, Donna, Lisa, and I became naturalized US citizens. Walter already had automatic citizenship by virtue of his being born in Boston.

How can one not feel so welcome as a citizen in our adopted country? The OR staff at Farren Medical Hospital reflects how the entire population of Franklin County adopted my family and me as one of their own.

Donna was a perfect fit to model Oriental clothes at a fund-raising event for the Greenfield hospital. Her pictures, together with those of other models, were featured prominently in the pages of *The Greenfield Recorder*.

210 High Street became too crowded for us when Donna's parents and Ima were staying with us at the same time. We wanted them to stay with us for as long as they wished, and so we decided to induce them to stay longer with more space for us all. The address 11 Crescent Street was closer to Main Street, where it was easy to walk to the library, post office, YMCA, and restaurants in the area. There were six bedrooms and four bathrooms in the main house. There was a carriage house behind the two-car garage that was made into a self-contained apartment complete with its own kitchen, a bathroom, and a bedroom in the bath. Behind this carriage house was an in-ground swimming pool. The property was almost an acre with a sloping backyard that made for a mini ski trail in the winter. We added a sunroom at the back to give us a summer-like ambiance even in the dead of winter.

Donna's mother died on September 17, 1985. Her passing is the only mournful event that happened so close to us. The deaths of my brother Pons, my beloved Apung Taqui, Donna's paternal grandfather, nephews Joey and Samuel, brothers-in-law Arthur and Perfecto all happened in the Philippines. Yet even remotely, we mourned for them in the same degree.

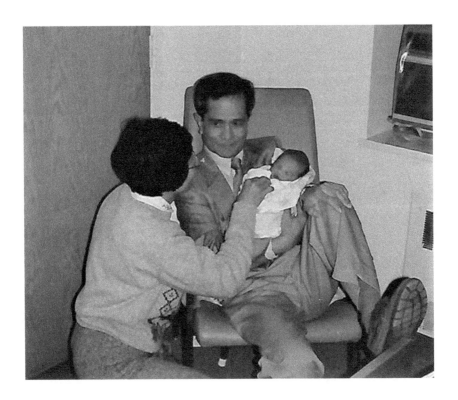

The normal cycle of life goes on. One dies and another one is born. Our firstborn grandson, JOSE PATRICK TIONGSON, made his appearance on March 5, 1991. He made a huge positive impact on our lives.

Peczon hosts reunion of Philippine doctors

By CHARLES L. KELLER
Recorder Staff

The next few days mark a milestone in the life of Dr. Jose D. Peczon of 11 Crescent St. — 25 years out of medical school.

It will be an unusual happening for Thomas Memorial Golf & Country Club in Turners Falls, too. About 100 Philippine physicians and their wives and children will wind up a three-day reunion there Thursday, enjoying the picturesque outdoor setting and activities at Thomas.

The Greenfield resident who practices oph-

thalmology at Med-Optics in Montague City will join others for the 25th reunion of the University of the Philippines' class of 1957.

The actual anniversary date won't come until December, Peczon told the Recorder, but it is summer here and "... since most of the class is practicing in this country, we have to organize the reunion here." It will be their first reunion since graduating.

Of the 86 graduates of that class, Peczon said 35 are practicing medicine in the United States. Six have died, including Dr. Robert A. Hendricks of Chicago, the only American

member of the class.

The reunion opened Tuesday at the Park Plaza in Boston. "We wanted to get out of the city in where we could have some athletic activity," Peczon said, so he helped arrange for the third day to be at Thomas, where swimming, golf and tennis can be enjoyed. They were to arrive at Thomas at about 11:30 a.m. Thursday. A dinner dance is expected to end the evening, Peczon noted.

The class attended the Philippine university's medical school. After graduation, they all entered various hospitals for internships

and then went on for special training in specialized fields.

Peczon said he and his co-chairman, Dr. Felipe Tolentino, an ophthalmologist and surgeon in Boston, are the only two from the class to settle in New England.

"They're coming from all over," Peczon said. "One is even coming here from Guam. It's really getting quite exciting, not having seen them all for 25 years."

Peczon said about 10 of his classmates have become full professors, teaching at medical schools.

I hosted the first major reunion of my UPCM class of 1957—the SILVER JUBILEE.

Most members of UPCM class of 1957 attended the reunion for the first time during this Silver Jubilee celebration that started in Boston and ended in Greenfield. It was the start of more class reunions averaging about once in every two years, a unique accomplishment that none of the other UPCM classes could claim. As class president for life, appointed by my close friend Mutya, I took my responsibility seriously. Now in the twilight of our lives, at least a dozen of the class survivors meet in a virtual Zoom chatroom at least once a month.

On my fiftieth birthday, Donna surprised me with a catered party at our home. As you can well imagine, my lifetime partner meticulously paid attention to the details, choosing the food provided by a caterer, which included caviar (to which I developed allergy in later years), champagne, and other foodie stuff. The guest list was a microcosm of Greenfield society. Life cannot be better than that.

A blonde, dressed appropriately, sang me the birthday song capped by a kiss on the cheek. That may have popped a balloon. I do not remember that well. Champagne can dull one's memory.

Donna can be rightfully called a triathlete. Her daily routine starts with a one-mile swim in the nearby YMCA, a set of one or two tennis doubles with her friends, and a two- to three-kilometer jog with me when I came home from the office. We participated in one five-kilometer race sponsored by the YMCA. Donna came THIRD in her age category. I came in second from the last in all age categories. The one who came in last was the local undertaker who got a humorous write-up in the local paper. Had I been that unlucky racer, I wonder what the sports page editor could have written. Local eye doctor, first in cataract surgery, last or lost in a foot race?

Walter graduated from Deerfield Academy on May 30, 1982. With him in the same class was a Rockefeller whose uncle gave the commencement speech. In the graduating class one year ahead of Walter, the present King Hussein of Jordan was a member.

Lisa got her high school diploma from PINE RIDGE SCHOOL in Williston, Vermont, in 1983. For her graduation present, I took her mom and brother on a two-week tour of Switzerland.

A&E   The Recorder, Greenfield, Mass., Thursday, May 11, 2000

Greenfield Classic Day set for Saturday

By MICHAEL PUFFER
Recorder Staff

Festival

GREENFIELD — The Greenfield Business Association is offering a chance this weekend to celebrate those things that have made Greenfield special.

This year's Classic Day celebration Saturday will be at the Greenfield Energy Park on Miles Street.

Elvis will rise again to croon, visitors can learn to swing dance, poets will read, and many activities incorporating local history and the evolution of Greenfield will be offered free.

The event came about seven years ago, after the town repelled the advance of Wal-Mart, said organizer Jodi Kramer. At that time, the Greenfield Business Association decided to sponsor an event that would highlight those things that continue to make Greenfield a special and distinctive town, she said.

Kramer said she expects 2,500 people to visit the Energy Park for this year's event. "We wanted to have a festival to celebrate Greenfield and what a classic town we have," she said. "And just to expose people to our area."

The "Spotlight on Greenfield" presentation honoring local heroes will tie the event together, said Kramer. This event, beginning at 11:45 a.m., will spotlight the achievements of Greenfield natives, with many of these local heroes on hand to

Dr. Jose Peczon, the inventor of a microsurgical device used to treat cataracts worldwide, will be on hand, as will 15-year-old dancer Lindsay Dunn. Dunn has been featured on "Good Morning America" and was one of four dancers, out of 4,000, chosen to work with film director Spike Lee on an upcoming production. Also attending will be Masha Arms — a woman who broke into the world of photography during the Depression when men ruled the scene, Terri Cappucci — a photojournalist who documented the anti-Apartheid movement, 1981 Academy Award nominee Steven Alves, film editor for the documentary "The Garden of Eden," and several others.

Joel McFadden Designs will host a diamond-cutting demonstration from 9 a.m. to 5 p.m. featuring master diamond cutter Maarten de Witte from Hearts on Fire Diamond Company.

A walking tour of the historic architecture and changing face of Greenfield will be directed by Professor Lawrence Buell of Greenfield Community College at 1 p.m. beginning in front of the Northeast Sustainable Energy Association building at the Energy Park on the end of Miles Street.

John P. Prangie, M.D., of Pioneer Valley Ophthalmic Consultants P.C., will offer free eye examinations at his Sightmobile at the Energy Park.

A month before I formally retired from private practice, *The Greenfield Recorder* ran a piece about GREENFIELD CLASSIC DAY. This was to honor Greenfielders who had distinguished themselves in their field. I was cited for my invention of an IA needle for cataract surgery.

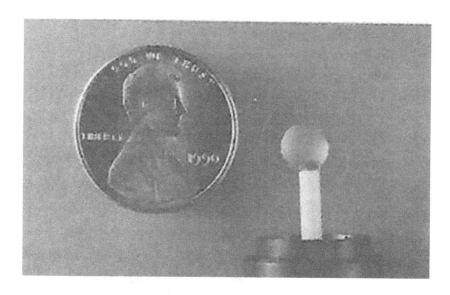

Using the same successful design as this artificial intraocular lens, I asked a manufacturer, Mentor ORC of California, to make a similar one but of a smaller diameter that can be inserted via a smaller corneal incision. Later models were foldable, making it possible to insert them in even smaller incisions. Progress in the design of these lenses is ongoing. If I were to start all over again, with 20/20 hindsight, I would choose ophthalmology over all the other medical and surgical subspecialties. There is a magical, fully satisfying sensation by a cataract surgeon witnessing the happy faces of almost all patients who regain near-perfect vision after the surgery. Many happily "complained" about seeing all the wrinkles on their faces which they did not see before!

Col. CHARLES KADES was a lawyer under the command of Gen. COURTNEY WHITNEY, who, under the order of Gen. DOUGLAS MACARTHUR, was tasked with rewriting the Japanese Constitution. That new constitution provided the framework that paved the way for a peaceful nation to shed its militaristic stance. During the last two or three years of his life, I made him happier by restoring his vision to a near-normal state using a secondarily implanted intraocular lens. Previously, he had ordinary cataract operations to both eyes without internal replacement of the lens, and he had to depend on spectacles with high power and distorting lenses which gave him less than fully satisfying results. I discovered that when he came to see me at GEC. For me, a Filipino boy who grew up in a tiny town in Luzon, a witness to some of the horrors perpetuated by the Japanese invaders, to be given the rare opportunity to rehabilitate the vision of the lawyer who rewrote the new Japanese Constitution that made Japan one of the most peaceful in the world is way beyond my wildest dreams.

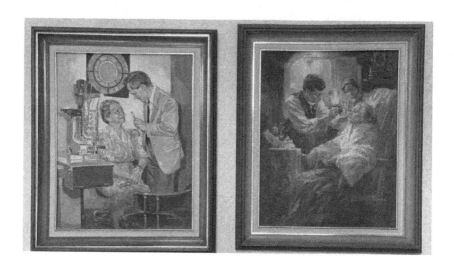

Hanging in my den in Dove Canyon, California, are these two paintings, painted by the same artist, LEONARDO, depicting the loving care of sons to their mothers. On the right is Philippine national hero, Dr. JOSE RIZAL, one of the first two ophthalmologists in the Philippines. In one of his books, he described the difficulties which he encountered when he operated on his mother's cataract. In part, he attributed this to a lack of total cooperation of his patient. Dr. Jose Peczon, the one depicted in the left painting, encountered no such difficulty. He and his mother had the benefit of modern technology. Life is all about timing, isn't it?

Four generations of firstborn mothers were among my many patients; APUNG TAQUI, my maternal grandmother; IMA, my mother; ZON, my older sister; and GRACE, Zon's oldest daughter, all had eye surgeries by my hands. The older three had cataract surgeries; the youngest had a refractive surgical procedure. I jokingly told her that she should have allowed me to do cataract surgery in one eye, although her eyes were not cataractous, to correct her nearsightedness, just for the purpose of getting myself listed in *The Guinness World Records*. No deal, she said. In all seriousness, I did several patients with no cataracts but had a high degree of nearsightedness or the opposite, farsightedness, that would have been difficult to correct with reshaping of the corneas alone. (That is the principle behind refractive surgery.) Removing clear lenses and replacing them with appropriately powered intraocular lenses resulted in more than satisfactory results. Few ophthalmologists dare perform that controversial procedure, probably even at the present time.

I was still a resident in ophthalmology in PGH when I had the opportunity to operate both eyes of my beloved Apung Taqui. At that time, intraocular lenses were not yet known in the Philippines and even in the United States. One surgeon at the Moorefield Hospital in London did perform some experimental ones, which mostly ended up in disastrous results that gave these early artificial lenses a bad reputation. Nevertheless, Apung Taqui was happy to regain vision, which she lost from mature cataracts. I was happy that I could at least do that for her in return for all the loving support, financially and morally, to help me get through medical school.

Who could have predicted that the serious-looking lad on the right would someday in the future operate on the eyes of his mother and two sisters? Our national hero, Dr. Jose Rizal, certainly did not have that opportunity.

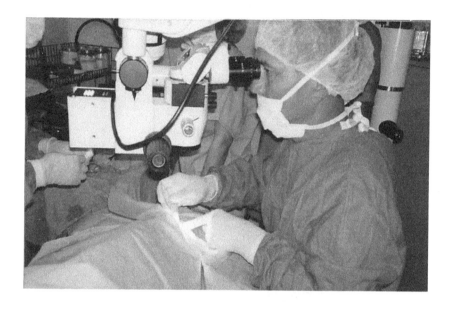

In the Mobile Eye Clinic, I performed the first cataract surgery with lens implantation on an indigent patient done on a purely outpatient basis in the Philippines.

Rev. Henry Bartlett handling First U.P. Pres. Murray Bartlett retirement Gold Omega Watch to Jose D. Peczon, M.D., UPCM 1957 in presence of Rev. Dr. Feredico Agnir, A.B., U.P. 1959 11 Crescent St., Greenfield, MA 1982

The odds that a gold Omega watch given on the retirement day of the first president of the UP (established in 1908), Murray Simpson Bartlett, to be in the possession of his only heir, his nephew the Rev. Henry Bartlett, who happened to be in Greenfield, Massachusetts, where he was a patient of a UP alumnus practicing ophthalmology and to have that watch eventually returned home to the Philippines is an awfully long shot. But it happened. Fred Agnir and I are proud UP alumni.

Murray Bartlett Watch

Foxtail Lane has a minuscule carbon footprint because of solar panels on the roof, storage batteries of unused electricity in the garage, and a fully electric car. The monthly electric bill is in the negative range, despite running the central AC 24/7 and charging the Tesla S for local trips. Blackouts do not affect the house at all because of the stored electricity in the batteries. This is a picture of how renewable green energy should be. Eventually, it will be available to most homes because, as in the case of computers, smart TVs, and iPhones, technology will keep on getting better and cheaper. I predict a more robust economy, based on renewable energy, in the coming years, and internal combustion motor vehicles will become museum pieces.

Two Kenyon sisters, Donna and Alysia, among my very first patients, starting all the way back to Boston, had this tree planted in my honor on the front lawn of the Greenfield Public Library upon my retirement in 2000. I guess you can call that a live growing memorial.

2   The Recorder, Greenfield, Mass., Friday, June 23, 2000

Greenfield doctor of 40 years to have tree planted in his honor

Sometime this year there will be a new tree planted on the grounds of the Greenfield Public Library. The tree will honor Dr. Jose Peczon, local opthalmologist, who is retiring today.

"I was six years old. I was his second patient when he began practicing at the Boston Eye & Ear Hospital," said Donna Hyland of Springfield. "He came to Greenfield shortly after that. Today I'll be his last patient in Greenfield."

Hyland, whose family has hereditary glaucoma, said that was 40 years ago. Peczon He had taken care of her late father and has taken care of her sister, Alesia Barbaro of Ludlow. As a child, Hyland had to undergo surgery by Peczon for her glaucoma.

"We've known him for 40 years. He's like a member of the family," Hyland said. "With his going, it's like losing a safety net. Without him, we probably would be blind right now. He'd always be there with a hug or a pat on the back, even if he had to tell us bad news."

Hyland told me she is planning to give Nancy Buchanan, co-chairman of the Friends of the Greenfield Public Library, a check to purchase a tree "to honor Dr. Peczon's involvement in the community."

"It's symbolic," said Hyland, who has been a reading teacher for 25 years. "I feel and my family feels a great loss."

Peczon and his wife, Donna, will be leaving the area to move to southern California to be near their son and daughter.

A private party for the Peczons will take place on Sunday at the grounds of his office, 33 Riddell St.

Irmarie Jones
Just Plain Neighbors
774-4954

As expected, *The Greenfield Recorder* had this to say about me and the tree planted in my honor.

My Dear Friend,

How can I ever begin to thank you for all you've given me? You have been one of the very best things that has ever come into my life. When I first came to the Greenfield Eye Center I had no idea how much it would change my life. I was offered a job, an education and a work environment that will never be matched. We had a second family to come to each day we arrived at work. You took such good care of us. Can you remember going to Andy's school musical? How many employers would do that? Not many. You see...you never really were just and employer. You have always been a friend.

Thank you for the best job I have ever had. Thank you for a career I love. Thank you for never being critical and always being a great teacher. Thank you for the weekends at Killington, the summer parties, the Christmas parties, the bonuses, the flowers, the visits in the hospital, the lunches, the desk from your office, the video equipment, the nickname Q.W. Thank you for the experience of seeing the West Coast and Disneyland and Rodeo Drive and The Beverly Wilshire.

Thank you for the trip of a lifetime and showing me a part of the world I would never have been able to see without you. You have given me memories that I will always treasure.

No matter how far away you go, you will be in my heart forever. You are family and I love you.

Gail
Q.W.

All GEC employees were happy to work for us not only for the generous salaries and bonuses we gave them but for the way we treated them like family. "I enjoyed every day I went to work in the office," Charlene Sulda and Nancy Moriarty said. Gail articulated the same sentiment with a letter she wrote me when I retired.

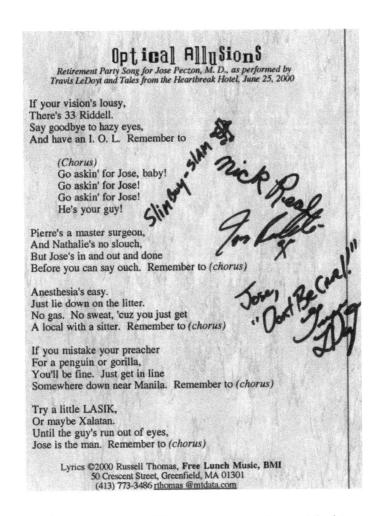

Optical Allusions

*Retirement Party Song for Jose Peczon, M. D., as performed by
Travis LeDoyt and Tales from the Heartbreak Hotel, June 25, 2000*

If your vision's lousy,
There's 33 Riddell.
Say goodbye to hazy eyes,
And have an I. O. L. Remember to

    (Chorus)
    Go askin' for Jose, baby!
    Go askin' for Jose!
    Go askin' for Jose!
    He's your guy!

Pierre's a master surgeon,
And Nathalie's no slouch,
But Jose's in and out and done
Before you can say ouch. Remember to *(chorus)*

Anesthesia's easy.
Just lie down on the litter.
No gas. No sweat, 'cuz you just get
A local with a sitter. Remember to *(chorus)*

If you mistake your preacher
For a penguin or gorilla,
You'll be fine. Just get in line
Somewhere down near Manila. Remember to *(chorus)*

Try a little LASIK,
Or maybe Xalatan.
Until the guy's run out of eyes,
Jose is the man. Remember to *(chorus)*

Lyrics ©2000 Russell Thomas, **Free Lunch Music, BMI**
50 Crescent Street, Greenfield, MA 01301
(413) 773-3486 rthomas @mtdata.com

A colleague, Dr. Russ Thomas, presented me with this song he wrote about me. I love it.

In less than a year, I won the Men's Senior Club Championship at the Dove Canyon Country Club. Even to myself, it was hard to believe, wasn't it? Tiger Woods, I am not. A happy golfer, yes.

On October 15, 2000, Donna won the Women's First Net Division in the golf championship. All her life, she always applied her best effort to anything she does. Donna's trophy (pasted on).

WALTER and RINA produced three granddaughters that Donna and I tried to spoil as often as we could.

I met our second grandchild MICHAELA AMOR TIONGSON, the day Donna and I arrived on the West Coast after an eight-day long automobile drive from Massachusetts. We knew that more grand-children would be coming soon.

Here are the reasons why we pulled out of Massachusetts and became California dreamers. Grandchildren, clockwise, from the top: JOSE PATRICK TIONGSON, MICHAELA AMOR TIONGSON, CHARLIE PAGE PECZON, HALEY ADRIANNA PECZON, and BRIANNA DANIELLE PECZON.

Grandchildren, from the left: HALEY, BRIANNA (tall one), CHARLIE, LOLO, LOLA, PATRICK, and MICHAELA.

Hi, Uncle Joe!

I'm pleased to tell you that your recent visit here
has proved to be very fruitful. Dr. Agulto has finally
made it a policy to forego medical clearance for
patients undergoing cataract extraction. Everyone was
saying it's about time this was implemented but then
nobody in authority was doing something about it. So
now we can fasttrack our objective of decreasing the
cataract backlog in the country. We owe it to you.

I've also succeeded in convincing my batchmates to do
lens extraction under topical. You wouldn't believe
how amazed they are that they could finish the
procedure without the patient feeling any pain. Still
there are some patients (men mostly) who feel
discomfort during the operation but they are in the
minority. I also did DCR under local, and again my
assists are in awe.

The patients that we operated on are all doing fine
with their visual acuities ranging from 6/6 to 6/9.
The DCR patient is happy since she is not tearing
anymore. The pxs who underwent phaco have all got good
visions, and are raring to have their other eyes
operated on. But then we have to learn to do small
incision ECCE before we are allowed to learn phaco.
I'm confident that that won't take long.

Thank you again for all the things you taught us and
the changes you brought about. We're hoping that on
your next visit you could help polish our techniques
in phaco.

Even in retirement, I keep returning to the homeland to try to
give back to the Filipino people from whom we can never separate
ourselves. At the PGH Eye Department, I continued to share my
knowledge and experiences with the younger eye doctors in training.
One of them is Don, the youngest son of my brother Pons. His email
dated February 9, 2003, articulates it well. The residents in training benefited, and more importantly, patients received better care at
much-reduced cost.

We started with a tiny lovable VW Beetle in 1959. Now in retirement, we drive around California in this Tesla Model S, Elon Musk's all-electric car that does not emit any kind of gas emissions. We believe science which warns us of the danger of human activities that play a large part in global warming. In our small way, we are doing our part to minimize the world's carbon footprint. We have solar panels on the roof that provide all the electricity to supply our domestic needs, store excess energy into Tesla-made storage batteries, and provide free charging to the car when parked in the garage. On the road, we also enjoy free charging of the car batteries from strategically situated Tesla Superchargers that can allow us to drive all the way to the East Coast if we choose to. You can see that I am an enthusiastic fan of Tesla cars and renewable green energy because I believe in new technology that improves the lives of all humans while helping to preserve our planet. Choosing to adopt the implantation of artificial lenses inside the eye even when it was frowned upon by the establishment, I am doing exactly the same thing with the new and exciting transition to green renewable energy consumption. I am certain that history will prove me right again.

Northwestern Luzon Chapter of the
Philippine Academy of Ophthalmology

In association with

Invites you to a lecture on

SMALL INCISION CATARACT SURGERY
AND PHACOEMULSIFICATION
TECHNIQUES, PEARLS AND TIPS

Dr. Jose Peczon, Fellow AAO
Guest Speaker

Saturday, Jan. 31, 2004
Conference Hall, Lorma Medical Center
San Fernando City, La Union

My efforts to impart new knowledge in ophthalmology were not limited to PGH. In the provinces, I tried to help too.

Our grandchildren and their parents helped Donna and me to celebrate our fiftieth wedding anniversary on a Carnival cruise ship on September 6, 2008.

Relatives and friends from the Philippines, Australia, and several US states came to help us celebrate special events in September 2018. Our oldest grandchild, PATRICK, married SAMI LEE, Donna had her eighty-fourth birthday, I had my eighty-fifth, and we had our sixtieth wedding anniversary. The Dove Canyon Country Club house was the venue.

I told relatives and friends that for the past sixty-five years, dating and married life, we have not tired of always holding hands. It was for romantic reasons, in the beginning, I told them, now there is still romance in it but there is also the extra benefit of preventing each other from falling! Romantic and practical, you can call us.

Fifty-one years ago, Donna, Walter, Lisa, and I came to Greenfield to settle down. We did not choose the town. Instead, the town chose me among a long list of possible ophthalmologists on the roster of the Massachusetts Selective Military Draft Board. That allowed me to escape the fog of war in Vietnam. We also found our home.

Just before being wheeled on a hospital gurney to the operating room at the Memorial Hospital in Mission Viejo, on September 5, 2019, I took this picture of Donna with that typical dynamite smile of hers. She was unafraid even with the knowledge that the surgery she was about to undergo carried a lot of risks. She had me promise not to let her suffer unnecessarily if something went wrong. It was the most difficult decision I made in my life, but I kept my promise to her. She left me on September 9, three days after her eighty-fifth birthday and the sixty-first anniversary of our tying the knot together for life. Now I must continue life without her physical presence, but the countless happy memories we shared will live on.

Postlogue

A complete renovation of a twenty-four-bed room for orphaned boys, St. Andrews Dormitory, was started at the White Cross Orphanage in San Juan, Manila, in February 2020 to honor the memory of Donna whose love for children is common knowledge among family and friends.

Under the capable supervision of our niece, Maria Antonia Orlina-Leong, the work was completed in March 2021 under difficult conditions due to the COVID-19 pandemic. Family funds, supplemented by many relatives and friends who contributed donations in lieu of flowers, were used to finance the entire project.

About the Author

Jose David Peczon, MD, is a retired ophthalmologist living in Orange County in California. He graduated from the University of the Philippines, College of Medicine, in 1957. During the third year of medical school, he met his future partner in life, Donna Ibanez Villaflor, a student nurse enrolled at the School of Nursing at the Philippine General Hospital in Manila. Jose's widowed mother, a pharmacist, was the driving force that steered him to a career in medicine. She was also largely responsible for encouraging him to marry Donna earlier rather than later. Donna and Jose went on to seek further postgraduate training in their respective fields in America. Their lives together spanning sixty-five years is one that is full of happy memories. It is a story that Jose wants to share with his family, friends, and the general public.

Printed in the USA
CPSIA information can be obtained
at www.ICGtesting.com
LVHW040756250424
777839LV00006B/2